STRANDED

STRANDED

ROCK AND ROLL
FOR A DESERT ISLAND
edited by
GREIL MARCUS

ALFRED A. KNOPF
NEW YORK
1979

Since this page cannot legibly accommodate all permissions acknowledgments, they will be continued on page 304.

Grateful acknowledgment is made to the following for permission to reprint previously published material:

ABKCO MUSIC INC.: Excerpts from "Stray Cat Blues," "Parachute Woman," "No Expectations," "Sympathy for the Devil," "Dear Doctor," "Salt of the Earth," and "Street Fighting Man." All songs written by Mick Jagger and Keith Richard. All songs copyright © 1968 Abkco Music, Inc. Reprinted by permission. All rights reserved.

BEEFHEART MUSIC: All songs from the *Trout Mask Replica* album, copyright © 1969 by Beefheart Music. Used by permission.

BLUE SKY RECORDS, INC.: Excerpts from "Personality Crisis" and "It's Too Late" by David Johansen and Johnny Thunders. Excerpts from "Frankenstein" by Syl Sylvain and David Johansen. Reprinted by permission.

FORT KNOX MUSIC COMPANY, CARLIN MUSIC CORPORATION, AND MUZIEKUITGEZERIJ ARTEMIS: Excerpts from "School Girl" by Lowman Pauling. Copyright © 1954—Fort Knox Music Company. Excerpts from "Say It" by Lowman Pauling. Copyright © 1957—Fort Knox Music Company. U.S. and Canadian rights administered by Fort Knox Music Company. United Kingdom rights administered by Carlin Music Corporation. All other rights administered by Muziekuitgezerij Artemis. Used by permission. All rights reserved.

LIBRARY OF CONGRESS CATALOGING IN PUBLICATION DATA
(Main entry under title:)
Stranded: rock and roll for a desert island.
Discography: p.
1. Rock music—Addresses, essays, lectures.
I. Marcus, Greil.
ML3534.S8   784   79-2225
ISBN 0-394-50828-9
ISBN 0-394-73827-6 pbk.

CONTENTS

My thanks to Robert Gottlieb,
Wendy Weil, Darlene Pond, and
James Raimes for their advice
and support.   —G.M.

INTRODUCTION

The premise of this book was simple: ask twenty writers what rock and roll record they would take to a desert island. It's an old question and a good one; absurd, but irresistible. When I began to call up people I thought would be interested and asked them that question, asked them to contribute, the response was enthusiastic, but in many cases for a reason I hadn't anticipated. "A great idea," said one person after another. "I feel like I've been living on a desert island for years."

Rock and roll, black music altered in one way or another by white culture, began in the early and mid-fifties as something like a secret, the apprehension of a strange, wildly various, and undeniable new sound. By about 1955 it had achieved the status of a rumor. The arrival of Elvis Presley turned rock and roll into a deeply shared culture, the password of millions, a means to identify and delight, and the advent of the Beatles intensified that process beyond all expectation. One listened in a lot of ways, but one always listened as a member of an audience; ten years ago one would have said as a member of a generation, or a community.

For many reasons—some of them having to do with rock and roll itself, some of them having to do with political facts of life—

this is no longer so true. As happened in the late fifties and early sixties, with the disappearance of rock's founders, the music and the audience lost their center in the late sixties, when the Beatles disbanded and Bob Dylan eased up; in any case, the music had lasted far too long to be the possession of any identifiable generation, and the audience had likely grown too big and broad for any center. Rock and roll, as culture, lost much of its shape. The mass movements of the sixties, which for many brought a sense of common endeavor and shared fate to almost every aspect of life, fragmented; people who before took pride identifying themselves as members of a group, no matter how unorganized or spectral, found that they could best identify themselves by their names, and life became more private, more isolated.

Rock and roll has never been remotely monolithic—there have always been countless performers to pin your hopes on; though one may have found identity as a member of an audience, one also found it by staking a place in that audience, defining one's self against it—but in 1965 virtually no one who cared about rock and roll could fail to care about the Beatles, just as in 1956 you had to have an opinion about Elvis. For a long time now, there has been no single figure one has felt compelled to celebrate or denigrate. People have staked out their territory in rock and roll, but they don't feel much like members of anything big enough to take over the world—which, as Robert Christgau points out in his piece on the New York Dolls, is what rock and roll is supposed to do.

The objects of the obsessiveness that has always been part of being a rock and roll fan, or a rock and roll critic, are no longer obvious—which means, for one thing, that while one's sense of the music may not have perfect shape, it's probably a lot richer. I'm sure that if this book had been written ten years ago, the Beatles and Bob Dylan would have not only appeared in it but perhaps dominated it, and not just because their records (in Dylan's case, his most exciting) were newer then. At that time, the very idea of shared obsession was often controlling; that there is no one now around whom rock and roll turns, no one who defines it, makes the rest of rock and roll more visible—and more compelling.

The choices the writers of this book have made (their ultimate record) are, many of them, quirky—at least within the context of official rock and roll history, certified masterpieces, or already cleared common ground. As shared obsession becomes less possible, one joins smaller audiences—one feels allegiance to punk, or to soul, or to one's part of the country, or to one's generation—or one is thrown back upon oneself. Captain Beefheart, an obsession that can (as Langdon Winner almost insists, *must*) be nurtured in isolation, may speak more vitally to the state of things than an obsession with the Beatles, which, after ten years, may seem chimerical, if it hasn't simply worn out. Albums become less touchstones than companions, though of course writers and fans continue to try to turn them into touchstones; artists become less symbols than figures with whom one can carry on a long-distance, perhaps lifelong, dialogue, and one grows dubious about making anyone into a symbol.

I chose the writers for this book because they were to me clearly the best people to write it, and because they were the people I most wanted to work with. They, however, didn't necessarily choose to write about the album they thought was "the best": their number-one choice on the all-time list that critics are always being asked to compile, and that everyone else compiles for their own pleasure. I asked for those lists: the Beatles did show up (not *Sgt. Pepper*, which today seems artificial where *Rubber Soul* still seems full of life), as did Bob Dylan and most everyone else you might expect. (The absence of Chuck Berry or Elvis from this book is as scandalous as the fact that the Beatles are missing, and as sensible.) The records most often mentioned were Dylan's *Highway 61 Revisited* and *Blonde on Blonde, Chuck Berry's Golden Decade* (or *Greatest Hits*), *James Brown Live at the Apollo, Rubber Soul*, Elvis Presley's *Sun Sessions*, the Rolling Stones' *Let It Bleed* and *Exile on Main Street*, none of which anyone chose to write about, and Van Morrison's *Astral Weeks*, which Lester Bangs claimed. The essays that follow, all written specifically for this book, have more to do with what these writers care about than with what they think deserves the first spot in the Hall of Fame; they're fans' statements, among other things, written out of involvement more than judgment, and they mean to tell tales not everyone has heard, or that have yet to be told at all. The long annotated Discography that ends the book—

a history of rock and roll in records—is my attempt to give everyone who's rightly earned it a place in the romance.

In her piece on Bruce Springsteen, Ariel Swartley says an interesting thing about his characters: they "live on islands close enough to shore to see the mainland, too far away to make the crossing light or easy." This book begins on the islands where so many feel stranded these days, but what it is about, finally, is the effort to make that crossing: less to head off into exile with a single piece of rock and roll than to bring it home, along with a story good enough to make others want to listen.

—GREIL MARCUS
Berkeley, December 2, 1978

STRANDED

THE SEA'S ENDLESS, AWFUL RHYTHM & ME WITHOUT EVEN A DIRTY PICTURE

NICK TOSCHES

Call me Gilligan. As I confront in earnest the problems of divine retribution, way-out sex, and the value of the Folk Mass, so I confront the desert-island question.

I must say that the idea of being marooned somewhere with neither whiskey nor Jewish girls troubles me greatly, and I believe, as the nightmared child believes in morning and its peace, that the God of the New Testament shall see to it that I am accompanied upon the rough-hewn raft of my solitude by at least a case of Tulamore Dew and La Louise in Diorissimo ultrasheer, off-black pantyhose. But, Lord, I am a humble man, and would settle for Carstairs and my first wife.

And what book should I take with me from the lending library of poetic justice? Perturbed by the fate of the Russian ivory-hunter in *Heart of Darkness*, who was stranded with naught to read but *An Inquiry into Some Points of Seamanship*, I have given the matter much thought, and have chosen Richmond Lattimore's translation of Pindar's *Odes* (Chicago, 1947), with issue number twenty-six of *Leg Art* (San Pedro, 1976) concealed between its pages. And Mr. Kurtz be damned.

But the phonograph record. Ah, the record. Presuming that some dolt and colleague, less dignified with the meter and metaphor than myself, has elsewhere in these pages brought something not wholly unlike wit to bear upon the Las Vegas odds against encountering electric circuitry on an uninhabited island, I shall ignore the opportunity for runny-nosed humor—reminding all who would not of Goethe's remark to Chancellor von Müller, "The possible will be attempted only because we have postulated the impossible"—and instead, sacrificing at the altars of charm and hyperbole as little honesty as possible, speak from the heart. Together, in my bathroom, like this.

The record I would take is *Sticky Fingers*, by the Rolling Stones. There is something about the dullness of my choice that bothers me; but *Sticky Fingers* it is. The Tullamore Dew, La Louise, the *Odes, Leg Art*—of these things I am sure beyond doubt. But *Sticky Fingers* is a choice as mysterious and as difficult to explain to myself as to anyone else.

At first, I thought of bringing a Jerry Lee Lewis album. The Killer has been a constant inspiration to me, and I've always believed that he's the last man to have been touched by the Holy Ghost of Gnosis. The powers of his music—that loud, unspeakable philosophy of his Horus-Snopes soul; the search through mania and excess for that unknown, unknowable sin without which there can be no redemption or damnation more thrilling than any redemption or damnation known to the gelt rest; the pitting within of good against evil without knowing, maybe even caring to know, or refusing to know, one from the other—are more than rock 'n' roll, or whatever you want to call it. They are powers of light and dark, wickedness and strength, and they are powers that can cure and heal and cause miracles. The trouble is that Jerry Lee has never made a great album, largely because of Jerry Kennedy, the member of the Nashville mediocrity conspiracy who produced his work from 1968 to 1978. For these sins, as sure as the Venerable Bede deals three-card monte in the hereafter, Jerry Kennedy will pay. And I will disembark upon my desert island without the music of Jerry Lee Lewis.

Then I thought of the Chieftains, and how I love to play *Bonaparte's Retreat* in the middle of the night, and how I could listen to it forever. But there is something too eerie, too wraithful in the Chieftains' wedding of pagan joy and Gaelic mourning. To be left alone with such music, especially after the whiskey ran out, could be quite dangerous to my spiritual well-being, the stability of which has not commonly been likened to a large rock. Besides, it is rare for me to hear the Chieftains without thinking of (a) La Margaret, the prodigious mucus of whose lust I was anointed with while "An Chéad Mháirt den Fhomhar" filled the Nashville night and the first chill hours of 1978 with the caws of estrangement, and (b) the Bells of Hell, that New York bar where I sat, leaning toward 4 a.m., hugged by perniciousness, listening to the Chieftains' sullen jukebox magic, night after wasted night. No, it simply wouldn't do.

I turned to the Doors, to their reduction of all to sex, death, and rhythm. Before I decided which Doors album I would bring, I realized that, in solitude, I wouldn't want to be with the voice of someone so newly dead. I wanted a *memento vivere*, not a *memento mori*. For the same reason, I resolved not to bring Lynyrd Skynyrd's *Gimme Back My Bullets*, an album I listen to far more often than *Sticky Fingers*.

I listen to Randy Newman more than I listen to anyone else, but while Randy Newman's songs give me more pleasure, and impress me more, than anyone else's, I don't think one of his records could much assuage my solitude, for his are songs of people and people's delicate mysteries (of which I would not care to be reminded on my unpeopled isle), and little of his work reaches, with word or rhythm, into the greater, indelicate mystery—Τα Μυστηριον DeLuxe—which makes and vanquishes the lesser mysteries. And here even I cease to understand what I'm saying; so let's move on.

The Rolling Stones supplied the soundtrack for much of my grown-up life. When I first heard "(I Can't Get No) Satisfaction," I was fifteen years old, and had never gotten laid. I remember sitting with my *citrulli* friends on the concrete steps of a store, where one could either play the numbers or buy dog food, beer, cigarettes, and the full line of fine Contadina products, on the corner of Clendenny and Miller in Jersey City, smoking two-cent loosies, and hearing that new Rolling Stones song blare from a transistor radio. It was unlike anything else to be heard that summer of 1965. Lurid, loud, and concupiscent, it was at once a yell of impotence and of indomitability. Its conspiratorial complaints sanctified our frustrations, and its vicious force promised deliverance. It gave us power over girl-creatures, and made of our insignificant, wastrel cocks spigots of wordless insolence—which, of course, we had always wanted them to be. I was arrested for the first time that summer, for D&D.

When I first heard "Have You Seen Your Mother, Baby, Standing in the Shadow," I had taken five blood-orange capsules of Dexedrine and was riding with friends through the streets of Hoboken, looking for girls who would let us share the miracle of physical love with them. It was the first really cold night of the fall, 1966. The apocalyptic dissonance of the record struck me first, and then the surly notion of throwing at the face of the neurotic, castaway girlfriend the image of her mother, and sneering, in afterbreath, at the girl's pregnancy. Swathed and speeding, we prowled with the windows shut against the black coldness, looking for feminine throats in the shadows, where there were none, listening to that, smiling terribly, and feeling, with something like orgasm, our existences contract beatifically into that terrible smiling.

In the late summer of 1969, I wasn't thinking of music. I had then terminated two years of bliss, or its reasonable facsimile, with La Dominique, the lovely daughter of Perpignan and of the sea, upon the small of whose lithe back I had painted a perfect Day-Glo Ronsonol can, its spouter cocked, like the slender finger of Botticelli's *Calumny*, toward the dimple of her dextral shoulder, and within the penetralia of whose softness I had, for seven-times-seventy nights, studied the craft of prostatial eloquence. I was employed as a paste-up man for Lovable Underwear in New York, devoting my creativity to tasks such as the production of cordate stickers for pantyhose packages which bore the legend, "No bag! No sag!" I knew contentment. One night I went into Ojay's Bar on Ninth Street near Avenue A, right around the corner from Ed Sanders's Peace Eye Book Store. I stood at the bar between a moist short man with dried blood on the front of his shirt, at whom the bartender frequently glared, and a young couple who hissed at one another in clipped cadences of wrath—there was a journey to Pennsylvania, to visit someone's relatives, involved; also a matter of stingy behavior regarding the sharing of egg rolls. And from the jukebox came the lewd, commanding sound of Charlie Watts's cowbell, making with a stick and a piece of copper a truer, greater rhythm than most can make with a wealth of electric equipment. I realize now that "Honky Tonk Women" was welcome detumescence for the sixties, and a surly, languid waking from the restless sleep of ideology. It strutted its indolence, as one who nods off while fucking. As "Satisfaction" had been innocent in its discontent, "Honky Tonk Women" was wise in its slavering contentment. It washed my mind —indeed, washed Ojay's and the slow river of dark night that ran without—in a perverse peace; and before the evening was over, it had become my favorite song.

And I will tell you of crab music, and of much else besides. In the spring of 1972, my friend Charlie and I were living in Tampa, and were without money. Charlie had been working for Budweiser and wanted to get fired so that he could lay back for a while drawing unemployment. With that end in mind, he had sat down with a crisply sharpened Budweiser pencil, a Budweiser Clydesdale calendar, and a small pad of Budweiser stationery. To be eligible for unemployment benefits, he needed a minimum of twenty work-weeks under his belt. After checking, double-checking, and triple-checking, he had circled upon his Budweiser Clydesdale calendar the date that would mark his hundredth day of loading Budweiser beer into Budweiser trucks. The hundred-and-first day was to have been M-day. There was only one sure way to be canned at his job. On his first day at work, his supervisor (a man who, it is said, listed "Gum" as his hobby on a job application) had informed Charlie that anyone stupid enough to crack open a ceiling sprinkler valve while operating a forklift would immediately receive his walking papers. Such was the Budweiser *lex non scripta*. Two in the past had been careless enough to transgress, and they had both been fired before—and here came the phrase the supervisor savored—the first drop of water hit the floor. Thrilled by the notion of whiling away the summer drinking Georgia peach wine in the Clearwater sand, Charlie had arrived at work on M-day, mounted a forklift, scooped up eight feet of clanking Budweiser cases, looked to be sure his supervisor was nearby, elevated the lift to its maximum height, drawn a bead, and proceeded to smash into a sprinkler valve. The next afternoon, while sitting in the downtown unemployment office, certain errors in his computations had come to light. Pencil, pad, and calendar notwithstanding, Charlie had somehow fallen short of the hundred-day mark by eleven days. His reply to the lady at the unemployment office included strange allusions to the miracle of the loaves and feverish indictments of those who would manufacture defective calendars.

As for myself, I had been fired from my job as editor of *TV Weekly* ("The Bay Area's Only TV Magazine"), for a number of devious deeds, such as fabricating an exclusive interview with Joan Blondell, in which La Blondell confessed that she had cooked and eaten her three-year-old daughter. ("'It tasted like *blanquette de veau*, which I love,' said the former star of ABC's *Here Come the Brides*, indicating with coy fingers the bloated, sixty-year-old flesh of her midsection, which mutely testified to the love she professed.") The publisher, who was also a local disk jockey, told me, upon delivering my final paycheck, that I was deranged. I told him, in response, that I planned to blow his bowels asunder with my AMP .44.

Charlie and I sat and thought. Between us, we had ninety dollars in folding money and a pint jar of pennies and dimes. We owed ninety-eight dollars for the rent and fourteen for the electric. It was then that we conceived Grab-a-Crab.

Our closet contained thirty cases of beer, conservative estimate, which Charlie had stolen from Budweiser over the months. We decided that we could load the trunk of our car each morning with beer and boiled crabs (which we were to harvest from Tampa Bay), and drive to the Courtney Campbell Causeway, where, parked on the side of the road, we would sell our goods to the beach traffic. For a dollar, you'd get a crab and a beer. Perhaps we would include a few saltines to fancy things up. Since paper plates and napkins were to represent our only overhead, profits would be considerable. Soon, Grab-a-Crab franchises would proliferate along the Gulf. We would acquire great wealth, wed lovely girls with hyphenated names and masochistic streaks, sire children with strange, Nordic noses. Money would lose its value, but greed would not. I would sit, high above Newark, gazing into the night and pondering the meaning of it all:

Charlie dead by his own hand; the woman of my life's summer locked in a home for the sweepingly insane. I sip the fine Armagnac, watching passion pull at the face of La Contessa. She grasps my arm. I look into her eyes and see something I would never dare betray unto words. She speaks, and the sound of her voice makes me think of the Aegean and that night in Kálimnos, how many years ago?

"Fuck me," La Contessa says. "Fuck me till blood runs down my leg."

To celebrate the birth of the Grab-a-Crab empire, Charlie and I ate many micrograms of psilocybin and lay by the sea. A crab—the Magna Mater of all crabs—marched from her saline source and danced at our feet. She reared up and snapped her claws, commanding silence throughout the garden of God. In the distance, the voice of a he-child whined, "I don't want no hamburger. I want a crab, mommy! I want a crab!" As the child's voice faded, the crab spun around and marched back into the sea. And from somewhere came, quite loudly, the Rolling Stones' "Sympathy for the Devil," a record perfectly suited, we realized at once and forever, to the hermetic dance of crabs. The song's demonic owlings whistled through us as day became night, and we felt fate to be a faithful wife at our feet, and we felt blessed.

But we discovered that it took nearly two hours to pluck a lone crab from the gazpacho of pollutants that is Tampa Bay. We knew pain and emptiness, and eventually we knew eviction. I soon found myself, thick newspapers wrapped around my legs with wire, hunting snakes in the Everglades. Doctor Haast of the Miami Serpentarium, the nation's largest dealer of antivenin, paid two dollars per foot for live rattlesnakes and cottonmouths; more for coral snakes, America's only neurotoxic reptile. And there was a standing reward of a thousand dollars for anyone who could bring in a rattlesnake over six feet long. One morning, hung over unto the point of apoplexy, I was bit on the shin, right through the real-estate section of the Sunday *Herald*. Next to me in the emergency ward was a boy who held a Maxwell House coffee can to his neck, to catch the blood that dribbled from a cut in his throat. In his lap was a cassette recorder playing the new Stones album, *Exile on Main Street*.

And from there things got worse. But I was young. I got over it.

[Here occurs a pause, the gravity of which mere indentation could only hint at, but which additional leading would render too melodramatic.]

The Rolling Stones have always been looking over my shoulder, and I feel comfortable with them. I probably would not play *Sticky Fingers* too often on my desert island, but I know it would, like Pindar, like *Leg Art*, fulfill a need finely. Whenever I felt as if I were missing something back home, I could play "Bitch" or "Dead Flowers" to inspire cynical estrangement. "Moonlight Mile" would be perfect for staring out into the white-capped nothingness. For a spiritual anthem, I'd have "You Gotta Move," that song of sacred fatalism written by my father, Fred McDowell, and the Holy Ghost, and done best by the Rolling Stones. And should the days of solitude run into years, I might even figure out the lyrics of "Sway."

And when that devious-cruising *Rachel*, in her retracing search after her missing children, finds me, I will tell all about it. You can kill Grab-a-Crab, but you can't kill the dream. No, never.

"IT'S TOO LATE TO STOP NOW"

VAN MORRISON (WARNER BROS. 2760)
1974

M. MARK

A few months before she died at age 91, my grandmother gave me a memorable lecture on the value of disobedience. The night before her funeral, I gave my grandmother a goodbye gift. That evening her house was filled with kneeling people. I slipped away from the reverent whispers and walked the streets of Greene, Iowa; then I began to run, knocking over every garbage can in sight, creating clamor and frenzy among neighborhood dogs. I would have liked to give her a wake. The Irish, as everyone knows, are adept at mourning—we're famous for our funerals. My grandmother was Irish to her soul.

Three years later, when I was fifteen, W. B. Yeats came into my life, and with him the image of a wondrous moonlit dance—figures whirling and leaping, falling down, clambering back up, and once in a great while leaving the ground. On the periphery of the vision stood other figures: those who watched. I knew right then that I didn't want to be an observer and wrote a passage in my diary repudiating the English in me and vowing to pursue extravagant passions. I had begun to understand that being Irish implies a willingness to go too far, to risk it all—which includes the risk of making fools of ourselves. The hope of the indomitable Irishry is that if we're foolish, it will be on an impressive scale.

Van Morrison is Irish, Irish to his very soul. His songs take me home. If I were to be banished to some warm and sunny place with a single record to keep me company, I'd choose one of Van's. The music is a peculiar mix of moonstruck story-telling and bar-band groove, country blues and R&B and gospel and jazz and soul. It's mystical Celtic poetry with a rock and roll beat and all the contradictions that amalgam implies—body and soul music which takes itself very seriously half the time. Unless the relentlessly balmy weather impaired my perspective, Van's music would remind me to take an occasional look at myself—dancing, dreaming—and have a good laugh.

A few weeks ago at dinner with a friend, I held forth on V. Morrison and W. B. Yeats and my conviction that they share something more complicated than their status as Irish visionaries. My friend the Jewish visionary agreed, but both of us had trouble finding the words. We sat in the restaurant attempting to define a gesture: left hand over left shoulder, a fluttering movement, allusive and elusive and quicker than the eye. The pitcher winds up; before the ball leaves his hand, a great pitcher does something akin to music. A dove appears in the magician's hand, then flies away.

There's another version, of course. Both Morrison and Yeats are acquainted with the mystic and both sing the ancient ways. That coat covered with embroideries out of old mythologies would fit Van just fine. In his early poetry, Yeats created an iridescent faeryland inhabited by the Sidhe, a gentle race who spent a lot of time dancing beneath the moon. Morrison has his gypsies singing 'round the campfire, living in time out of mind. He also has a timeless lovers' landscape: woods and fields and waterfalls and secluded lanes. Yeats summons up Cuchulain, Conchubar, Aengus and Fergus, the Red Branch warriors, the Fenian tales; he summons up an ancient Ireland and, in his late poetry, a Byzantium where souls clap hands and sing. Morrison sings of Caledonia, an ancient land which sounds like home to him, a land where his ancestors made a brand new start and where bagpipes gave birth to the blues.

If the devil makes a covert appearance in Yeats's grappling with his sexuality, angels dominate most of Morrison's work. In this respect his is a soul sensibility: sexual connection as salvation and rebirth, lovers as guiding lights, the profane as sacred, as wholly holy love. But here as elsewhere Yeats and Morrison speak the same language. Both worship romantic love; both delight in it and define it as the crooked thing; both have loved and pined and publicly whined. And both get away with more sentimentality than any writer should expect to. Yeats and Morrison know how to make extreme romanticism work. They have fanatic hearts.

And they use language in an extraordinary way. The associative authority of their words—the power to evoke—is mystical call and response. Even when Morrison and Yeats are wandering-witted fools (and they are, on occasion), they can touch us in places we don't know how to defend. This alchemy is sometimes clothed in straightforward conversational language, sometimes in symbolism. Through night and the moon and ships in search of harbors, through dancing and singing, through astral bodies and astral weeks, they speak of embracing both Thanatos and Eros, of naming the fear and going beyond.

They seek what Yeats described as "images that constitute the wild,/The lion and the virgin,/The harlot and the child." The lion is a significant image for both of them. Yeats speaks of a dream that a lion dreamed till the wilderness cried aloud; Morrison listens to the lion in his soul. Yeats again: "A vast image out of Spiritus Mundi/Troubles my sight: somewhere in sands of the desert/A shape with lion body and the head of a man." The lion is both a resident of the Great Mind and a guide to it, one of those immensely potent archetypal symbols. When the music or the poetry turns magic, the borders of our minds shift, just like Yeats said they would, and art takes on the authenticity of dreams that know their own meaning better than we ever will. This, needless to say, is the stuff of transcendence.

Comparing one of our greatest poets to a rock star is, needless to say, the stuff of absurdity. There's the obvious high/pop incongruity, and the fact that one wrote *Words for Music Perhaps* and the other writes words for music exclusively; there are other incongruities as well. Yeats was a Dublin aristocrat who spent all his life in Ireland and felt at home among the stately swans at stately Coole. Morrison is a Belfast street kid with a pilgrim soul, an exile who writes with obsessive yearning about Cyprus Avenue, a place of trees and money and mansions on hills. Yeats belonged with

Lady Gregory inside the house shaken by land agitation; Morrison has always been outside, with the agitators if not of them.

Still, Yeats paid those visits to Mme. Blavatsky, the Theosophist necromancer, and Morrison has been known to extoll the virtues of Rolfing. They share something—and it has to do with what Edmund Wilson called the dreaming and mocking Irish mind. Yeats and Morrison want to believe in magic. They search for unity, but view the world through an aesthetic and philosophical filter that creates oppositions. Their struggle to come to terms with unresolvable conflicts is what puts the lion and the moon in their poetry.

Yeats spent most of his life worrying about action versus contemplation and rationality versus mysticism; he even devised a theory of interpenetrating opposites. In *The Vision* he laid out his ideas on Husks and Daimons as if he truly believed in them—though every few paragraphs the twentieth-century man, the Protestant man in Yeats, would announce that the supernatural beings were only poetic symbolism. Yeats also wrote the famous line about making rhetoric out of our quarrels with others and poetry out of our quarrels with ourselves. Van Morrison sings amid uncertainty, too. His music is defined by the quarrels he has with himself, and his art depends on oppositions of the most fundamental sort: black-white, open-closed, real-surreal, parts-whole. Without these contradictions, he would be an interesting musician; because of them, he's a great one.

Van Morrison is Leadbelly and Otis Redding, Brendan Behan of the pub brawls and St. Brendan of the quest. He's a white soul singer with the black Irish blues; he sings in a way that affirms his musical roots and transforms them into something altogether his own. In his category of music, the bat, ball, and vacant lot belong to him. Because jazz and the blues and R&B and soul are part of him, Van's music has nothing to do with borrowing or imitating. In his best songs, all the elements are there, now one in ascendance, now another—intertwined, suspended, playing off each other, creating resonances in the space where they merge or clash.

Van has excellent taste in roots. As a child, he listened to his father's Leadbelly collection, then moved on to Bo Diddley and Little Richard. In the mid-sixties, before and during the rowdy blues-raunch days with Them, he assimilated Ray Charles's sound. It's clear that he has also listened to Bobby Bland, Muddy Waters, Willie Dixon, Sonny Boy Williamson, John Lee Hooker, James Brown, Chuck Berry, Hank Williams, Bob Dylan, and the Rolling Stones (not to mention the Holy Ghost). It's clear, too, that he has been heard—by Bruce Springsteen, Graham Parker, Bob Seger, Phil Lynnot. In a sense, Van's got family. But he has trouble getting home. When he sings, "It's a long way to Belfast," the line rings true. He could do a great cover of Bobby Bland's "Lead Me On": "You know how it feels, you understand/What it is to be a stranger, in this unfriendly land."

Van has spent most of the last ten years in America, the country that gave birth to the music that gave birth to his. He tried to find love here, to make it all blend. After marrying Janet Planet, his California flower-child Maud Gonne, he went to Woodstock for some heavy-duty utopianizing with the Band, who were on a similar quest for lost and found American dreams (perhaps because all but one of them are Canadian). Van was in a dreamland, a condition that intensified both his ambivalence about being Irish and the Irishness itself. (Which isn't as contradictory as it sounds. An illustration: When I lived in Iowa, my wardrobe and vocabulary were as sophisticated as possible, befitting one bound for the Big City; now that I live in New York, my wardrobe consists of jeans and my vocabulary is littered with phrases like "real good," befitting one reared in the heartland. I don't recall deciding to make these changes.) Roots are a complicated business. Real complicated.

Neither the marriage nor the utopia worked out, but for a while Van was content. *His Band and the Street Choir* and *Tupelo Honey* prove it. They're his rendition of Dylan's family-man music; and, like *New Morning*, they're short on transcendence. The acknowledgment of unalterable homelessness and the struggle against it are essential to the awesome poetry of Van's masterpieces, *Astral Weeks* and *Veedon Fleece*; he wrote the music for both of them during visits to Ireland. From 1971 to 1976 he lived in California, which in brogue sounds a lot like Caledonia. After his marriage fell apart, he told an interviewer, "I never fit into California. It's strange I stayed here so long." He moved to England, home of his country's ancient enemies. In 1978 he moved back to California.

More contradictions: Van is a fine lyric poet who has trouble with words. Going through clips at Warner Bros., I ran across a homemade bio from the late sixties, awkward and typo-ridden. At the bottom Van had scrawled a note to his agent: "Perhaps you could add or subtract these facts." Realizing that the sentence needed fixing but apparently not quite knowing how, he'd stuck a "to" after "subtract." He gets his music from another part of himself—out of the medium's mouth or the slipstreams of his mind. (Joyce, whom he calls a soul writer, turns up in his lyrics, as do Joycean puns and mystical Catholic terror.) The songs just come to him, Van says, and often he doesn't know what they mean. Like Mrs. Yeats with her automatic writing, he receives messages and passes them on. His singing is intense because it's the language he really knows—it's his native tongue and his release.

At its best, Van's music transcribes an intensely personal vision; his profession is an intensely public one. Because pop culture implies mass audiences, he searches for hit singles as well as the lion in his soul. And he finds them. "Here Comes the Night," "Mystic Eyes," "Gloria," "Brown Eyed Girl," "Domino," "Wild Night," "Jackie Wilson Said," and "Wavelength" are rock and roll hits from a man who would never be mistaken for a rock star. Van is short, pudgy, gloomy, uncharismatic, uncharming. He tends to disappear between albums, he gets defensive during interviews, and at concerts he can never think of anything to say between songs.

Van is capable of giving transcendently wonderful concerts and transcendently awful ones. He has earned his reputation as an erratic performer—galvanizing an audience with his passion, or standing rigid, clutching the mike stand as if he'd only just decided not to enter the abyss, covering his eyes with his hand, turning his back like an Irish folk singer having a private relationship with his song, attempting to hide behind shades and a less than convincing simulation of cool, sending out waves of distrust and hostility, walking off stage in mid-set. There's nothing Brechtian or punkish about this alienation—it's too raw and self-punishing to be part of the act.

Although he wants to touch his listeners directly and deeply, he feels violated by their presence. He needs a measure of distance to come close, and he finds it through the wonders of modern science.

Records allow Van to obliterate distance. And second-degree distancing—records played on the radio—is even more intimate for him. The radio as receiver as sexual and emotional current as connection is one of his central images. (*Wavelength* has a twist: "We're on the telephone and we're connected.") Van takes this imagery seriously. He's lived it. After *Astral Weeks*, he was down and out in Boston—few friends, little money, some whiskey. He spent his evenings telephoning DJs to request blues songs. One afternoon he heard something on the radio—"The Weight," as he recalls, or "I Shall Be Released"—and in response wrote "Brand New Day." The rest of *Moondance* followed.

Another come-close-keep-your-distance convolution has to do with content and form. Many of Van's songs are about the pursuit of direct emotional response, about breaking through barriers, shedding psychological armor, recovering innocence. These messages are delivered in a formal, mannered vocal style. His voice is a remarkably flexible instrument: it can be a saxophone or a guitar or a violin, gentle, sweet, rich; it can be hard and untouchable. He's a master of dynamics—from a whisper to a scream or from a line as fluid as the ocean to a percussive staccato. He pushes and pulls at words, he scats and wails and stutters. "Just-a like going home," he sings, and "leavin-uh me behind."

Some of his mannerisms—dropping the first or last word in a line, for example—come from the blues. Many of them come from gospel and soul; Ray Charles, Otis Redding, and James Brown leap out of his mouth from time to time. So does Wilson Pickett, with whom Van is seldom compared—perhaps because he lacks the Wicked's arrogance (Van aims for 100 percent but would never revile 99½). For the Morrison inflection on "all right," listen to "In the Midnight Hour"; for the "huh" that can be either a sexual grunt or a small sad laugh, listen to "Mustang Sally." Van also does idiosyncratic variations on jazz mannerisms: he uses hypnotic repetition to create emotional intensification, and he uses verbal fragmentation to create unity. He takes songs apart in order to make them whole, isolates words and syllables, repeats them, scatters them in the air. When this technique works, the parts coalesce in magic-lantern shapes.

Unity of another sort has eluded Van. For a few heady months in 1963 at Belfast's Maritime Hotel, he belonged to a group caught up in the spirit of shared purpose and communality. But by the time Them began to make a name for itself, Van was being backed by a revolving crew of studio musicians. Since then, he's been a star singer with a more or less faceless band. He doesn't aim to be an outsider, but he's not cut out to be a communard. His back-up musicians change from album to album, partly because he wants different sounds at different times, partly because he's notoriously difficult to work for. The bands aren't able to build the sort of wholeness that musicians achieve after they've lived with one another for a while. Still, in Van's best music, all the instruments, including his voice, are wholly integrated. They become one big instrument, perfectly tuned, expertly played.

There's more. All of Van's songs—the rockers, the romantic ballads, the mystical reveries—are of a piece. All of them are about his search for the right ways to say the right things, ways of caging the lion or setting it free. In spite of or because of the internal contradictions, all of Van's music is part of one song, one great incantatory hymn of praise and propitiation. Which is why it's ridiculous to take a single album (a mere verse in the supersong) to the desert island.

Which is why I refuse.

When the editor of this book—a soulful man, but temporarily an agent of the English—instructed me to choose one Van Morrison record, I took the quantitative approach and "*It's Too Late To Stop Now*," Van's only double album. But one is clearly not enough. (Did I mention that the Irish have a deep and loving relationship with excess? Did I mention that we tend to be pugnacious?) Out of good manners and a knowledge of who's got the upper hand, I'm willing to limit myself. To a degree. The following are nonnegotiable demands. If I go to the island, they go too.

Them (1965, about the time Dylan was bringing it all back home). "Gloria," of course: an all-time rock and roll classic of the growls-and-balls variety. "Mystic Eyes": chilling graveyard imagery and a guitar that sounds like a weapon. "One Two Brown Eyes": bossa nova beat and devastating lyrics (when Van sings, "I'm gonna cut you down to size," you know he's not gonna do it with his sharp tongue). "Don't Look Back": a blues ballad by John Lee Hooker, touching precisely because it does look back, with tenderness, without meaning to.

Them Again (1966). "It's All Over Now Baby Blue": a fine cover, sadder than Dylan sings it. "My Lonely Sad Eyes": romantic, naive, with Dylan's habit of crowding more syllables into a melodic line than seems probable. "I Can Only Give You Everything": Van sings "I trahee and I trahee" (Q: Who was he listening to? Hint: I'll leave this cut behind if I can take *Out of Our Heads*). "Bad or Good": Ray Charles-flavored gospel rock. "Bring 'Em on In": Van's first I-was-walkin'-down-the-street-checkin'-out-the-boats-in-the-water song.

Blowin' Your Mind (1967). On his own, with mixed results: the second side is a mess, the first side a conceptually brilliant whole containing a masterpiece. "Brown Eyed Girl": playful sunlit imagery of lovemaking in the grass ("Do you remember when we used to sing shah lah lah lah lah lah lah lah-lah lah-lah-tee-dah, lah-tee-dah") with a hint of darkness near the end ("So hard to find my way now that I'm all on my own"). "He Ain't Give You None": darkness intensified, obsessive blues, an edge of desperation. "T.B. Sheets": the masterpiece, out of a great tradition (Leadbelly's "T.B. Blues," Hooker's "T.B. Sheets") into the viscera. A ten-minute exploration of claustrophobia and of purgatory (where, in Yeats's terminology, outraged souls confront one another again and again until the outrage is expiated). Van, who once had tuberculosis, wrote these blues out of fear; every time I hear him cry "Gotta go," part of me believes that neither he nor I will get out of the song alive.

Astral Weeks (1968). An album without which desert-island survival is impossible. Every cut goes with me. "Astral Weeks": an infinitely gentle celebration of sex as rebirth—beautiful flutes and strings, romantic imagery that goes straight for the Spiritus Mundi, and in the middle a disturbing passage filled with muted accusation. "Cyprus Avenue": Van contemplates little girls and craziness way up on way up on way up on the avenue of trees. "Madame George": a novelistic work of genius. More scenes from Cyprus Avenue, with George—whose name may be Joy—falling into (or inducing) a trance. The boy, Van, says goodbye—"Gotta go"—and as he leaves, "the room is filled with music laughter music dancing music all around the room." "Ballerina": a song which Van says may be about a hooker (he's not sure, it doesn't matter) and which haunts like a beautiful dream or a nightmare. "Slim Slow Slider": guitars and eerie horns create another dream, more haunting still. Death and bereavement hover above Ladbroke Grove.

Moondance (1970). Into the mystic, on the mellow side. "Stoned Me": quintessential Morrison, stoned just like goin' home by a summer shower. "Crazy Love": an incredibly sweet acknowledgment that her fine sense of humor is something to love . . . I'll take every cut on the first side, with the exception of "Moondance," a jazz song about which Van once said, "Frank Sinatra wouldn't be out of place singing that." Well, exactly. Its replacement: "Brand New Day" from side two.

His Band and the Street Choir (1970). Pleasant melodies, playful hooks, and as Van himself said in an interview, not much going on. I'll settle for "Blue Money," a pun-filled song about time and cash. Take five, honey.

Van the Man. A classic bootleg recorded mostly at concerts in 1970 and 1971. "Just Like a Woman": an unembellished, deeply felt version I like better than Dylan's. "Moondance": loose and easy and very peaceful. "Caledonia Soul Music": eighteen minutes of mesmerizing guitar, mandolin, piano, and Van's voice, which hums like an ancient tenor horn and chants, "Caledonia soul music/Tell me what it is." What it seems to be is something that lolls in the air, delights, and soothes.

Tupelo Honey (1971). More scenes from the marriage. "Wild Night": the one lonely song on the album, a mix of fear/despair/ epiphany and unstoppable beat—the wind catches your feet (sends you flying, crying) and the inside jukebox roars out just like thunder. "You're My Woman": slow, powerful R&B that builds for intense

lovers-as-shining-lights imagery and then recedes. "Tupelo Honey":
child of "Crazy Love," every bit as sweet as.

Saint Dominic's Preview (1972). Post-marriage toughness and
grace. "Jackie Wilson Said (I'm in Heaven When You Smile)":
(a) neatly deals with the sacred/profane dichotomy; (b) rocks out.
"Redwood Tree": catchy tune, uplifting story about a boy, his dog,
his dad, and what they may have learned. "Almost Independence
Day": Van singing like a guitar (with a Moog) (for a bit too long)
about boats, harbors, fireworks—about America. "Listen to the
Lion": something like what Yeats had in my mind when he wrote,
"my language beaten into one name."

Hardnose the Highway (1973). Turgid Vietnamese-peasant-sees-
dove-of-peace cover art, leafy imagery that connotes the Small Mind,
and a self-righteous ditty called "The Great Deception" ("Have you
ever heard about the great Rembrandt/ . . . he didn't have enough
money for brushes"). Everybody scrapes bottom sometime. A pass.

Veedon Fleece (1975). A magnificently gentle album of Gaelic
mysticism, lit from within—recorder, flute, and guitar music that
sounds centuries old and utterly newborn. I'm taking every cut and
giving special praise to a few. "Linden Arden Stole the Highlights":
the mournful tale of a man who loved the little children and took
the law into his own hands. "Who Was That Masked Man?": a
sad, high vocal like Curtis Mayfield gone to heaven and lyrics like,
"Oh, ain't it lonely/When you're livin' with a gun." "Bulbs" and
"Cul de Sac": uptempo, filled with puns and mystery. "You Don't
Pull No Punches but You Don't Push the River": blues sensibility,
more puns and mystery, and a search for apocryphal fleece.

Period of Transition (1977). Too loose, too self-conscious (assis-
tance from Dr. John), short on evocation, but with a Memphis/New
Orleans groove that makes me more forgiving than I ought to be.
"The Eternal Kansas City": a chorus out of "You Can't Always
Get What You Want," a lonesome question asked again and again
as if persistence might actually help, homage paid to Charlie Parker
and Billie Holiday. "Joyous Sound": energetic gospel rock. "Flamingos Fly": an old Morrison song that points toward the mystic.
"Heavy Connection": in remembrance of Percy Sledge.

Wavelength (1978). Mystical imagery (nights, stars, dancing) but without the big risks and short on magic. First-class commercial music. "Wavelength": a very good rock and roll song. "Kingdom Hall": a not at all bad rock and roll song (its literal-minded command to throw away all inhibitions, though, is typical of what happens when the language of the edge is brought back to a safe place). "Santa Fe"/"Beautiful Obsession": written with Jackie DeShannon in 1968, the old rich melodic patterns and a new ending that takes Van's fondness for protracted fadeouts to its logical conclusion—a whole new song, in fact. "Take It Where You Find It": Lost Dreams and Found Dreams in America, Part 132, not quite into the mystic.

The Last Waltz (1978). "Tura Lural Lural (That's an Irish Lullabye)": a Bing Crosby chestnut as impassioned blues-rock. "Well, it's often in dreams that I wander . . ." By the time I knew my grandmother, she lived in town, but this song seems to be about the farm she worked for nearly fifty years. Someone—my grandmother? my mother?—is rocking me outside the kitchen door. I am a child, capable of being wholly comforted. This is what the old Spiritus Mundi is all about.

Over the centuries, the Irish have learned that life is easier if you placate the boss:

"It's Too Late to Stop Now," my desert-island album, was recorded in L.A. and London in 1973. It's not Van's greatest (live records seldom are), but it's a good deal more than a *Greatest Hits Jr.* The band is excellent. And large. And fancy. In addition to standard-issue piano, organ, guitar, bass, and drums, it has prominent saxes, a trumpet, three violins (first: Nathan Rubin, concert master of the Oakland Symphony), a viola, and a cello. They play fine. More to the point, they play fine rock and roll. (Opposition, tension, art.)

Since rock and roll started out to be a revolution against everything safe and smooth and processed, raw edges are as close to its true spirit as anything is. Live albums omit the overdubbing and let you listen to the singer clearing his throat; they also let you listen to the audience listening to the band (which, in a variation on one of Van's lines, is listening right back at them). Live albums are about people touching other people, about intercourse. Because of Van's built-in distancer, the audience side of the intercourse on "*It's Too Late to Stop Now*" has more to do with respectful enthusiasm than abandoned ardor. (When they do get a dialogue going, the comments—and the decibel level of same—are reminiscent of those you'd expect at a first-rate jazz concert.) The album has little extraneous chatter, no tedious stretches of applause, and almost none of the slightly off-the-beat clapping that can make live albums painful. Spontaneity hasn't been used as an excuse for sloppy sound.

All that, and an intelligent selection of songs that draws on six of Van's records and five of the musicians he learned from. Like most live albums, this one's short on concept—but not on structure. The shape corresponds to a line Van improvises on "Cyprus Avenue": it's about a process. Each of his albums synthesizes the past, and each adds up to more than the sum of its parts. "*It's Too Late to Stop Now*" restates the past and resynthesizes it in another dimension. Van listens to several lions on this album, and to several of his lions' more or less domesticated relatives. He gets into the mystic, he gets down, and he gets down to basics, which is to say roots.

CAT'S CRADLE: (NO NEED TO) FEEL LIKE A FATHERLESS CHILD. On one-third of the cuts, Van gives us context; he sings four blues and two soul covers. Although Van's post-Them sensibility has little to do with such blues preoccupations as sex and the devil, he obviously feels right at home singing black American blues, particularly if the music is rural and electrified. "Help Me," by Sonny Boy Williamson, is raw country boogie; Van's version takes you out on the dance floor and back to the Biscuit Boys. His cover of Williamson's "Take Your Hand Out of My Pocket" is the only one on the album that sounds emulative—as a result, the bitterness seems forced and the arrangement tricky.

No problems at all with the slurred, low-down vocal on Willie Dixon's "I Just Want to Make Love to You," a much recorded song (by, among others, Muddy Waters, B. B. King, Bo Diddley, Chuck Berry, Etta James, Lou Rawls, the Stones). Dixon played bass for Muddy Waters in the fifties and wrote "Hoochie Coochie Man" and

"Little Red Rooster"—blues for a Chicago shouter. Van shouts hoarsely, sings a duet with a guitar, and demonstrates his mastery of dynamics. (I JUST. wanna make. *Love. to You.*) "Ain't Nothin' You Can Do" was done by Bobby Bland with a soulful balance of dignity and despair that builds toward agonized cries. Van's version has a more complex arrangement, a stronger groove, and (apart from the first few lines, which sound strangely reassuring) a rougher approach.

He also roughens up his soul covers. "Bring It on Home to Me" is gritty and hungry and miles away from Sam Cooke's sad gentleness. For his tribute to Ray Charles, Van includes "I Believe to My Soul," which Ray wrote in the days before his impeccably dressed soul began frequenting the middle of the road. Ray sings, "I think I'm gonna have to use my roar," and follows through on the threat with a gospel chorus; Van does it with horns. "These Dreams of You" is another tribute, a song Van wrote after dreaming about Ray Charles. It has blues lyrics, an R&B groove, and an odd but characteristic shape—the song begins in anger, sketches several hostile encounters, and ends with an angel-filled lullabye/love song. There's also a tribute within the tribute: Stagger Lee and Billy the Lion come out of the mythology of black American music and into Van's nightmares ("Dreamed we played cards in the dark/And you lost and you lied").

STRAY CAT: FEEL LIKE A STREET FIGHT. (Or, as Carl Perkins put it, "Rave on, cats!" This is rock and roll.) The Beatles sang, "Here comes the sun"; Van, with Them, sang, "Here comes the night," and immediately won my heart. Too bad it isn't his song. It was written by wheeler-dealer Bert Berns, who brought Van to the U.S. for *Blowin' Your Mind* (and who showed the Isleys how to Twist & Shout). The *Them* version begins with a great "WOW! Here it comes!" but gets mired in a popsy sound; this version is vitiated by strings and a too moderate tempo. Nothing could vitiate "Gloria," which comes complete with dirty guitar, dirty vocal, and orgasmic screams. Listening to it, you know that Jesus died for somebody's sins—Van and G,L,O,R,I,A are likely candidates. "Domino," from *Street Choir*, isn't in the class of "Wild Night," but you can't sit it out. Good hot sax and horns, some intriguing laissez-faire psychology, and a line which gets at a primary need in Van's life: "Just wanta hear some rhythm and blues music on the radio. Uh huh. All right."

HOUSE CAT: FEEL LIKE STAYING HOME. This otherwise well-balanced album is short on ballads about hearth and cream and love sweet love. "Warm Love," written after Van's divorce, has a banal story about picnicking amid "green grass so tall" sung in a distinctly nonloving staccato. But later in the song Van's voice becomes a horn that twines among other horns and he sings fluent variations on "it's everpresent everywhere."

LION: FEEL LIKE GOING HOME. (Or, as Yeats put it, "A passion-driven exultant man sings out/Sentences that he has never thought." This is the mystic.) In these songs, Van makes his own blues. "Cyprus Avenue" sends him back to Belfast in pursuit of Nabokovian pleasures and pain. On *"It's Too Late To Stop Now"*—which has a less soulful, more sketchy version than the one on *Astral Weeks*—he leaves out "No one can stop me from lovin' you, baby/ So young and so bold/Fourteen, yeah I know." Like most of the mystical songs, "Cyprus Avenue" alternates between sharply perceived scenes and abstract passages about emotions. It calls up familiar imagery—autumn, trees, lonesome trains that take lovers away, wine that eases the loneliness, olden-day ladies returning from olden-day fairs. The song ends with an invocation: dozens of sanctified changes rung on "You were standing there in all your revelation."

"Saint Dominic's Preview" is also about Ireland—about being far from home during troubled times. The title is related to a mass for Irish peace held at St. Dominic's church in San Francisco, where Van was trying to make a new life. The imagery is glancing, oblique, and for the most part forlorn: people determined not to feel anyone else's pain, freedom marchers who feel the pain but can't solve the problems, a celebrity who has to face reporters and his own worst smile, orange crates scattered at the Safeway supermarket in the rain. Violins and horns take flight in beautiful and intricate patterns; the music sounds like a lament.

The two *Moondance* songs are lighter and more hopeful. "Caravan" cuts between gypsies 'round the campfire and a twentieth-century love story in which difficulties are illuminated/eliminated when electric lights and radios are turned on. The music is lush and contrapuntal: Vivaldi as soulman. (Listen to the first few bars of "Caravan" for an illustration of that gesture my friend and I tried to define.) "Into the Mystic" is a great song about finding connection and going home—except that part of the time Van seems to be singing, "When that foghorn blows/You know I *won't* be coming home." (His lion thrives on ambiguity.) Near the beginning, a violin soars high above the rest of the music, then floats down, a leaf. Near the end, horns modulate from brassy to majestic, accompanied by quick, high, flighty violin figures. A song to rock the soul.

In "Listen to the Lion," Van's love comes tumblin' down (it's obviously the midnight hour), he searches his soul for the mysterious leonine thing, his tears like water flow. The words are clichéd. The song is utterly magical. Listening for the lion, he hears the Holy Ghost and chants in tongues—glossolalia, ecstatic utterance that sounds not unlike a roar. The song ends with a leap back in time; we sail from Denmark way up to Caledonia, and for a little while we can believe in the possibility of mystical rebirth.

Now about this lion. It's more than a sound—something like living up to the blues, something like what Yeats had in mind when he wrote about climbing to a place swept bare by the salt sea wind. The lion is related to extremities and dislocation and questing, to big questions and possibly big answers. It's related to defenselessness and instinctual response.

Late one night, the prisoners described in *Cold Stone Jug* go beyond the level of desperation they've learned to live with. First one, then another, then dozens of them begin to bay at the full moon. The next day they pretend it didn't happen. In "The Cat and the Moon," Yeats writes of a black cat who stares at his nearest kin and dances to the elemental music of the night: "Minnaloushe creeps through the grass,/Alone, important, and wise,/And lifts to the changing moon/His changing eyes." The cat and the moon are the lion.

There's another kind of defenselessness: the intensity which comes from discarding self-protection because you figure that you don't have a choice or that you've got nothing left to lose. Robert Johnson singing out of his demons. Janis Joplin crying, "It ain't fair!" Neil Young—drunk, angry, off-key—mourning his friends in "Tonight's the Night." Eric Clapton, on his knees, finding the blues at the beginning of "Layla." The lion also has something to do with the overwhelmingly beautiful music after the piano break in "Layla"—pain accepted and transcended, the peace that lies on the other side of despair.

Leadbelly dealt with his demons in bed and in jail and on the run. Unlike Robert Johnson, he lived long enough to reach a place where demons seemed like home to him and he could be calm. In "Good Night Irene," he sings the line about sitting down by the fireside in much the same way he sings, "Sometimes I get a great notion to jump in the river and drown." He also sings, "You gotta ride it like you find it." Van Morrison has a version of that attitude: "You don't pull no punches but you don't push the river, you don't pull no punches and you don't push the river."

My grandmother was fond of taking solitary moonlit walks and listening to baseball games on the radio; she could recite fantastical fairy tales and Cub RBIs. The summer she turned ninety, her doctor suggested that she might consider eating more sensibly—say, toast and tea for lunch. Most days she had toast and tea . . . and half a dozen radishes. My father, her son-in-law and friend, sometimes played a lonesome harmonica late at night. Their friendship was based on a shared fondness for wisecracks. One day, watching her eat radishes, he said, "Don't they come back on you?" She grinned. "Come back better every time."

Willie Mae Thornton sang with the blend of resignation and rebelliousness and pride that poor people learn early on. She made a wonderful recording of "Hound Dog," that consummately silly imitation black song (written by white men) which earned Elvis buckets of money. It earned Big Mama Thornton about fifty cents. In the middle of her version of the song, with a neat mixture of drollery and rue, she turns to her guitarist and says, "I like your tan." The lion has something to do with humor that encompasses pain.

In the end, of course, it gets away, as lions ought to. Leadbelly once remarked that black people like the blues because they were born with them. He added, "Now everybody have the blues. Sometimes they don't know what it is." Van Morrison sings, "There's something going on/It fill you up, it fill you up, it fill you up now./ Well you don't know what it is,/But you don't know what it is,/But you don't need to know."

One night last year, "Into the Mystic" was playing; I was dancing. The music built for "I want to hear it, I don't have to fear it, and I want to rock your gypsy soul." On about "want to rock" I came down from a leap—the sort of maneuver I've been unable to do since ruining my knee on ballet ten years ago. The leap was not physiologically possible. It happened. I limped for a few days afterwards, but it didn't matter much: for an instant, I left the ground.

Step right up, just like a ballerina. And step right up and step right up. Ballerina. You're going somewhere and I know you won't be back, I know you're dying (a girl at play that, it may be, had danced her life away, for now being dead it seemed that she of dancing dreamed). Could you find me? Would you kiss my eyes? Lay me down in silence easy, to be born again (grown nothing, knowing all) in another place, in another time, you go out, you come back. Gotta go. Come back. (Come back better every time.) Looking for a brand new start, for a brand new . . .

Or: *Shah lah lah lah lah lah lah lah-lah lah-lah-tee-dah. Lah tee dah.*

BEGGARS BANQUET

THE ROLLING STONES (LONDON PS–539)
1968

SIMON FRITH

I've had the Rolling Stones' *Beggars Banquet* ten years already and it still makes me laugh. It's the cleverest record the Stones ever made and the subtlest, and it includes all the usual arrogance, dance, and dirt. If I ever stopped learning from *Beggars Banquet* I could still jump up and down to it and reminisce. I don't know how Mick Jagger became the symbol of rock and roll but he did and I've had to think about him and his band and his music more than I've had to think about anything else in rock.

Which isn't to say that I've ever been much of a Rolling Stones fan. In the days when people paired off and cool people were Stones people, I was a Beatles fan—they were more comfortable—and later, when the Stones became The Greatest Show on Earth, I couldn't get a ticket. I've only seen them once and that was later still, a routine show featuring Percy the Plastic Phallus and Billy Preston dancing. I wasn't that impressed. Over the years I've bought few Stones records and liked fewer; "Satisfaction" remains, for me, the most overrated record ever. Mick Jagger and Keith Richard were the first stars I ever interviewed but even that was a mistake—I'd been hoping for a few words with Andrew Loog Oldham.

Even then, in 1965, I was asking Johnny Rotten's question:

"Who cares?" My Stones pose was weariness, a pose I've feigned pretty well ever since. But it's a pose that's taken effort to maintain and reflects a furtive obsession. Making sense of rock has meant making sense of the Stones and when *Beggars Banquet* came out in 1968 I changed my usual habits—bought this white album, left the Beatles' white album on its parallel shop floor pile. The Beatles still made more comfortable music but *Beggars Banquet* was the most interesting record I'd ever heard.

Most rock records aren't difficult to understand. They draw on commonplaces of community and adolescence: easy listening, good dancing, simple emotions, and sharp images. From this point of view *Beggars Banquet* isn't difficult either, just a mainstream Stones LP, party music with a sneer and a leer. But its cleverness makes the difference. The Stones, as intellectuals, share an acute, almost contemptuous grasp of their own paradoxes: British makers of American music, white romancers of black culture, middle-class triflers with working-class urgencies, adult observers of youth, aesthetes of body music. *Beggars Banquet* is the celebration of the contradictions of British rock culture.

Which means, for a start, that the Stones are not musical geniuses. They're solid and insistent (the best rhythm section in rock) but their talent is hard-working rather than magical; theirs are craftsmen's skills, with craftsmen's loving knowledge of the tools of their trade. The basis of the Stones sound is not an up-front flashiness, but the background rhythms; Brian Jones's contribution to *Beggars Banquet* is unclear but since he's been gone the Stones have used journeyman guitarists, Mick Taylor and Ronnie Wood, comrade artisans, nothing startling.

It's up to Mick Jagger to carry the charisma and the result is mannered; on record Jagger continually cuts back from his own emotions, mocks his own pretentions as a white blues singer. Irony is implicit in his Stones persona. Similarly, as writers Jagger and Richard are efficient but self-conscious. Their songs rarely take the breath away—no images to haunt like Bob Dylan's, no language as beautiful as Smokey Robinson's, none of John Lennon's plain talk. The Stones tend to vulgarity, to the slyly pounding use of rock clichés. The magic of the Stones lies in their transformation of the ordinary into the extraordinary and if this transformation is hard to grasp analytically, it clearly rests on their awe-inspiring commitment to rock and roll itself.

The Stones have commented on this themselves, but "It's Only Rock 'n Roll" was a shoddy record, evading the questions it raised. Keith Richard is "only" a rock and roll star (the only rock and roll star?) but it is a life, not a pose, a life that is disturbing and not much to be envied. The spirit of Keith Richard, gaunt and bad-toothed, a never-sleeping swirl of sound, hovers over the uneasy dreams of all rock fans, and this haunting image can't be exorcised by boogie clichés. It needs more sensitive, more cerebral expression and *Beggars Banquet* is the Stones' most intellectual account of their rock and roll values.

Hedonism is usually taken as the basis of these values—rock and roll and sex and drugs and if it feels good, do it. But hedonism isn't really what the Stones are about. Sex is the key to their pleasure (they've rarely celebrated drug use, hippie-style) and the Stones' pleasure in sex is notorious. *Beggars Banquet* includes one of Jagger's most explicit sexual performances, "Stray Cat Blues." Over a seedy blues backing he slurs a smug commentary on young groupie sex: "Bet your mother don't know you can scratch like that!"

What's erotic about this track is not its abandon but its detachment. Jagger isn't wheedling these girls up to his rooms, he's taking their presence for granted. It's not his needs he's worried about, but their plain expression, without romantic or psychological frills. The music is sensuous in its very laziness: this isn't a boogie band's masturbation fantasy, a simulated urgency, it's a blues, and Keith Richard's chord changes are churned out with a sure solidity, a sexual certainty that is much more disturbing than a rock guitarist's usual phallic come-on. As Jagger's vowels get longer and longer, more and more insidious, it becomes obvious that his contempt is less for the girls involved—children going about their pleasure business—than for the straight world that can only experience such simple sex as cheap, nasty, titillating.

And so Jagger plays the part of the leering seducer, parodies the Jagger image his listeners need to measure against their own respectability. The Stones' own sexual morality is expressed not in "Stray

Cat Blues" but in "Parachute Woman," a clearer statement of sexual need. It's solid again, R&B thrust and chorus, but Jagger is deeper-voiced, uses his harmonica to make the traditional demanding sound and says matter-of-factly what he wants. Lyrically, the song is unimpressive—standard blues metaphors without much resonance, wit or point—but emotionally it makes clear the Stones' claim to adult status. Their case is made without musical rhetoric, teenage self-pity, or male drama. "I'm in for a spell of paradise" is an assertion, not a dream; life on the road and the morality of the moment. A sexist song but without sexist consequence, because what is being expressed is not sexual pride but emotional disinterest.

Most popular songs are love songs, but love is too sociable a concept for the Stones. They've made love songs, but they're atypical. "Angie," for example, is dependent on the language and sentiment, the pretty tune and vapid rhythm, of pop convention. The best Stones songs about love are non-love songs, statements of non-involvement, no commitment. "No Expectations" is the Stones' finest non-love song. In an acoustic blues of great tenderness, Jagger never once pulls back from his argument that "love is like water, that flashes on a stone." Spells of paradise are conveyed now by a stately but inexorable musical movement. The emotional point is that a traveler's life is incompatible with domesticity: no ties mean no expectations, no expectations mean no ties. The argument is descriptive, not moral: the road and the home each have their own decencies, loyalties, and self-respect, neither life is better than the other. The music is dignified, the slide guitar adds pathos. What is involved here is not hedonism, or even self-indulgence.

In the beginning, Andrew Loog Oldham decided that the best way to sell the Stones was in shock horror headlines. Out went Ian Stewart (looked too much the car-cleaning suburban man) and in came silly album sleeves. The Stones soap opera has run ever since and Oldham's original pranks have had sinister consequences, projecting the Stones into their roles as the villains of Altamont, the idols of decadent chic. The dumbest track on *Beggars Banquet* is "Sympathy for the Devil." Jagger as Satan wends his way through famous dark events from the Crucifixion of Christ to the assassinations of the Kennedys. Lyrically, the song is idle in the extreme. The images are strung together with little rhyme or reason—is the Russian Revolution really equivalent to a Kennedy assassination? Jagger indulges in some surprisingly glib moralizing. "After all," he smirks, "it was you and me."

Bullshit. It wasn't him or me that killed the Kennedys. Any interesting point the song might make about popular obsessions with evil and violence is lost in the swirl of "ooh oohs," in the falsetto riffs. Any sense of doom is undercut by the song's jolly beat; lyrical portentousness is punctured by the chirpy percussion. "Sympathy for the Devil" has been heard as the *Macbeth* of rock music, a song with the mysterious power to impel new dark deeds, but that's not how the Stones play it. If "Stray Cat Blues" is a cosmic commentary on their supposed sexual appetites, "Sympathy for the Devil" is a comic comment on their supposed outrageousness. It's funny, sure enough, and as a piece of devilcraft it's about as disturbing as *The Omen* and much less upsetting than *Beggars Banquet*'s other religious song, "Prodigal Son."

I've always lived a decent, sober, careful life, and I've always found the story of the prodigal son the most unpleasant in the New Testament. It's straightforward enough: A father has two sons. One day the younger one asks for his share of the property, gets it, converts it into cash and takes off for a good time. Eventually, when he has squandered it all "in reckless living," is destitute and starving, he goes back home again. His father sees him coming, rejoices, kills a fatted calf to celebrate the prodigal's return. The older brother, who has meanwhile been working dutifully for his father, keeping the family income going, is dismayed and won't join the feast—his father has never celebrated his *good* behavior. "But," his father remonstrates, "your brother here was dead and has come back to life/Was lost and is found."

As a parable of forgiveness, I suppose this is okay but the secular emotion it inspires (at least in all of us who identify with the older brother) is resentment. In the same circumstances I'd sulk even worse. The Stones, of course, identify easily and naturally with the prodigal. The version of the tale they chose—written by black sanctified singer Rev. Robert Wilkins—is a blues story: simple, unadorned, detached. Jagger narrates in the first person. He is the prodigal son, returning to his father, not expecting the fatted calf but not surprised by it either. For the prodigal the whole affair is neither emotional (as it is for his father) nor is it instructive (as it is for his brother); it is just another episode in the prodigal life that creates its own morality as it goes along.

The Stones' performance of the story is stately and without tension; their self-assurance is stunning. The real point of the Stones soap opera turns out to be that they get away with behavior most of us daren't risk for fear of the consequences. They take the risks, get away with them, and don't much care either way. Sex and drugs and rock and roll: no expectations but no consequences either, and for the rest of us, engaged in constant behavioral calculus, it is the Stones' lack of interest in moral accounting and not their supposed "sinfulness" that is shocking.

1968 was a good year for the Stones to consider the story of the prodigal son. It was a very moral year. Counter-culture and counter-politics came together with an intensity of self-righteousness that even the Stones had to respect. The year did, in a sense, mark the Stones' return to their domestic base. After the arty indulgence of *Their Satanic Majesties Request,* "Jumpin' Jack Flash" and then *Beggars Banquet* reached back to the values and sounds of the Stones' R&B dance music days. These records had an Englishness, a provinciality, that belied the Stones' international aura. But the 1968 problem for the Stones was not to respond to some notion of the people's morality. They never renounced their success or their style; they weren't, whatever happened, John and Yoko. The Stones' problem in 1968 was, rather, that their reckless living had exhausted their resources. They needed to go home again and going home, in this context, meant a grappling with a notion of collectivity. Politics was much more of a challenge than psychedelia. The counter-culture had given the Stones another version of individualism and indulgence; counter-politics posed the problem of joining.

Their response was "Street Fighting Man," their finest single and the cornerstone of *Beggars Banquet.* On the surface, "Street Fighting Man" is an ironic commentary on the Stones' own position in 1968: their detachment from everyone else's passions, their doubts about the effectiveness of such passions in sleepy London town, their own cop-out—"What can a poor boy do, but to sing in a rock and roll band?" But beneath the lyrical commentary is a more subtle musical commentary. "Street Fighting Man" makes a direct link between rock and roll and politics that qualifies the wry alternatives of the lyrics. Rock's beat is made military, its steadiness and uniformity are emphasized, its power and vigor become ominous. The Stones borrow a Pete Townshend device, opening with strummed rhythm guitar before thundering in with the sustained sounds of electricity. The transformation of rock language into militaristic marching music reverses the point of the lyrics: the argument is not that rock is a source of revolutionary energy and solidarity (the Yippie suggestion) but that revolution in its 1968 youth expression had no more solid basis than the community of rock and roll consumers. Politics, the Stones concluded, is just a matter of style. If marching in the streets was collective behavior, it was still no more meaningful than any other form of rock and roll behavior. The oblique reference is to "Dancing in the Street," Martha and the Vandellas' 1963 hit, but while that dancing record later took on resonance for black rioters in the streets, the Stones' "Street Fighting Man" was only a dance record. The street activities of 1968 became, in the Stones' sneer, just another metaphor for self-indulgence. The Stones had come home, but only to scoff.

For Mick Jagger, son of the middle class, London School of Economics student and elitist, the biggest joke has always been his fans' romanticization of the working class. His own false cockney accent and all-purpose dumb prole pose have been a useful way of keeping the press distant, but the Stones' music has rarely expressed any affection for workers. The normal line is a bohemian contempt for the commonplace and a long-standing Stones convention is the jokey redneck song. On *Beggars Banquet* we get "Dear Doctor"—"Oh help me, dear doctor, I'm damaged"—sung in nasal harmonies to a raucous bar-band backing. And we get to laugh at some poor dolt who's got involved with a wedding. The theme is not sympathy for a victim of the tension beween love and freedom, but contempt for someone who can only suffer such tension passively. The track has a musical coldness that only a highly intellectual rock band could manage.

Most of the time the Stones have got away with their contempt for everyone else because it answers the snobbery of their audiences, but in 1968, when everyone in Europe was busy identifying with the proletariat, this position needed justification. The Stones' most touching 1968 song was "Jigsaw Puzzle," an all-purpose Bob Dylan-style number, instant pop in which Jagger tries to persuade us that he does have a social critique, that he too has been an outcast all his life. It's the jigsaw puzzle of life—the Stones' imagery is from a bad sermon, a series of familiarly resonant pictures: the tramp on the doorstep, the bishop's daughter, the queen shouting, "What the hell is going on?" Desolation Row again and just as meaningless but less literate and not as witty. Funnier, though—by the time we get to the twenty thousand grandmas screaming which side are you on we might as well be listening to the Bonzo Dog Band. Jagger sings convincingly, the rhythm section is masterful in its persistence, and the result is monoto-rock that I could listen to forever.

As sociology, however, "Jigsaw Puzzle" is silly—the Stones don't need to make their political points through poetry. Oscar Wilde once remarked that he favored socialism because it would free him from the burden of having to worry about other people. The Stones' position is the same, and the imagery of "Jigsaw Puzzle" is misleading. The Stones are voluntary outcasts and their attitude toward other outcasts isn't solidarity but curiosity and amusement. *Beggars Banquet* the album is called, and the inside sleeve makes the message plain—the Stones as beggars, gorging on the illicit fruits of some bourgeois kitchen. The picture is straight from a Buñuel film. But unlike Buñuel, the Stones don't see their grotesques and losers, their exiles on mainstreet, as sources of grace or honesty but rather as the objects of aesthetic titillation. The value of outcasts is simply in their contrast to the ugliness of the mundane, or even, in 1968, to the working class.

In 1968 the Stones were too bright not to make their own comment on capitalism but their critique was exclusively aesthetic. Capitalism is condemned for its ugliness; the working class are especially exploited because they are especially ugly. "Factory Girl" is an acoustic song, almost a folk track, with Jagger again taking the worker's voice—but stolid now, not jokey. He's waiting for a girl with curlers in her hair, with stains all down her dress, but he's waiting patiently, his feet are getting wet. The girl is described without emotional comment; there's no suggestion that she's worth anything more than the description, no reference to qualities under her curlers or even under her dress. The song is profoundly unerotic and it is not clear what our response is meant to be. The simple strummed sound and Jagger's easy vocal suggest an innocence, but an innocence to be pitied rather than admired or enjoyed. This factory worker is pathetic, a far cry from 1968 political myths, and the Stones' music, for once, has no anger in it. The irony involved is more a matter of distaste than outrage. "Is this the working class you want us to march with?"

The Stones return to the theme in *Beggars Banquet*'s closing track. "Salt of the Earth" is a drinking song. It combines the militaristic musical references of "Street Fighting Man" with the music hall references of "Factory Girl" and comes straight from a pub. A hearty melody, a solid sound, and Jagger ringing the changes, drinking to hard-working people and uncounted heads and back-breaking men and common foot-soldiers and stay-at-home voters. The music builds up the sense of jolly community and only slowly does its irony seep through—this emotion is false, these are the emptily patronizing phrases the ruling class has mouthed through the ages. When Jagger steps out of the chorus it is to make a different point about the people: "They don't look real to me, in fact they look so strange . . . " And still the music builds, the chorus soars, until, as the populism peaks, the Stones have achieved the maximum distance between what the music feels like and what the music means. The references as they echo back across the album—references to marching in the street, to working-class power, to styles of collectivism—are plain and sour.

Which is why I've never really been a Stones fan. I've always heard them as petit bourgeois jesters, who've taken delight in standing morality on its head but retained a touchy egotism, a contempt for the masses that they share with any respectable small shopkeeper. Their rebellion has been a grand gesture, an aesthetic style without a social core. It is a politically ambiguous position and the Stones' sharp worldliness has always been confused by childishness, sexism, a surly individualism. The British punk point—"No more Stones in '77!"—rests on the angry argument that however excitingly the Stones say it, they have nothing socially significant to say.

I share the instincts of this argument, but then I listen to *Beggars Banquet* again and know that the punks have got it all wrong. The Stones' best music remains the source of rock's greatest energy and joy, and even for the punks—especially for the punks —the Stones remain the greatest symbol of rock and roll possibility. It's back to my own Stones problem: bad politics, good rock and roll—how to reconcile them? The punk cliché is that the Stones were politically okay once, but got rich and famous and irrelevant. This is nonsense. The Stones haven't changed their position from the day they started; their rock and roll may have got worse but their politics were never any better. Which leaves only one other possibility: good rock and roll *equals* bad politics. Don't the grace and power and dignity of *Beggars Banquet* depend on its social detachment?

I've spent ten years of my life avoiding the conclusion and I'm quite happy to spend the rest of my life at it. I mean, if I had to choose between rock and Marxism I'd choose rock, but I still don't think the choice is necessary because *Beggars Banquet* moves me, makes me laugh, but it has also made me think, about rock, about politics, and, for all the Stones' snooty bohemianism, their account of their world fits my account of mine. It even illuminates it.

Beggars Banquet is constructed around a series of paradoxes but all its puzzles rest on the central ambiguity of the Stones' history: are they earnest, hard-working craftsmen or dilettante, pleasure-seeking playboys? This ambiguity isn't unique to the Stones. All popular entertainers work at our play, dedicate themselves to our relaxation. The importance of the Stones is that they take pleasure completely seriously. Their commitment to it is total and the result is neither hedonism nor outrage but an awesome self-sufficiency. *Beggars Banquet* makes its own comment on the Stones' stardom, on their lives of glamour and excitement; the music has a pathos, an appreciation of the false promises of pleasure that has been matched in rock only by Elvis Presley.

And it is in this respect that Stones music is political: not as an analysis of conflict or exploitation, certainly no commitment to party or class, but powerful and critical all the same. Punk's political ideologues, like sixties politicos before them, measure musical seriousness by reference to reality; my point is that play is as much a reality as work—and the Stones have played more seriously than anyone else. *Beggars Banquet*, so intense in its pursuit of pleasure, lays bare the weight borne by our notions of love and sex, the secret melancholy of life in the consumer collective. These are as much effects of current capitalism as dole queues and boring jobs and material squalor and the Stones' pleasure perspective gives us a new sense of them, a sense strengthened, not weakened, by the Stones' own aesthetic stance. In other words, the function of the Stones' rock and roll dedication (which, in 1968, seemed cynical) is not self-indulgence or escape but defiance. *Beggars Banquet* celebrates the reality of capitalist pleasure and denies its illusions. No expectations, a lot of laughs—the Stones' strength derives from their prodigality, from their denial of consequence.

The Stones aren't an activist band—"Street Fighting Man" is still the fairest comment on that—but this no longer bothers me. Like them, I no longer believe in the political possibilities of counterculture—no useful revolution is going to announce itself through stereo headphones. I value the Stones differently. As the poets of lonely leisure they've made more sense of my "free time" than anyone else, and I can't live my nights and weekends without them. *Beggars Banquet* is pre-revolutionary art and can't get me *complete* satisfaction. But what the hell, it's the best there is.

PRESENTING
THE FABULOUS RONETTES
FEATURING VERONICA

THE RONETTES (PHILLES PHLP–4006)
1964

JIM MILLER

Don't want to spend my life,
    living in a rock 'n' roll fantasy
Don't want to spend my life,
    living on the edge of reality
Don't want to waste my life,
    hiding away anymore.
                    —Ray Davies,
                        "A Rock 'n' Roll Fantasy"

Her motel was down the strip from the shopping center where the Ronettes were appearing. This was her first tour in almost ten years. In 1964, the Ronettes had headlined at the Brooklyn Fox and the Copa and toured with the Beatles and Rolling Stones. In 1973, they were playing suburban clubs catering to dimly-lit memories.

A colleague had invited me to help interview Veronica, lead singer for the Ronettes and once upon a time wife of Phil Spector, the world's greatest rock and roll producer. In their heyday they had made sublime records together. But after she married him in 1966, the Ronettes disbanded, and Veronica virtually disappeared. In the following six years, Spector cut only two singles with her—

records that scarcely approached the glories of "Be My Baby," the Ronettes' first and biggest hit, released in 1963.

She was staying in a suite with her mother, who chaperoned our interview with the same discreet care she must have once devoted to the career of the original Ronettes—a trio consisting of her two daughters, Estelle and Veronica Bennett, and their cousin, Nedra Talley. Veronica's family was committed to entertainment. Her grandmother, who insisted that Ronnie learn three-part harmony with Estelle and Nedra, helped launch their career as "The Dolly Sisters"; later, they were called Ronnie and the Relatives. Billed as the Ronettes, the trio eventually found themselves dancing and singing with Joey Dee at the Peppermint Lounge, warming up audiences for Murray the K at the Brooklyn Fox, singing back-up on records by Bobby Rydell. Ronnie was scarcely sixteen.

One day, Estelle dialed a wrong number and got Phil Spector on the phone. After apologizing, she discovered that Phil had heard of the Ronettes, needed singers for a Crystals session, and would the Ronettes be interested in coming over? Or so the story goes.

Veronica greets us sweetly. Weary of living the life of a caged parakeet with Spector and hopeful of resurrecting her career as a singer, she has fled his sanctuary for a tour of the East Coast oldies circuit—venues numerous enough to sustain five different versions of "The Original Platters," depressing enough to dissuade all but the most desperate from making it a way of life.

Her teased hair cascades around eyes that are no longer quite hidden beneath a mountain of mascara. On stage, she still plays to the image of the tough chick. But in her room, she seems vulnerable, girlish, and rather at sea in the world. After confiding my own incurable passion for "Be My Baby," she thanks me with a kiss on the cheek.

On a desk lay several boxes of matches with gold-on-black block lettering: VERONICA ESTELLE NEDRA. Ronnie explains that Phil had gotten a number of these boxes made for the group's debut at the Copacabana, but that since few people outside the industry had attended that engagement and the extra boxes were cluttering the house, she had decided to bring some along to use on this tour.

Phil had not wanted her to make the trip. He disapproved of having his wife cheapen herself in nightclubs. He didn't like her exposing herself to the seamy side of show biz. Despite her pleas, he had also refused to reissue the one Ronettes album he had released on Philles, his own label, in 1964. Veronica said she felt sorry for the fans. I said I felt sorry for her.

After seeing her act at the oldies club, I felt even more sorry. Sounding like Helen Reddy with inflamed adenoids, she staggered through a set handicapped by a plodding pick-up band. Without the strings, horns and handclaps, "Be My Baby" and "Walking in the Rain" were empty. But she gamely went through the motions, relishing what little applause she won. Such recognition was a tangible symbol of her autonomy, proof of her independence from Spector. Several months later, they were divorced.

The main memento I carried away from our encounter was an autographed copy of *Presenting the Fabulous Ronettes Featuring Veronica*. For years, I coveted this album. In what I count as my greatest find as a collector, I had discovered a copy in 1970, in a supermarket cut-out bin. Ronnie was very obliging, signing my copy "To Jim, Very nice to meet You, Love always, Ronnie S. Ronettes." She drew an arrow from her name to her picture on the cover—as if she could be mistaken for anyone else.

But then, the album that presented her as an idol had also put her in her place. If the cover proclaimed "Featuring Veronica," the label, dropping her name, stated plainly, "Producer: PHIL SPECTOR." Ronnie might be elevated on a pedestal and Phil might even marry her, but for the record there was no question who was in command. Larry Levine's liner notes set the tone: "When I first met The Ronettes I didn't think they were going to be a very good group. Phil had said to me, 'I found this group, they're good looking, but they don't sing too well.' So I said, 'Well, why bother?' He said, 'I kind of promised their mother.' "

He had already proven himself as producer, entrepreneur, megalomaniacal mogul of pop. He had created his own record company. With the Crystals, Darlene Love, a small band of crack

Los Angeles sessionmen, arranger Jack Nitzsche, and engineer Larry Levine, he had forged his own unique "wall of sound." He was rock's most eccentric version yet of the self-made man.

His real gift was his ear for music. A child of fifties rock and roll, a composer and singer on a number one record at the age of seventeen, an understudy on the hits produced by Jerry Leiber and Mike Stoller for Ben E. King and the Drifters, Phil Spector cultivated a street-wise flair for image and melody. He was after a new concept in recorded sound. He took as prototypes uptown producers like George Goldner, uptown performers like the Chantels and Frankie Lymon, Brill Building songsmiths like Doc Pomus and Mort Shuman, Gerry Goffin and Carole King. Uninterested in merely emulating them, he was obsessed with outstripping them, doing what they had done, but doing it unimaginably better, making rock and roll records that were more refined, more direct, more sophisticated, and more powerful than anything anybody had ever heard before. With an astonishing mélange of raw instinct and Tin Pan Alley panache, he pushed "teen-feel" pop past adolescent sit-coms and straight into the heart of a sonic blitzkrieg that could have but one architect: Phil Spector, *auteur*, *artiste*, self-crowned king of rock and roll.

What Spector heard in Veronica's voice is hard to say. Under the kindest of circumstances, it is an unsteady instrument. Her wavering vibrato wobbles off pitch; her diction is slurred; her timing awkward. Yet in this ungainliness and in the native forcefulness of her voice, Spector encountered the sound of sincerity. Handed the most banal moon-June lyrics, Ronnie made them feel brand new, simply by sounding so anxious to please. She claims to have been in awe of Frankie Lymon. It shows in her expression of romantic sentiments with pre-adolescent innocence, an incongruity all the more seductive coming from a voluptuous 18-year-old dressed to kill.

Spector fell in love, not with Veronica Bennett, struggling singer, but rather with the sultry *chanteuse* he tried to transform her into. For a producer who specialized in throwaway albums, *Presenting the Fabulous Ronettes* shows signs of caring—and not only because it collects five of Spector's best singles. Ronnie brought a human presence to Spector's grandiose vision. In her voice, Spector found a challenge, and also a way of resurrecting the most shopworn sentiments with a conviction that was both pure and powerfully erotic—a rock and roll Lolita for the airwaves of America.

He chose to present her, not in the urban melodramas he had perfected with the Crystals, but instead in a succession of un-adorned lyrics about love, written with the help of Ellie Greenwich and Jeff Barry, Barry Mann and Cynthia Weil, Vin Poncia and Peter Andreoli. His first single with the Ronettes, "Be My Baby," introduced the group with a glorious thunderclap of percussion. As if on the brink of losing herself, Veronica strains to hit her notes—an impassioned struggle surrounded by a clatter of castanets and Jack Nitzsche's string arrangement, scored for subliminal cellos until the magisterial break for full orchestra. The air of incandescence is only amplified by Ronnie's slightly breathless urgency.

Presenting the Fabulous Ronettes puts that song in a new context. On one level, of course, the album is simply a glorified greatest hits package. It would be a classic even if it only contained Spector's first five Ronettes singles: "Be My Baby," "Baby, I Love You," "Breakin' Up," "Do I Love You," and "Walking in the Rain." Spector was forced to do battle with the British Invasion in his sequels to "Be My Baby." Released in the same year that saw the Beatles transform the nature of rock, none of them sold particularly well. Yet in retrospect it seems clear that Spector was staking his claim to rock and roll immortality, driven by the fresh competition and the feelings he could articulate through Ronnie's voice.

The album's first cut, "Walking in the Rain," was also Phil's last real hit with the Ronettes. It gives stately expression to the theme that dominates the album as well as the string of singles: Ronnie's yearning for The Boy—the Perfect Man who will make life right. "I want him/And I need him/And someday, some way, whoa-oh-whoa, I'll meet him." Ronnie's "whoa-oh-whoas" pack a world of meaning. Here, as on "Baby, I Love You" and "Be My Baby," they are executed with a clumsiness that defines a kind of chaste rapture, the ineffable longing of someone who is incurably romantic but not quite in command of the appropriate etiquette.

As the lyric makes clear, Ronnie will not settle for just any boy. He'll be shy, dreamy, willing to share wishes under a starry sky— and because he'll be all these things, she'll know that he's The One.

This record is Ronnie's show. She faces Spector's gulch of glitter—which includes peals of thunder and the plip-plop of puddling water—and rises above it, largely by throwing herself without reserve into the lyrics. As with all of Spector's singles, the instrumental track took hours to perfect, with Phil rehearsing the rhythm section until a platoon of instruments meshed seamlessly, locked into an ineluctable riff kicked along by drums and percussion, sweetened with legato strings, anchored by the ubiquitous buzz of baritone saxes. Ronnie's vocal, by contrast, was cut in one take— and in that contrast lies one secret of this album's power.

Except for a feeble version of "What'd I Say"—a ringer that throws Ronnie's limits into unflattering relief—*Presenting the Fabulous Ronettes* is of a piece with the hits that form its heart. The sequencing mixes the singles with two dreamy ballads, "So Young" and "When I Saw You," both awkwardly sung with great feeling, in a delicate shimmer of strings and echo. Also included are two songs, "You Baby" and "Chapel of Love," that could have been singles. The spirit of "You Baby" is summed up in the marvelous naiveté with which Veronica pouts "uh" on the fade; it has a serenity most of the other songs don't even try for. "Chapel of Love" evokes a different mood. Surrounded by an armada of rattles, the anarchy of Spector's vocal arrangement sounds simultaneously irreverent and soulful—a far cry from the rather timid hit version cut by the Dixie Cups several months later. While a bass man goes bomp like a Jew's harp gone berserk, a falsetto hovers uncannily in the distance, like some refugee from "Over the Mountain." There is a slightly daft informality about the cut, as if the tension of longing—and Spector's search for the perfect single—had abruptly been relaxed. Here at last the quest for The Boy finds its issue. It seems only fitting that "Chapel of Love" closes the album.

The appeal of these records is difficult to dissect. In the single-mindedness of his play with surface elements—in his attempt to concoct cavernous sonorities, in his search for a monolithic epiphany of melody and rhythm fused in one drum beat—Spector contrived a veil that both solicits and defies analysis. To rationally account for this hermetically sealed universe of superficial splendors would be to dissolve its essence. A certain trashiness and an aura of magic are both integral aspects of Spector's achievement.

What brings me back to these records is the inexhaustible density of their surface. Each listening reveals a new profile, a fresh nuance. Spector's productions invite an obsessive response that I have willingly given them. Each time I listen, I scan the backdrop of instruments, hoping to throw into relief what by design is dimly perceived—like the harmonica on "Breakin' Up," or the hammering harpsichord triplets on "Walking in the Rain." Spector's was an aesthetic of excess, and unpacking the litter of his imagination has given me hours of solitary pleasure. He made records to get lost in —and that, I think, is the key to his appeal.

Rock works on many levels: as shared enthusiasm, public entertainment, communal experience; but also as secret fantasy, private escape, a personal obsession. The public aspect is easier to celebrate: memories of drive-ins and love-ins can service nostalgia for years to come. The private aspect—the way rock has entered the existence of persons who date their lives and measure their desires by it—is less easily represented, perhaps because it suggests that beneath the flashy surface lies an obsessive solipsism: the real basis of America's popular culture.

Phil Spector was reclusive enough to know all about the obsessive possibilities of rock; and like Brian Wilson after him, he refined his private fantasies to the point of implosion. His records gradually became more intricate, more convoluted, more garbled with echo. And when an audience could no longer give him the gratification of admiring the sounds inside his head, he simply stopped recording them.

For the self-satisfied hermit, rock is not really about sex or dancing or living dangerously, but instead about daydreaming, imagining, fantasizing all these things in their immaculate perfection and impossible abundance. The narcissistic rocker lives life at one remove, and perceives it through a filter of unthreatening stereotypes. Phil Spector might have never felt at ease making love or dancing or having fun in the customary ways. But in those fantastic miniatures he affectionately called "little symphonies for the kids," he was free to create his own utopia of love, dance and fun, a world where he was in complete control. On his records, he could let his imagination run riot, building a personal paradise out of rock and roll bric-a-brac, the unlikely ambitions of a self-taught perfectionist, and, on the Ronettes records, the instinctive eroticism of his fantasy princess.

The plentitude of this world was a fiction. It existed only through the records he made. By fulfilling her function in his musical *mise-en-scène*, Ronnie could flourish. But once they were actually married—in the same year he virtually retired from recording—her star went into eclipse. She disappeared in Spector's Bel Air castle. "It was like being in the dark all the time," Ronnie explained ten years later. "You're on stage, you're with the bright lights, you're with people and having fun, traveling and seeing the world, and all of a sudden everything turns black. I lived in twenty-three rooms. Phil went out annually, so that meant I didn't go out either. I stayed home a lot. And it was like my whole world for five and a half years. I must have been walking in a daze."

Ironically, it was the source of her unhappiness who helped her create the indelible image of bliss she will be remembered for. When Phil's romantic fantasies took flight with Ronnie's anxious singing on the album they made together, it was precisely his narcissistic absorption in his runaway imagination, his icy command over her touching attempts to evoke worldly happiness, that made for such a curiously moving metamorphosis of the most common-place desires. Veronica's struggle to fill the role he cast for her lent resonance to the simple dreams she expressed, just as Spector's effort to create great rock and roll gave that struggle grandeur and meaning. She brought to Spector's fantasy-land the element of authenticity and the possibility of disenchantment. With a stroke of her wavering voice, she let us all in on the hopeless fragility of her fondest wishes. Darlene Love, Tina Turner, even the Righteous Brothers fulfilled their appointed parts in Spector's scripts with more skill and finesse. Ronnie, though, believed in what she sang, and tried desperately to make it seem real. Amid Phil's sandcastles of sound, she was able to turn clichés into fragments of feeling.

Through early adolescence, I believed in the same clichés Veronica and so many other rock stars voiced. But those clichés were merely pawns in a larger strategy of isolation and escape. In the beginning, rock mattered to me as an untroubled world of serene romanticism and exotic mysteries. The first time I heard rock and roll, I was visiting an older cousin. It was late at night, and I was dozing in the top bunk of his bed, while he stayed up to catch the local imitation of Alan Freed's "Moondog Matinee." At 11:00 his radio emitted a succession of echoed howls and the distant strains of "Night Train," followed by a babble of disc jockey jive and "Don't Be Cruel." Lying in the dark, staring at the ceiling, and wondering what it was all about, I had the sense of entering another world. I sought that feeling of wonder again. For a long time, it was something I didn't want or need to share with anyone else. I fled school for the sanctuary of my room, where I could summon a world with a choice of singles. That was what rock and roll meant to me.

Because it connects with that experience, I return to *Presenting the Fabulous Ronettes*. There I have always found my most primitive desires renewed in Phil Spector's never-never land of rock and roll romance. Meeting Veronica confirmed what I already knew: that vision of romance is cruel in its unreality. Yet every time I hear "Be My Baby," I smile.

THE WILD, THE INNOCENT AND THE E STREET SHUFFLE

BRUCE SPRINGSTEEN (COLUMBIA 32432)
1974

ARIEL SWARTLEY

The band's playing and the singer's singing
something about going home.

—"Incident on 57th Street"

It must have been the summer of '65 when Sandy's, our late night rendezvous, closed down and the action moved across the street. The Cave & Pit was in tune with the times—two entrances and a wall down the middle that divided more than the bar and burger halves of the establishment. You didn't just go in one door or the other; you picked a side and made a stand: dope or booze, freak or straight, FM or AM, dove or hawk. Lines were drawn down the middle of everything, including old friendships. But down in back where the jukeboxes were, there was a connecting door that was always open. And standing in that doorway you were on the firing line in the loudest confrontation of them all—the battle of the bands. Nightly the Kingsmen fought it out with Dylan, party boys against the prophet, Louie knocking at the gates of Eden. Usually I knew which side of the wall I belonged on (and where I couldn't get served). But back between the Wurlitzers I was caught out on the fence, wanting both: the visions and the dumb exuberance, a prophet and a party, rock and rock and roll.

It still seems like the perfect combination. A kind of ethical hedonism, an enlightened savagery, a wise naiveté. An American dream out of Fenimore Cooper or Mark Twain—but I don't want to talk about history. All I want is for a voice to come out of the wilderness and the stereo to crackle in flames like the burning bush. I don't want to have to ask, "Are you talking to me?" I want to know. And then I want to dance. In other words, I'm going to be a sucker for someone who takes rock and roll as a religion, and romanticizes the hell out of mundane details. For someone who says "Sparks fly on E Street when the boy-prophets walk it handsome and hot." Bruce Springsteen wins my heart with the first line of *The Wild, the Innocent and the E Street Shuffle,* wins it over and over again. Used to be only rock critics took lyrics that seriously and turned the romance of the streets so explicitly into myth. But while Springsteen's making his pronouncements the horns are waggling their hips and sassing him. And just when you think the song's going to collapse under the weight of its verses, the party-time chorus shouts the immortal instruction: "Everybody form a line." Then the only thing left on anybody's mind is the latest step—the E Street Shuffle or the Bristol Stomp. James Joyce meets the Dovells? Creation myths from The Land of a Thousand Dances? Yes, I say. Yes. Yes.

With its mumbled lyrics, its street slang, nicknames, and local references, the song, "The E Street Shuffle," seems as deliberately insular as the kids it's describing. But then dance songs have always flaunted their authenticity and traded on an exclusivity that's an open invitation: learn the steps, join the crowd, they're doing it in Philly, instructions included. Springsteen's insularity is just as artificial and provocative a barrier. The narrator doesn't figure you know the neighborhood—he points out the spots of interest—but he assumes you're on his side. It's an assumption that's hard to resist, as rock and roll has always understood. From the start its appeal has been partisan (call it anti-intellectual, anti-establishment, provincial, chauvinistic, ageist, sexist, all or none of the above—doesn't matter). All you have to do to join is want to. Having gotten you to buy into the rock and roll myth, Springsteen invites you to examine it. He plays with associations the way he plays with overtones on the guitar: picking at them while he's playing a line and just letting them ring.

Nice word, "shuffle." It applies so well: to the motion of the corner boys, their heel-and-toe strut before the girls, their ironic and provocative defiance of authority. And to the wild cards and jokers who fan out when the cops come, only to rearrange themselves at another hangout. It's all a dance—Little Angel changing partners, the dos-si-dos with the riot squad, the poses and the posturing and the attitudes. The cosmic E Street Shuffle. Even Leonard Bernstein saw the light: put the corner kids on the stage, wrapped them up in literary allusions, and orchestrated the thing. But Springsteen leaves the dance on the street where it lives. He is a participant as well as an observer, and he takes the details as seriously as their metaphoric possibilities. The song's final scene has the hypernaturalism of a closing shot in a grade B western: "He slips on his jeans and they move on out down to the scene— all the kids are there." That string of adverbs is as deliberate as a walk into the sunset. It's a hero's exit, except the boy-prophet's on his way to the hop. For if it's all a dance, it's also *just* a dance, and that's enough. Springsteen's laughing like the party's starting and all his oldest friends have just walked in the door and he picks up a guitar and twangs out lines the Ventures would have killed for.

Smack dab in the visionary tradition of Dylan and Van Morrison, Springsteen's got the former's faith that words, stretched and piled on fast enough, are music; the latter's feel for the grinning warmth and greased motions of R&B. Listen to Springsteen and you know he's listened to them both, and also to garage bands, Little Eva, one-shot singles, late-night TV giveaway deals. He hasn't only learned from masters. But it's not the knee-jerk nostalgia of teen-scene verité he's after in his authentic dialogue and his blasts from a past that never seems so bright except in retrospect. He treats rock and roll history as our common language, our shared mythology, and thereby reinforces rock and roll's promise of community. Spectoral echo, (James) Brownian motion, Dion-ysian brawl—he triggers memories like you were a jukebox and he was the man with all the quarters; plays it like a slot machine and wins. Hell yes, he exploits rock and roll's past, just like he exploits the language itself

—turning it inside out, digging for the metaphors under the surface of conversation.

The Wild, the Innocent and the E Street Shuffle is Springsteen's most extravagant and most easygoing album. He insists you can have rock and roll both ways—even the title makes it clear. Two value judgments and a dance step—what's going on here is synthesis. But Springsteen's double vision doesn't have an ironist's cruel double edge. Sure, characters in his dramatic monologues reveal themselves. The narrator of "Sandy" is an adolescent loser, the kid whose shirt gets stuck in the fun-fair ride, leaving him stranded and looking like a fool. You'd think he was ruining his chances with the girl: he can't stop telling her about his humiliations, about the girls who led him on, about the waitress that got tired of him. He can't even hand her a line without blowing it: "I promise I'll love you—forever?" Springsteen's voice squeaks incredulously. Oh, there'll always be another girl; adolescence is something you grow out of. But that's cold comfort and Springsteen's offering something warmer and more immediate: the moon is rising, the organ notes twinkle like stars, the "sha la las" are triumphant and irresistible. The chorus promises romance despite the odds.

"New York City Serenade" opens with a piano riff as night dark and extravagant as the song's title, as glitteringly arrogant as the city itself. A marching band tootles at the beginning of "The E Street Shuffle," fat and self-important. Springsteen doesn't just establish a mood or a groove; his songs begin with gaudy overtures —instrumental trailers for the story that's to follow. The piano in "New York" is stilled by a single acoustic guitar note coming soft and startling like an unexpected kiss; the marching band is taunted by a cheeky guitar and an electric piano line that sprints away before they can retort. The action begins before Springsteen sings a word. When his voice finally comes, it seems to be fighting its way through the elaborate arrangements, the flood of words, determined to get to you, to grab you, to convince you. Intimate against the grand scale of the songs, compelling in its compulsion to be heard, Springsteen's voice is that of a man possessed. His techniques are those of a master storyteller: the whispers to get your attention, the shouts to bring you to your feet, the teasing expectations. He builds songs into an ache of tensions, laying on strings like whips, applying pressure with drawn-out horn notes; dissolves the tensions in chants as rowdy as a Bronx cheer. But release is only temporary: he pulls the next phrases taut, the percussion threatens, the horns renew their urgency. Springsteen's timing reels you in through the artifice and sentimentality in "Wild Bill's Circus Story." The verses, spun out wide-eyed, filmed in ever slower motion, lead you on, "past the kids, past the sailors, to his dimly lit trailer/And the ferris wheel turns and turns like it's never going to stop." He delays the punch line till the last possible second, then spits it out in a rattle of phlegm and tobacco juice: "Hey sonny, wanna try the big top?" Who wouldn't be a fool for a tall tale? Springsteen's one himself. Sprawling, methodical, impassioned, and manipulative, *The Wild, the Innocent and the E Street Shuffle* teeters on the edge of melodrama and slips into rapture. "Ooh, ooh, ooh, it's all right"; "Good night, it's all tight, Jane." Springsteen's final choruses are incantations. Benedictions. Acts of surrender. He's caught up in his own spells.

If Springsteen is a storyteller, so are his characters. In some sense hustlers, both he and they live by their lines, by their powers of persuasion (and self-persuasion), by their ability to transform prosaic material into something shining. His stories are set in a self-absorbed, circumscribed world of adolescents, small towns, closed communities, where appearances count and reputations are as unshakable as a nickname. No one travels Springsteen's streets incognito. He identifies them all: Spanish Johnny, Lover Boy, Jazz Man. Even nouns. They aren't modified, they're christened: fire trails, rude boys, bruised arms, blond girls. More than descriptions, the adjectives, like nicknames, have the force of characterizations. Say "the girls were blond" and you're talking about the color of their hair. Say "blond girls" and they're something special, blond all through, a race apart. It's the old rosy-fingered dawn trick: the epic-maker's device for turning ordinary words symbolic and loading details down with implication. But it's not like the songs lay out in neatly knitted metaphors (or plots)—one tug and they're unraveled. They come at a rush and you grab what you can. Still, the implications are felt. The omnipresent compounds in "The E Street Shuffle"—double-shot, sweet-sixteen—drag at the verses like heels scuffing the pavement. Each stretched-out line ambles on, coolly oblivious to the insistent jab of the horns, the frenetic blather of wah-wah and percussion: "But the boys are still on the corner loose doin' that lazy E-Street shuffle." The rhythm of the words is as nonchalant as the boys, and it's only when Springsteen finishes "shuffle" with a wheeze and a gasp for breath, that there's any suggestion that that cool costs an effort to maintain. Sometimes the implications are felt in the sheer weight of words: "with bruised arms and broken rhythm and a beat-up old Buick—" ("Incident on 57th Street"). They beat up on the line till it's punch-drunk, so that the phrase that steps out clear when the dust settles seems all the more defiant "—but dressed just like dynamite."

Spanish Johnny's clothes and cornerboy's shuffle are gestures falling somewhere between courage and bravado, between a hustle and a good story. Johnny plays the gallant promising Janey he'll take her away from the battles on the street, but she's got his number: "Those romantic young boys/All they ever want to do is fight." She knows they're not going anywhere. The corner is "The E Street Shuffle," the boardwalk in "Sandy," the hometown alleys of "Kitty's Back," even the traveling midway of "Wild Bill's Circus Story," the tenement neighborhood of "Incident on 57th Street," the back roads and parent-and-school-dominated world of "Rosalita" —Springsteen's settings are territories in limbo. Satellites of the metropolis, overshadowed, robbed and ruined; resort towns begging to be invaded, dependent on other people's leisure and mobility; home turf staked out and fought for but never owned. And adolescence itself. Like the "man-child" or the "boy-prophet," neither one thing or the other. All of Springsteen's characters live on islands close enough to shore to see the mainland, too far away to make the crossing light or easy.

But isolation is chosen as well as imposed. Caught in the middle, challenged from the outside, each community is self-protective, fiercely partisan. When Kitty comes back, it's almost too good to be true, for her departure was a double betrayal, forsaking the hometown and the kids in the alley for marriage and the big city, power, prestige, and opportunity. Her return not only vindicates her small-town admirer, but all of those who've never left. And their victory is as sweet and keen-edged as the notes of Springsteen's guitar. Yet her defection raised doubts and questions that still hang like the sax's final whistling high note. As envied and disdained as a resort visitor, as threatening and tempting as the city, adulthood glimmers just over the horizon too. And like the Corner or the Street, it has to be claimed. The final song on the album confronts growing up and the metropolis head-on: "New York City Serenade" is a rite of passage. Enticing with its jazz and drugs and promises of plunder, dangerous—"a mad-dog's promenade"—the city is a domineering mistress, sneering like Fishlady that cornerboys are too easy, grinding supplicants in their own insignificance. In her hostile, garishly-lit embrace, manhood becomes a matter of self-assertion—"I'm a young man walking real proud for you"—and self-respect: "Sometimes you just have to walk on."

But then, he dosen't sing the line quite straight; there's a gulp in his voice, an exaggeration to his drawl. Dangers over the horizon, oppression at home—what's a poor boy to do? One solution is obvious, and Springsteen concedes the point so fast you trip over it in the album's most explicitly autobiographical cut. In "Rosalita" he's no street fighting man, and no more under the thumb of circumstances, adults, and authorities than any other kid. When he comes to the door he may be a truant, a hot-rodder, and what your mother would call a bad influence, but rock and roll is his guarantee of respectability. Hell, that record company advance is probably a lot bigger than Rosie's father's salary. There's an edge of mockery that keeps Springsteen's heroism honest. He's found the perfect escape: work that's fun, rebellion that's legitimate, eternal youth, a name that's known not just on the corner but on the global street, all that stuff. But however much he romanticizes rock and roll as an ideal or a code, he only plays the star in fun. Sometimes it seems like he's deliberately burying his voice in the mix, as if to deny that he's anything but another member of the band. Sometimes it seems like he and the other guys have never left the corner at all.

Certainly the songs seem like they were filmed on location, or

maybe it's just that the settings feel almost like characters themselves. Springsteen is a compulsive recorder of detail—the sheets
"damp with sweat," the girl "bopping down the beach with a
radio." But it's not like you'd call him a realist. Sometimes it
seems as though he's looking back at the corner through a rearview
mirror—the streets turned shimmery and the action blurred by the
speed at which he's traveling. It's not just that the language slips
out of the colloquial into the high-flown. It's as though he's caught
up in the rhythm and led on by his own words to more and more
audacious leaps. From neat tricks like putting hard girls on easy
street, to metaphors that are high wire acts: "Let the black boys in
to light the soul flame." (I mean, I always figured that phrase had
to do with turning the radio to an R&B station. But?) And finally
he skips beyond probability and any tidy interpretation to visions:
Of "golden-heeled fairies" fighting with .38s (and it's anybody's
guess what kind of fairies). Of "barefoot street boys" throwing
down their switchblades and kissing each other goodbye. Visions
of the natural order he's been at pains to record turned on its head.
But then, calling the kids on E Street "boy-prophets" was a leap as
well. Springsteen's double vision, seeing the what-is beside, on top
of, through the what-could-be, is consistent enough to take on a
moral force. Like a hardboiled detective, he observes as though his
life depended on it, on recognizing the shift in stance that tells you
the other guy's about to go for his gun. And like the detective,
once he's established the facts, they're not enough. His characters
aren't presented as free agents: they're shown, if not as victims, at
least as products of an environment. And still, they're held
accountable for their actions. They can walk on or not. The choice
may be only a gesture, but the space between courage and bravado,
between a hustle and a good story, is also the place where appearances become truth. Where Fishlady's gibe is picked up and worn
as a badge of honor: "Hey babe, I'm easy, won't you take my arm?"
Where the only names that matter are the names you give or call
yourself.

Knowing the score is how you survive; knowing, for instance,
that midnight in Manhattan is not the time to get cute. Faith, on
the other hand, is how you manage—well—whatever it is that's

more than survival. Yeah, it sounds hokey, but faith in these songs isn't just some smarmy, self-help est-uary. It's nothing more or less than an act of imagination (like the songs themselves). Envisioning a junkman dressed in satin is as absurd as falling in love. The facts don't justify the faith; no loved one ever lives up to a lover's dream; still, no love ever survived on facts alone. So buy the vision. Believe the lady's sawed in half. Be willing to be made a fool. Listen to the junkman. If only every act of faith were just as easy.

Still, held in any kind of limbo, trapped in stupid circumstances, it's nice to hear him singing. Singing something about the towns I grew up in and the boys I loved. And why I left and why I care about them still. But I didn't grow up in towns much like the ones he describes. Or something about the songs I listened to and the beat I danced and turned around. But he remembers songs I thought were silly and tunes I never heard. Something then, about growing up. But I'm already grown. Aah, it doesn't matter. The band's playing and the singer's singing something about a prophet, something about a party. And rock and roll's going to take me home.

TROUT MASK REPLICA

CAPTAIN BEEFHEART (STRAIGHT STS 1053)
1969

LANGDON WINNER

Having lived in something of a shipwreck for the past several years, I understand that the question of which record I would want to play on a desert island must be taken literally. It is not a matter of what my favorite album happens to be. At issue is a kind of music rich enough, substantial enough to enable this castaway to endure a place of desolation over a very long haul. My own first requirement for any such record, therefore, would have to be its power to construct, furnish, and enliven a world in and of itself. In this setting almost all rock and roll records would be worse than useless. Their content so thoroughly presupposes the material and social circumstances of modern civilization that, except as cues to frustrated nostalgia, they could provide little joy, inspiration, or solace. There is only one album I know of that deliberately and successfully sets out to devise a special world of its own as if in defiance of the prevailing norms and fashions of contemporary society: Captain Beefheart's *Trout Mask Replica*. Created in isolation by a renegade artist/genius/madman and his band of unquestioning disciples, hermetic almost to a point of catatonia, yet challenging in every moment of its seventy-nine-minute duration, *Trout Mask* is a record uniquely suited to years and years of isolated listening.

Of course, in the decade since the album was released the vast majority of rock and roll fans have found it to be completely unlistenable. No record alienates the ear of modern America faster than Beefheart's magnum opus. Its guitars wail along in cacophonous jerks and starts that seem designed to offend our appetite for harmony and order. Beefheart's singing, actually an unrestrained bellering on most songs, shocks us with the visceral impression that the man is either angry or just plain deranged. Why would anyone sing in the voice people usually reserve for telling trespassers to get the hell off their property? The lyrics, similarly, appear either senseless or so thoroughly contrived for freaky effects that no one other than clinical psychiatrists could take them seriously. For those who were humming along to Crosby, Stills and Nash or *It's a Beautiful Day* when *Trout Mask Replica* was first issued, and for the millions who nurture themselves on a diet of Fleetwood Mac, the Eagles, and Linda Ronstadt today, Beefheart's music offers none of the qualities of a "good" record: engaging melodies; a solid, interesting groove; poignant hook lines; and an intelligible reflection of the life of the listener. One reason, then, that *Trout Mask Replica* would be my personal choice for a desert island is that a desert island is possibly the only place where I could play the record without being asked by friends and neighbors to take the damned thing off.

On its own terms, the popular judgment of the work is entirely justified. If the purpose of a phonograph record is to soothe us, to provide a beat for dancing, a pulse for making love, a set of themes to reassure us in the joys and troubles of life's daily commerce, then *Trout Mask* fails utterly. Anyone who tried to make love to these infernal rhythms, for example, would have to be carted off to a chiropractor. But if a record is legitimate in trying to overthrow our somnambulistic habits of hearing, seeing, and touching things, if it is valid in seeking to jolt our sensibilities and restructure the way we experience music and everything else, then Beefheart's strange collection of songs begins to make sense. Beneath the apparent chaos of its surfaces are structures of remarkable intricacy. Beyond the ugly noise that assaults us on first listening is a wealth of ingenious melodic and harmonic inventions. As one penetrates the apparent hysteria of its tunes and lyrics, one discovers a realm of surprisingly serene and happy freedom.

Trout Mask Replica wastes no time announcing its basic intentions. Where most popular records try to entice listeners with a catchy riff in their opening few moments, this one begins with a rugged test of endurance. Beefheart's Magic Band launches into a grating, off-center guitar line that sounds like a sawmill given a log too heavy to cut and slowly grinding itself to pieces. Beefheart enters howling a tune that, oddly enough, matches the music exactly: "My smile is stuck. I cannot go back t' yer Frownland. My spirit's made up of the ocean and the sky 'n the sun 'n the moon 'n all my eye can see. I cannot go back to yer land of gloom where black jagged shadows remind me of the comin' of yer doom."* Disgusted with the world we normally inhabit, he's gone in search of a new place, a homeland "where uh man can stand by another man without an ego flyin', with no man lyin' 'n no one dyin' by an earthly hand." Beefheart openly entreats his listeners to leave "those old worlds, take my kind hand" and join him on his mission. Although its tone is anything but alluring, the invitation is explicit. Beefheart is not concerned to build bridges for his audience or to make it any easier for anyone to come along. Either you're interested or you're not.

As the musical barrage of the first minute and a half abruptly subsides, we receive our first glimpse of the land to which we've been invited. Unaccompanied by any instruments, Beefheart begins crooning softly in an old granny's voice. "There's ole Gray with 'er dovewinged hat. There's ole Green with her sewing machine. Where's the bobbin at? Tote'n old grain in uh printed

---

* Among the innovations that characterize *Trout Mask Replica* are certain idiosyncrasies of spelling and grammar. Captain Beefheart regularly employs "uh" for the words "a," "an," and "of" and uses colloquial contractions such as " 'n" for the word "and," and "-in' " on words ending with "ing," to represent the sounds actually sung or spoken. I have used his spelling and punctuation here. The reader should consult the song sheet given in the first edition of *Trout Mask* but, criminally, left out of subsequent pressings.

sack. The dust blows forward 'n dust blows back." Memories of country life flood the woman's addled consciousness in a panorama of senility. "What am I gonna die?" she asks. "Uh white flake riverboat just flew by." At about its midpoint the song suddenly changes (or at least confuses) the gender of its imaginary singer as old grandma becomes an old geezer remembering his fishing expeditions. "Bubbles popped big 'n uh lipstick Kleenex hung on uh pointed forked twig. Reminds me of the bobby girls, never was my hobby girls," Beefheart moans, making up a distracted tune as he goes along. "Hand full uh worms and uh pole fishin'. Cork bobbin' like uh hot red bulb . . . Well I put down my bush 'n I took off my pants 'n felt free. The breeze blowin' up me 'n up the canyon far as I could see. It's night now and the moon looks like uh dandelion. It's black now 'n the blackbird's feedin' on rice 'n his red wings look like diamonds 'n lice."

The images in the song are those of a pleasant, unromanticized American landscape described in the motley vernacular of old time rural culture. Its lyrics reshuffle a set of experiences and expressions from everyday American life to sketch comic portraits in miniature. While the specific references to places, times, characters, colloquialisms, and material artifacts change throughout the album and while dark themes often intrude upon the comedy, Beefheart's approach to his subject matter remains the one we see at work here. He begins with elements that are ridiculously familiar to everyone and plays with them until he's produced extraordinary, unsettling effects. How he accomplishes this and what it all means is something I'll come to later. But for the time being it is sufficient to notice that the vision of *Trout Mask Replica* is fundamentally that of an American primitivist surrealist. The land he asks us to visit is one we already know very well. It is *not*, as many of his fans have supposed, outer space or the realm of late 1960s hippie, psychedelic weirdness for weirdness' sake. To accompany Captain Beefheart on this journey is to re-experience the nature and artifice of the American continent through a vast project of surrealistic reclamation.

If one is to enjoy *Trout Mask Replica*'s twenty-eight songs on a desert island or anywhere else, two major obstacles must be overcome: its music and its lyrics. Of these two, the music is by far the more difficult. Beefheart's desire to disconnect and reorder things according to novel principles extends to the way he employs instruments, voices, melody, harmony, and the song form itself. *Trout Mask* willfully violates almost every convention—technical and psychological—that gives music its appeal. We generally expect, for instance, that a rock and roll song will start off with a repetitive beat and keep it going, at least for a while. Beefheart delights in jamming these expectations. His songs begin a rhythmic pattern, let it run for a couple of measures, and then break it off only to strike up something completely different. In the two and a half minutes of the instrumental "Hair Pie: Bake 2," for instance, there are no fewer than fourteen separate beats and melodies quickly introduced, briefly run, and abruptly junked. Throughout the whole album, just when you think you've begun to groove on something, just when your toe starts tapping, it's vanished and something else has taken its place.

Trout Mask also tramples upon all normal standards for what is tuneful and harmonious. Its guitars and bass play in abrasive twangs, strangely pinched notes, and ringing discords. On many songs the melody is composed of a progression of guitar discords or even two separate but simultaneous discordant lines wandering in vermicular patterns. Beefheart's vocals, similarly, rely less upon the melody of any given tune than upon the music present in the way people actually talk. Thus, the singing—and it is definitely singing—on "Pachuco Cadaver" takes the form of the rising and falling emphatic tones of an Old West storyteller. Beefheart loves the voices of everyday American folks and changes his own *Trout Mask* voice to mimic and spoof as many of them as he can.

Now, rock and roll is (or at least has become) an extremely conventional music. Performers who observe its stylistic traditions most faithfully—Bruce Springsteen is the most obvious example at present—are the ones likely to win the largest following of fans and critics. Beefheart's notion of musical liberty, however, requires the transcendence of all deeply rooted habits. He refuses to use them in his playing. More importantly, he will not allow his listeners to depend upon them for satisfaction. The steady beat and pleasant melody are, as far as he's concerned, simply ways of lulling people to sleep. *Trout Mask* tries to achieve for a guitar, bass, drum, and vocal ensemble—the rock and roll band—the same degree of freedom, the same overstepping of traditional boundaries that John Coltrane achieved for the tenor saxophone in jazz. Its mistake, if one can call it that, is that it challenges too many conventions too quickly. Its songs leave most listeners in a state of unhappy vertigo. Is there *nothing* we can hold on to?

Whatever else may be said about Beefheart's music, it cannot be called sloppy. One feature that characterizes *Trout Mask* is its unbelievably thorough attention to detail. Every note of the guitars and even the noise of the drums is meticulously tailored and carefully controlled. The work is perhaps best seen as an attempt to sculpture sounds in the same way that Don Van Vliet (Captain Beefheart's real name) sculpted clay animals as a little boy. Each song hangs together as a long string of intricate effects one piled on top of another and balanced with a good supply of paste and baling wire. In "My Human Gets Me Blues," to cite merely one case, Beefheart fashions a delicate musical contraption and then, by playing the piece loudly at top speed, takes the thing out for a peak performance road test. Will this buggy hold together? the listener might well ask. It does and in fine style. Perhaps the best place to review the Captain's compositions would be not the rock press but *Popular Mechanics* or *Road and Track*.

Beefheart has stormed the castle of musical authority and brought about a personal revolution in its operating structures. He has devised his own ingenious way of writing songs, of using guitars, of singing, of playing drums, of combining voice and instruments, and of weaving the whole thing together. In its own terms and for its own purposes, the achievement is nothing short of dazzling. The ultimate success of any revolution, however, depends upon getting a good number of people interested in the changes you propose to make. That is something that Beefheart has never accomplished. With the exception of a few punk rock guitarists who have imitated *Trout Mask Replica* licks, most rock and roll performers have ignored his work. Even Beefheart's small but devoted cult following shows, by its generally inane behavior at concerts, little comprehension of what the man is trying to do.

But on a desert island none of this would matter. The listener always completes an artist's work. In this regard *Trout Mask* offers two features that other records do not: (1) an enormous variety of musical puzzles that require a considerable amount of time and concentration to figure out, and (2) a seemingly inexhaustible supply of unfinished ideas that one can fill in oneself. From fragments the record makes available, the castaway could begin to create whole new musicals, symphonies, island anthems, and the like. As my own lingering puzzlement gave way to unbothered pleasure, I could imagine myself sitting on a coral reef charting the rise and fall of hits contained within this one album. Flash: " 'Neon Meate Dream of an Octafish' edged out 'Sugar 'N Spikes' for the number one position this week as a new dance craze based on the last several bars of 'Pachuco Cadaver' swept the island!"

Even after a person has begun to understand *Trout Mask Replica's* music, its lyrics will pose an awesome barrier to enjoyment. Of the songs on the album, only "The Blimp," with its outrageous mock mass hysteria over the similarity between dirigibles and human breasts, ever won favor with rock fans. Recorded over a telephone, the voice of Magic Band member Antennae Jimmy Semens parodies the radio broadcast of the 1937 crash of the Hindenburg: "Tits! Tits! The blimp! The blimp! The mother ship! The mother ship! The brothers hid under their hood. From the blimp, the blimp! . . . Daughter don't you dare! Oh momma, who cares! It's the blimp! It's the blimp!" Rock audiences evidently liked this number as much for the simplicity of its words as for the fact that, unannounced, *Trout Mask's* producer Frank Zappa and a couple of the Mothers of Invention provide instrumental background on this one cut. But to be amused by "The Blimp" is one thing; to understand and take pleasure in songs like "Hobo Chang Ba" or "Pena" is quite another. How, after all, are we to penetrate the meaning of phrases like: "Whale bone farmhouse, cavorts girdled in latters uh lite, cavorts girdled in latters uh lite"?

Patient listeners eventually notice that *Trout Mask's* songs fall into a few roughly coherent clusters. There are about half a dozen tunes that describe more-or-less contemporary people involved in

more-or-less recognizable social situations.* Four numbers turn out
to be songs with a fairly explicit ecological or anti-war message.†
Two songs consist of extremely rapid free association fantasies
recited to wild musical accompaniment.** There are three straight
instrumentals, one conventional blues, and three song-poems that
stand out as mini-epics in an unfinished Beefheartian saga.†† Then
there are several songs, Beefheart's commentaries on one thing or
another, that simply defy any convenient classification. So much
for categories.

Typical of the lyrics on contemporary predicaments is "When
Big Joan Sets Up," a rugged song that treats the question of why
Americans are embarrassed about their bodies. As the band whips
up a fast, repeating two-bar riff, Beefheart roars: "Hoy, hoy. When
Big Joan comes out, her arms are too small, her head like uh ball.
She tied off her horse 'n galloped off into the moonbeams. She
pulled up her blouse 'n compared her navel to the moon." Big
Joan seems to be a friendly young lady, but she's afflicted by having
body parts that are the wrong size according to current fashion.
When she goes to the beach they laugh at her because her hands
are too small. "She ain't built for goin' naked, so she can't wear
any new clothes," Beefheart explains in truthful paradox. The
song points to the shame and glory of Southern California where a
person's freedom to enjoy the beautiful climate is limited by social
preconceptions of how people ought to look. Beefheart tells the
woman that since she's too fat to go out in the daylight, he'll sit
up with her all night (if she promises not to talk about her hands
being too small). "Hoy, hoy. Is she uh boy?" he shouts. The

* "Ella Guru," "Moonlight on Vermont," "Pachuco Cadaver," "Bills
Corpse," "Sweet Sweet Bulbs," "My Human Gets Me Blues," "When
Big Joan Sets Up," "Fallin' Ditch" and "She's Too Much for My Mirror."

† "Dachau Blues," "Ant Man Bee," "Wild Life" and "Veteran's Day
Poppy."

** "Neon Meate Dream of an Octafish" and "Pena."

‡ The instrumentals are "Hair Pie: Bake 1," "Hair Pie: Bake 2" and
"Dali's Car." The blues is "China Pig," and the epics in miniature are
"The Dust Blows Forward and the Dust Blows Back," "Orange Claw
Hammer" and "Old Fart at Play."

answer, of course, is yes. Big Joan is none other than Captain Beefheart recalling his own traumatic visits to the beach.

While many of the album's lyrics express love and contentment, the most powerful songs deal with the troubles and suffering of life. Clearly, something is wrong in the human world and Beefheart offers a number of explanations. "Bills Corpse" points to the way that parents, especially mothers, psychologically cripple their children by pushing them in directions contrary to nature. "She smiled and twisted, she smiled and twisted hideously looking back at once was beautiful," he sings in his most offensive rasping voice. "My Human Gets Me Blues" laments a more general condition of mutual estrangement between God and human beings. God, it turns out, is unhappy because people have always made him a boy and never let him have a doll to dress. For that reason, men and women on earth have been clothed in perpetual misery. "I saw yuh dancin' baby in your x-ray gingham dress. I knew you were under duress, I knew you under yer dress. Just keep comin' Jesus, yer the best dressed. You look dandy in the sky but you don't scare me."

On some cuts, Beefheart's criticisms are so explicit that they become protest songs of a peculiar sort. "I cry, but I can't buy your Veteran's Day Poppy," he announces during the record's last moments. "It don't get me high. It can never grow another son like the one who warmed me my days after rain." Another song, "Dachau Blues," dwells on the details of this century's mass carnage in images that even Beefheart fans find hard to stomach. "War One was balls 'n power 'n blood 'n snow. War Two rained death 'n showers 'n skeletons danced 'n screamin' 'n dyin' in the ovens." The song suggests that our age has been playing a lethal children's game with Satan. "They're counting out the devil with two fingers in their hands, begging the Lord don't let the third one land."

A central *Trout Mask* hypothesis is that because human beings vastly overestimate their standing in the natural order, they feel entitled to cause all kinds of destruction. The words to "Ant Man Bee" observe that only two creatures in God's garden, men and the ants, are unable to live in harmony with their fellows. Both species are aggressive organizers ready to wage war over a lump of sugar. While a number of songs bemoan the lack of peace in man's dealings with nature, "Wild Life" actually contemplates defecting to the other side. Things have gotten so bad that Beefheart is going "up on a mountain, find me a cave 'n talk the bears into takin' me in. Wild life," he concludes, "is a man's best friend."

Very few moments on the album, however, are devoted to Beefheart's biological politics. *Trout Mask* covers an astonishingly broad range of topics both serious and comical with surprises at every turn. By far the most elegant statement of all is "Orange Claw Hammer," one of Beefheart's epics in miniature, a song about an old sailor who returns home after thirty years at sea, walks down main street and, in his besotted, barnacled mind, believes he "recognizes" things and people. Borrowing the tune of a familiar sea chantey, Beefheart croons, "Uh little up the road uh wooden candy stripe barber pole 'n above it read uh sign 'painless parker.' Licorice twisted around under uh fly 'n uh youngster cocked 'er eye. God before me if I'm not crazy is my daughter." The old salt is overcome by mistaken feelings of affection and remorse. He offers to buy the little girl a cherry phosphate, and says he'll "take you down to the foamin' brine 'n water 'n show you the wooden tits on the Goddess with the pole out full sail that tempted away your peg legged father." The child, who must be totally confused, hears the sailor explain that many years ago he was shanghaied by a "high hat beaver mustache man 'n his pirate friend." Left behind, although time and place are lost in his delirium, were seven babies and a beautiful lass with brown skin. "Thirty years away," he says, "can make uh seaman's eyes, uh round house man's eyes flow out water. Salt water."

The song has no particular point. On one level it is merely a collection of fragmentary impressions held together by an extremely odd premise. But like so many of *Trout Mask*'s pieces, "Orange Claw Hammer" achieves an effect that goes far beyond anything specifically identifiable in the content of its lyrics. What we experience is a marvelous sense of comedy and compassion that derives from a resonance with myths and memories deeply buried in America's past. The song works not for what it says to us but for the way it joggles out an inherited store of fantasies about drifters, seaports, pirates, and the separation of fathers and children.

In the last analysis, the content of any given song on the album, even the content of the very best of them, matters much less than the pattern that informs Beefheart's lyrics as a whole. There *is* method in this madness, a victory of form over substance. Not that any particular methodology is being consciously applied; *Trout Mask Replica* is probably the one rock album least influenced by the application of a rational, step-by-step procedure. Consistently present, however, is a way of using language, a form of speech that sets words and the world spinning in a perpetual dance. While specific utterances in this tongue vary greatly in texture and complexity, the general approach can, like Beefheart's music, be grasped in fairly straightforward terms that can help overcome our discomfort at what passes before our ears.

Beefheart tries to engage his audience in a continuing change in the focus of imagination: from microscopy to telescopy to kaleidoscopy and back again. He inevitably begins with a microscopic moment in which something very small is inspected under his conceptual lens—a beetle's wing, a plume of smoke, the blue of a Bromo-Seltzer bottle, the diamond back of a rattlesnake, an automobile brodey knob, or some other object, color, shape, or sound. For one brief moment we examine that thing very carefully and endow it with the greatest possible significance. Little things take on an exaggerated importance; they contain, Beefheart believes, whole worlds within them. In the wink of an eye, however, the focus shifts to a telescopic point of view. Our attention is directed to some faraway object—the moon, the sea, a distant hill—or to some larger category of human experience—death, love, fear, longing or the passage of time. Once again a significance is bestowed upon the thing involved; we look at it and say, "Yes, there it is." But the telescope is almost never allowed to rest on distant or abstract objects for very long. Almost immediately the mind's eye is drawn back to the furnishings of everyday experience seen under Beefheart's rapidly scanning view finder. Things large and small, things of grave importance and of seeming insignificance, are given exactly equal status.

The overall effect of this movement is that we begin to experience the whole world as if through a kaleidoscope. A panoply of freely associated perceptions of sight, sound, taste, smell, and touch cross their normal boundaries and form new patterns. Visual images and audible textures trade places. Verbs become nouns and vice versa. Whole new words—"formaheap," "fedlock," "drazy hoop," and "bluesferbones"—are concocted to fill spaces left vacant by ordinary English. Natural creatures and artificial objects pair off in strange new matings to produce, if only for a brief second, amazing little beings that vanish like the quarks or charmed particles of modern physics. Butterfly droppings become little worms that soon transform themselves into the tucks and rolls of hot rod upholstery. Custards make ominous clicking sounds. An oriole's tail at twilight becomes indistinguishable from an orange claw hammer.

Most prominent of the kaleidoscopically generated hybrids is the trout mask replica itself. Shown waving "hello" on the album cover, the beast finally makes its appearance in "Old Fart at Play," a tune that portrays Captain Beefheart's surrealistic reclamation of everything under the sun as a perfectly acceptable way of life. The Old Fart (a little boy?) has never lost his love of things astonishing. He notices parts and pieces of the world that other people take for granted and has a grand time rearranging the environment to suit his fancy. One afternoon, just for the hell of it, he puts on his homemade wooden fishhead and pokes it through the kitchen window to surprise his mother. "Momma was flatten'n lard with her red enamel rollin' pen when the fishhead broke the window, rubber eye erect 'n precisely detailed," Beefheart observes in the voice of an old time yarn spinner. Through the holes of the mask the Old Fart sees his mother lick her lips like a cat, peck the ground like a rooster, pivot like a duck, and continue preparing food over a hot stove. As he looks on, a metamorphosis begins to take place in him. The mask grows more and more fish-like. The boundaries between man, artifact, and natural creature quickly vanish. His head grows the fleshy protuberances of a "very intricate rainbow trout replica." Is it fish? gizmo? funny? grotesque? Beefheart is the master player who will not let us pause long enough to figure it out. He tips his hand only for a brief second with the following confession: "The old fart inside was now breathin' freely from his perfume bottle atomizer air bulb invention. His excited eyes from within the dark interior glazed, watered in appreciation at his thoughtful preparation." There is no doubt as to the Old Fart's identity.

It remains a legitimate question whether any record, indeed any work of art, has the right to demand as much of its audience as *Trout Mask Replica* does. To enter the album requires an almost total suspension of all normal structures of perception, rationality and belief; we are asked to drop everything and come along. If we accept the invitation, there is no guarantee that to travel this path will not bring us to a destination equivalent to madness. Beefheart offers no warranty of safe passage; in fact, he cannot. Through it all, one must never forget that the single element that prevents this wild experiment from flying to bits is the power of one man's imagination. At the center of all the delightfully unrestrained playfulness is an awesome, if not downright dangerous, degree of control. The musicians on *Trout Mask*, the members of the Magic Band, eventually came to believe that whatever Beefheart's intentions may have been, their own personal autonomy was not enhanced by playing this music or by having their names changed to Zoot Horn Rollo, Rockette Morton, and the like. To a man, they all eventually left the group and went looking for a sense of selfhood that their participation in this ambitious quest for total freedom could not provide.

On a desert island, nevertheless, the question of why anybody in his right mind would willingly abandon a rationally constructed, smoothly functioning reality just to listen to a mere phonograph record would be irrelevant. One's accustomed reality would already have been lost and the task at hand would be to install a new one. In that case *Trout Mask Replica*'s otherwise crazy offer—to purge our senses and return us to the world as if it were something totally new, something entirely wonderful—would seem very attractive. And if it turned out that this project contained hidden elements of insidious control, so much the better! After I had listened to the album for a while, fathomed its music, deciphered its lyrics, and solved its puzzles, I could then take up the struggle against its tyranny. *Trout Mask Replica* would become an exquisite test of character, an opportunity to learn how the sources of liberation can be distinguished from the causes of enslavement.

VELVET UNDERGROUND: GOLDEN ARCHIVE SERIES

THE VELVET UNDERGROUND (MGM GAS 131)
1967–1969/1970

ELLEN WILLIS

1. I'll Let You Be in My Dream

A change of fantasy: I have just won the first annual Keith Moon Memorial Essay Contest. (This year's subject was, "Is Ecstasy Dead?") The prize is a fallout shelter in the bowels of Manhattan, reachable only through a secret entrance in CBGB's basement. It is fully stocked: on entering the contest I was asked to specify my choice of drugs (LSD), junk food (Milky Way), T-shirt ("Eat the Rich"), book (*Parade's End*), movie (*The Wizard of Oz*), rock-and-roll single ("Anarchy in the U.K."), and rock-and-roll album. The album is *Velvet Underground* (not to be confused with *The Velvet Underground*), an anthology culled from the Velvets' first three LPs. (My specially ordered version of this collection is slightly different from the original; for "Afterhours," a song I've never liked much, it substitutes "Pale Blue Eyes," one of my favorites.) The songs on *Velvet Underground* are all about sin and salvation. As luck would have it, I am inspecting my winnings at the very moment that a massive earthquake destroys a secret biological warfare laboratory inside the Indian Point nuclear power plant, contaminating New York City with a virulent radioactive form of legionnaire's disease. It seems that I will be contemplating sin and salvation for a long time to come.

2. I Love the Sound of Breaking Glass

In New York City in the middle sixties the Velvet Underground's lead singer, guitarist, and *auteur*, Lou Reed, made a fateful connection between two seemingly disparate ideas—the rock-and-roller as self-conscious aesthete and the rock-and-roller as self-conscious punk. (Though the word "punk" was not used generically until the early seventies, when critics began applying it to unregenerate rock-and-rollers with an aggressively lower-class style, the concept goes all the way back to Elvis.) The Velvets broke up in 1970, but the aesthete-punk connection was carried on, mainly in New York and England, by Velvets-influenced performers like Mott the Hoople, David Bowie (in his All the Young Dudes rather than his Ziggy Stardust mode), Roxy Music and its offshoots, the New York Dolls and the lesser proto-punk bands that played Manhattan's Mercer Arts Center before it (literally) collapsed, the anti-punk Modern Lovers, the arch-punk Iggy Stooge/Pop. By 1977 the same duality had surfaced in new ways, with new force, under new conditions, to become the basis of rock and roll's new wave.

There are important differences, both temperamental and musical, that divide today's punks and punkoids from the Velvets and other precursors and from each other; American punk (still centered in New York) and its British counterpart are not only different but in a sense opposed. Yet all this music belongs to a coherent genre, implicitly defined by the tension between the term "punk" and the more inclusive "new wave," with its arty connotations. If the Velvets invented this genre, it was clearly anticipated by the Who: Pete Townshend, after all, is something of an aesthete, and Roger Daltrey something of a punk. It was not surprising that the impulse to make music that united formal elegance and defiant crudity should arise among working-class Englishmen and take shape among New York bohemians; each environment was, in its own way, highly structured and ridden with conflict. And as a vehicle for that impulse rock and roll had unique advantages: it was defiantly crude, yet for those who were tuned in to it it was also a musical, verbal, and emotional language rich in formal possibilities.

The Who, the Velvets, and the new wave bands have all shared this conception of rock and roll; their basic aesthetic assumptions have little to do with what is popularly known as "art rock." The notion of rock-as-art inspired by Dylan's conversion to the electric guitar—the idea of making rock and roll more musically and lyrically complex, of combining elements of jazz, folk, classical, and avant-garde music with a rock beat, of creating "rock opera" and "rock poetry"—was from the rock-and-roll fan's perspective a dubious one. At best it stimulated a vital and imaginative eclecticism that spread the values of rock and roll even as it diffused and diluted them. At worst it rationalized a form of cultural upward mobility, concerned with achieving the appearance and pretensions of art rather than the reality—the point being to "improve" rock and roll by making it palatable to the upper middle class. Either way it submerged rock and roll in something more amorphous and high-toned called rock. But from the early sixties (Phil Spector was the first major example) there was a counter-tradition in rock and roll that had much more in common with "high" art—in particular avant-garde art—than the ballyhooed art-rock syntheses: it involved more or less consciously using the basic formal canons of rock and roll as material (much as the pop artists used mass art in general) and refining, elaborating, playing off that material to produce what might be called rock-and-roll art. While art rock was implicitly based on the claim that rock and roll was or could be as worthy as more established art forms, rock-and-roll art came out of an obsessive commitment to the language of rock and roll and an equally obsessive disdain for those who rejected that language or wanted it watered down, made easier. In the sixties the best rock often worked both ways: the special virtue of sixties culture was its capacity for blurring boundaries, transcending contradictions, pulling off everything at once. But in the seventies the two tendencies have increasingly polarized: while art rock has fulfilled its most philistine possibilities in kitsch like Yes (or, for that matter, Meat Loaf), the new wave has inherited the counter-tradition, which is both less popular and more conscious of itself *as* a tradition than it was a decade ago.

The Velvets straddled the categories. They were nothing if not eclectic: their music and sensibility suggested influences as diverse as Bob Dylan and Andy Warhol, Peter Townshend and John Cage; they experimented with demented feedback and isolated, pure notes and noise for noise's sake; they were partial to sweet, almost folky melodies; they played the electric viola on Desolation Row. But they were basically rock-and-roll artists, building their songs on a beat that was sometimes implied rather than heard; on simple, tough, pithy lyrics about their hard-edged urban demi-monde; on rock and roll's oldest metaphor for modern city life—anarchic energy contained by a tight, repetitive structure. Some of the Velvets' best songs—"Heroin," especially—redefined how rock and roll was supposed to sound; others—"I'm Waiting for the Man," "White Light/ White Heat," "Beginning to See the Light," "Rock & Roll"—used basic rock-and-roll patterns to redefine how the music was supposed to feel.

The Velvets were the first important rock-and-roll artists who had no real chance of attracting a mass audience. This was paradoxical. Rock and roll was a mass art, whose direct, immediate appeal to basic emotions subverted class and educational distinctions and whose formal canons all embodied the perception that mass art was not only possible but satisfying in new and liberating ways. Insofar as it incorporates the elite, formalist values of the avant garde, the very idea of rock-and-roll art rests on a contradiction. Its greatest exponents—the Beatles, the Stones, and (especially) the Who—undercut the contradiction by making the surface of their music deceptively casual, then demolished it by reaching millions of kids. But the Velvets' music was too overtly intellectual, stylized, and distanced to be commercial. Like pop art, which was very much a part of the Velvets' world, it was anti-art art made by anti-elite elitists. Lou Reed's aesthete-punk persona, which had its obvious precedent in the avant-garde tradition of artist-as-criminal-as-outlaw, was also paradoxical in the context of rock and roll. The prototypical rock-and-roll punk was the (usually white) working-class kid hanging out on the corner with his (it was usually his) pals; by middle-class and/or adult standards he might be a fuckoff, a hell-raiser, even a delinquent, but he was not really sinister or criminal. Reed's punk was closer to that bohemian (and usually black) hero, the hipster: he wore shades, took hard drugs, engaged in various forms of polymorphous perversity; he didn't just hang out on the corner, he lived out on the street, and he was a loner.

As white exploitation of black music, rock and roll has always had its built-in ironies, and as the music went further from its origins the ironies got more acute. Where, say, Mick Jagger's irony was about a white middle-class English bohemian's (and later a rich rock star's) identification with and distance from his music's black American roots, his working-class image and his teenage audience, Lou Reed's irony made a further leap. It was not only about a white middle-class Jewish bohemian's identification with and distance from black hipsters (an ambiguity neatly defined when Reed-as-junkie, waiting for his man on a Harlem street corner, is challenged, "Hey white boy! Whatchou doin' uptown?") but about his use of a mass art form to express his aesthetic and social alienation from just about everyone. And one of the forms that alienation took pointed to yet another irony. While the original, primal impulse of rock and roll was to celebrate the body, which meant affirming sexual and material pleasure, Reed's temperament was not only cerebral but ascetic. There was nothing resembling lustiness in the Velvets' music, let alone any hippie notions about the joys of sexual liberation. Reed did not celebrate the sadomasochism of "Venus in Furs" any more than he celebrated heroin; he only acknowledged the attraction of what he saw as flowers of evil. Nor did he share his generation's enthusiasm for hedonistic consumption; to Reed the flash of the affluent sixties was fool's gold. Like Andy Warhol and the other pop artists, he responded to the aesthetic potency of mass cultural styles; like Warhol, he was fascinated by decadence—that is, style without meaning or moral content; but he was unmoved by that aspect of the pop mentality, and of rock and roll, that got off on the American dream. In a sense, the self-conscious formalism of his music—the quality that made the Velvets uncommercial—was an attempt to purify rock and roll, to purge it of all those associations with material goodies and erotic good times.

Though it's probable that only the anything-goes atmosphere of the sixties could have inspired a group like the Velvets, their music was prophetic of a leaner, meaner time. They were from—and of—hard-headed, suspicious New York, not utopian, good-vibes California. For all Lou Reed's admiration of Bob Dylan, he had none of Dylan's faith in the liberating possibilities of the edge—what he had taken from *Highway 61 Revisited* and *Blonde on Blonde* was the sound of the edge fraying. Like his punk inheritors he saw the world as a hostile place and did not expect it to change. In rejecting the optimistic consensus of the sixties, he prefigured the punks' attack on the smug consensus of the seventies; his thoroughgoing iconoclasm anticipated the punks' contempt for all authority—including the aesthetic and moral authority of rock and roll itself.

Throughout this decade rock and roll has been struggling to reclaim its identity as a music of cultural opposition, not only distinct from but antagonistic to its own cultural conglomerate, rock. The chief accomplishment of the punks has been to make that antagonism explicit and public in a way that is clearly contemporary—that is, has nothing to do with "reviving" anything except the spirit of opposition itself. What is new in rock and roll—what is uncomfortable and abrasive and demanding—is the extent to which it insists on a defensive stance; the authentic late seventies note is nothing so much as cranky. Though the British punk movement was in some respects a classic revolt of youth—a class-conscious revolt, at that—its self-mocking nihilism is a classic crank attitude, while the American new wave makes up in alienated smartassism for what it lacks in shit-smearing belligerence. The power and vitality of the crank posture is attested to by the way it makes less discordant sensibilities sound corny, even to those of us who might prefer to feel otherwise. Bruce Springsteen may still pull off a credible mélange of fifties teenage-street-kid insurgency, sixties apocalyptic romance and early/mid-seventies *angst*, but he is an anomaly; so is Graham Parker, whose stubborn and convincing faith in traditional rock-and-roll values recalls John Fogerty's. Patti Smith, on the other hand, is a transitional figure, half cranky messiah, half messianic crank. The rock-and-rollers who exemplify the current aesthetic do so with wide variations in intensity, from Johnny Rotten (maniacal crank) to Elvis Costello (passionate crank) to Nick Lowe or Talking Heads (cerebral cranks) to the Ramones (cranks of convenience). (The Clash, one convolution ahead, is boldly anti- or post-crank—the first eighties band?) The obvious core of their crankiness is their consciousness of themselves as a dissident minority, but it's more complicated than that. Real, undiluted rock and roll is almost by definition the province of a dissident minority (larger at some times than at others); it achieved its cultural hegemony in the sixties only by becoming rock—by absorbing competing cultural values and in turn being absorbed, making a new rebellion necessary. What is different now is that for the first time in the music's twenty-five-year history, rock-and-rollers seem to accept their minority status as given and even to revel in it. Which poses an enormous contradiction, for real rock and roll almost by definition aspires to convert the world. So we are back to the paradox of the aesthete-punk. In some ways the crankiness of current rock-and-rollers resembles the disaffection of an earlier era of bohemians and avant-gardists convinced they had a vision the public was too intractably stupid and complacent to comprehend. But because the vision of rock and roll is inherently populist, the punks can't take themselves seriously as alienated artists; their crankiness is leavened with irony. At the same time, having given up on the world, they can't really take themselves seriously as rock-and-rollers, either. They are not only anti-art artists but anti-people populists—the English punks, especially, seem to abhor not only the Queen, America, rich rock stars, and the uncomprehending public but humanity itself. The punks' working-class-*cum*-lumpen style is implicitly political; it suggests collective opposition and therefore communal affirmation. But it is affirmation of a peculiarly limited and joyless sort. For the new wave's minimalist conception of rock and roll tends to exclude not only sensual pleasure but the entire range of positive human emotions, leaving only what is hard and violent, or hard and distanced, or both: if the punks make sex an obscenity, they make love an embarrassment.

In reducing rock and roll to its harshest essentials, the new wave took Lou Reed's aesthete-punk conceit to a place he never intended. For the Velvets the aesthete-punk stance was a way of surviving in a world that was out to kill you; the point was not to glorify the punk, or even to say fuck you to the world, but to be honest about the strategies people adopt in a desperate situation. The Velvets were not nihilists but moralists. In their universe nihilism regularly appears as a vivid but unholy temptation, love and its attendant vulnerability as scary and poignant imperatives. Though Lou Reed rejected optimism, he was enough of his time to crave transcendence. And finally—as "Rock & Roll" makes explicit—the Velvets' use of a mass art form was a metaphor for transcendence, for connection, for resistance to solipsism and despair. Which is also what it is for the punks; whether they admit it or not, that is what *their* irony is about. It may be sheer coincidence, but it was in the wake of the new wave that Reed recorded "Street Hassle," a three-part, eleven-minute anti-nihilist anthem that is by far the most compelling piece of work he has done in his post-Velvets solo career. In it he represents nihilism as double damnation: loss of faith that love is possible, compounded by denial that it matters. "That's just a lie," he mutters at the beginning of part three. "That's why she tells her friends. Cause the real song—the real song she won't even admit to herself."

3. THE REAL SONG, OR I'LL BE YOUR MIRROR

If the Velvets suggested continuity between art and violence, order and chaos, they posed a radical split between body and spirit. In this way too they were closer to the Who than to any other contemporaries. Like the Velvets, the Who were fundamentally ascetic; they too saw the world as hostile—particularly the world as organized by the British class system. Their defiance was cruder than the Velvets', their early music as hard and violent as any to come out of the new wave. But they were not cranks; they were determined to convert the world, and Townshend's guitar-smashing expressed his need to break through to his audience as well as his contempt for authority, including the authority of rock and roll itself. That need to connect also took another form: even before Townshend discovered Meher Baba, the Who's music had a side that could only be called religious. If it seemed, at first, surprising that the same band could produce music as uncompromising in its bitterness as "Substitute" and as miraculously transcendent as the "You are forgiven!" chorus of "A Quick One," it was no contradiction; on the contrary, it was precisely Townshend's sense of the harshness of life, the implacability of the world, that generated his spiritual hunger.

The same can be said of Lou Reed, except that "spiritual hunger" seems too self-important a phrase to apply to him; the Velvets' brand of spirituality has little in common with the Who's grand bursts of mystical ecstasy or Townshend's self-conscious preoccupation with the quest for enlightenment. It's impossible to imagine Lou Reed taking up with a guru, though he might well write a savagely funny (and maybe chillingly serious) song about one. The aesthete-punk and his fellow demi-mondaines are not seeking enlightenment, though they stumble on it from time to time; like most of us they are pilgrims in spite of themselves. For Townshend moral sensitivity is a path to spiritual awareness; for Reed awareness and the lack—or refusal—of it have an intrinsically moral dimension. While he is not averse to using the metaphors of illusion and enlightenment— sometimes to brilliant effect, as in "Beginning to See the Light" and "I'll Be Your Mirror"—they are less central to his theology than the concepts of sin and grace, damnation and salvation. Some of his songs ("Heroin," "Jesus," "Pale Blue Eyes") explicitly invoke that Judeo-Christian language; many more imply it.

But "theology" too is an unfairly pretentious word. The Velvets do not deal in abstractions but in states of mind. Their songs are about the feelings the vocabulary of religion was invented to describe —profound and unspeakable feelings of despair, disgust, isolation, confusion, guilt, longing, relief, peace, clarity, freedom, love—and about the ways we (and they) habitually bury those feelings, deny them, sentimentalize them, mock them, inspect them from a safe, sophisticated distance in order to get along in the hostile, corrupt world. For the Velvets the roots of sin are in this ingrained resistance to facing our deepest, most painful, and most sacred emotions; the essence of grace is the comprehension that our sophistication is a sham, that our deepest, most painful, most sacred desire is to recover a childlike innocence we have never, in our heart of hearts, really lost. And the essence of love is sharing that redemptive truth: on the Velvets' first album, which is dominated by images of decadence and death, suddenly, out of nowhere, comes Nico's artless voice singing, "I'll be your mirror/. . . The light on your door to show that you're home./When you think the night has seen your mind/That inside you're twisted and unkind/. . . Please put down your hands, cause I see you."

For a sophisticated rock-and-roll band with a sophisticated audience, this vision is, to say the least, risky. The idea of childlike innocence is such an invitation to bathos that making it credible seems scarcely less difficult than getting the camel of the gospels through the needle's eye. And the Velvets' alienation is also problematic: it's one thing for working-class English kids to decide life is shit, but how bad can things be for Lou Reed? Yet the Velvets bring it off—make us believe/admit that the psychic wounds we inflict on each other are real and terrible, that to scoff at innocence is to indulge in a desperate lie—because they never succumb to self-pity. Life may be a brutal struggle, sin inevitable, innocence elusive and transient, grace a gift, not a reward ("Some people work very hard/ But still they never get it right," Lou Reed observes in "Beginning to See the Light"); nevertheless we are responsible for who and what we become. Reed does not attempt to resolve this familiar spiritual paradox, nor does he regard it as unfair. His basic religious assumption (like Baudelaire's) is that like it or not we inhabit a moral universe, that we have free will, that we must choose between good and evil, and that our choices matter absolutely; if we are rarely strong enough to make the right choices, if we can never count on the moments of illumination that make them possible, still it is spiritual death to give up the effort.

That the Velvets are hardly innocents, that they maintain their aesthetic and emotional distance even when describing—and evoking—utter spiritual nakedness, does not undercut what they are saying; if anything it does the opposite. The Velvets compel belief in part because, given its context, what they are saying is so bold: not only do they implicitly criticize their own aesthetic stance—they risk undermining it altogether, ending up with sincere but embarrassingly banal home truths. The risk is real because the Velvets do not use irony as a net, a way of evading responsibility by keeping everyone guessing about what they really mean. On the contrary, their irony functions as a metaphor for the spiritual paradox, affirming that the need to face one's nakedness and the impulse to cover it up are equally real, equally human. If the Velvets' distancing is self-protective (hence in their terms damning) it is also revelatory (hence redeeming); it makes clear that the feelings being protected are so unbearably intense that if not controlled and contained they would overwhelm both the Velvets and their audience. The Velvets' real song is how hard it is to admit, even to themselves.

That song in its many variations is the substance of *Velvet Underground*. This album can be conceived of—non-linearly; the cuts are not at all in the right order—as the aesthete-punk's *Pilgrim's Progress*, in four movements. ("Sha la la, man, whyn't you just slip away?" I can hear Lou Reed say to that.)

ONE: WORLDLY SEDUCTION AND BETRAYAL. "Sunday Morning," a song about vague and ominous anxiety, sums up the emotional tone of this movement: "Watch out, the world's behind you." "Here She Comes Now" and "Femme Fatale," two songs about beautiful but unfeeling women (in the unlovable tradition of pop—not to mention religious—misogyny, Lou Reed's women are usually demonic or angelic icons, not people), sum up its philosophy: "Aah, it looks so good/Aah, but she's made out of wood." These songs underscore the point by juxtaposing simple, sweet, catchy melodies with bitter lyrics sung in flat, almost affectless voices (in "Sunday Morning," Reed's voice takes on a breathiness that suggests supressed panic). "White Light/White Heat," a song about shooting speed, starts out by coming as close as any Velvets song does to expressing the euphoria of sheer physical energy; by the end of the trip the music has turned into bludgeoning, deadening noise, the words into a semiarticulate mumble.

TWO: THE SIN OF DESPAIR. "Heroin" is the Velvets' masterpiece —seven minutes of excruciating spiritual extremity. No work of art I know about has ever made the junkie's experience so powerful, so horrible, so appealing; listening to "Heroin" I feel simultaneously impelled to somehow save this man and to reach for the needle. The song is built around the tension between the rush and the nod— expressed musically by an accelerating beat giving way to slow, solemn chords that sound like a bell tolling; metaphorically by the addict's vision of smack as a path to transcendence and freedom, alternating with his stark recognition that what it really offers is the numbness of death, that his embrace of the drug ("It's my wife and it's my life") is a total, willful rejection of the corrupt world, other people, feeling. In the beginning he likens shooting up to a spiritual journey: he's gonna try for the Kingdom; when he's rushing on his run he feels like Jesus' son. At the end, with a blasphemous defiance that belies his words, he avows, "Thank your God that I'm not aware/And thank God that I just don't care!" The whole song seems to rush outward and then close in on itself, on the moment of truth when the junkie knowingly and deliberately chooses death over life —chooses damnation. It is the clarity of his consciousness that gives the sin its enormity. Yet that clarity also offers a glimmer of redemption. In the very act of choosing numbness the singer admits the depths of his pain and bitterness, his longing for something better; he is aware of every nuance of his rejection of awareness; he sings a magnificently heartfelt song about how he doesn't care. (A decade later Johnny Rotten will do the same thing in an entirely different way.) A clear, sustained note runs through the song like a bright thread; it fades out or is drowned out by chaotic, painful distortion and feedback, then comes through again, like the still small voice of the soul. Reed ends each verse with the refrain, "And I guess that I just don't know." His fate is not settled yet.

THREE: PARADISE SOUGHT, GLIMPSED, RECOLLECTED. This movement consists of four songs about world-weary sophistication and the yearning for innocence. "Candy Says" defines the problem: "I've come to hate my body and all that it requires in this world/. . . I'd like to know completely what others so discreetly talk about." "Jesus" is a prayer: "Help me in my weakness, for I've fallen out of grace." In "I'm Set Free," the singer has his illumination, but even as he tries to tell about it, to pin it down, it slips away: "I saw my head laughing, rolling on the ground/And now I'm set free to find a new illusion." In "Pale Blue Eyes," the world has gotten in the way of the singer's transcendent love: "If I could make the world as pure and strange as what I see/I'd put you in the mirror I put in front of me."

Musically these songs are of a piece. They are all gentle, reflective. They all make use of the tension between flat, detached voices and sweet melodies. They all have limpid guitar lines that carry the basic emotion, which is bittersweet: it is consoling to know that innocence is possible, inexpressibly painful that it always seems just out of reach. In "Pale Blue Eyes," a tambourine keeps the beat, or rather is slightly off where the beat ought to be, while a spectacular guitar takes over completely, rolling in on wave after wave of pure feeling.

FOUR: SALVATION AND ITS PITFALLS. "Beginning to See the Light" is the mirror held up to "Heroin." I've always been convinced that it's about an acid trip, perhaps because I first really heard it during one and found it utterly appropriate. Perhaps also because both the song and the acid made me think of a description of a peyote high by a beat writer named Jack Green: "a group of us, on peyote, had little to share with a group on marijuana   the marijuana smokers were discussing questions of the utmost profundity and we were sticking our fingers in our navels & giggling." In "Beginning to See the Light," enlightenment (or salvation) is getting out from under the burden of self-seriousness, of egotism, of imagining that one's sufferings fill the universe; childlike innocence means being able to play. There is no lovelier moment in rock and roll than when Lou Reed laughs and sings, with amazement, joy, gratitude, "I just wanta tell you, *everything* is all right!"

But "Beginning to See the Light" is also wickedly ironic. Toward the end, carried away by euphoria, Reed cries, "There are problems in these times/But ooh, none of them are mine!" Suddenly we are through the mirror, back to the manifesto of "Heroin": "I just don't care!" Enlightenment has begotten spiritual pride, a sin that like its inverted form, nihilism, cuts the sinner off from the rest of the human race. Especially from those people who, you know, work very hard but never get it right. Finally we are left with yet another version of the spiritual paradox: to experience grace is to be conscious of it; to be conscious of it is to lose it.

CODA: I'D LOVE TO TURN YOU ON

Like all geniuses, Lou Reed is unpredictable. In "Street Hassle" he does as good a job as anyone of showing what was always missing in his and the Velvets' vision. As the song begins, a woman (or transvestite?) in a bar is buying a night with a sexy young boy. This sort of encounter is supposed to be squalid; it turns out to be transcendent. Reed's account of the odd couple's lovemaking is as tender as it is erotic: "And then sha la la la la he entered her slowly and showed her where he was coming from/And then sha la la la la he made love to her gently, it was like she'd never ever come." Of course, in part two he almost takes it all back by linking sex with death. Still.

What it comes down to for me—as a Velvets fan, a lover of rock and roll, a New Yorker, an aesthete, a punk, a sinner, a sometime seeker of enlightenment (and love) (and sex)—is this: I believe that we are all, openly or secretly, struggling against one or another kind of nihilism. I believe that body and spirit are not really separate, though it often seems that way. I believe that redemption is never impossible and always equivocal. But I guess that I just don't know.

DESPERADO

THE EAGLES (ASYLUM 5068)
1973

GRACE LICHTENSTEIN

The Eagles' *Desperado* is a bit like the shard of prehistoric Indian pottery I once found in New Mexico—a fragment of Americana whose private associations are for me as valuable as the thing itself. More than any rock album in my collection, *Desperado* conjures up visions of the Western United States as I saw it and lived in it for several years, as well as the desperate state of mind I was often immersed in when I listened to the record.

Pretentious in spots, trivial in others, deliciously melodic throughout, the album spells out a connection between the popular music my contemporaries have produced and the heritage, musical and historical, upon which they draw. I know I can hear it over and over without tiring of it, the way I can look at my pottery endlessly. Unlike so much of my favorite rock music (Beatles, Rolling Stones) it is quintessentially American, and when I'm away from home the album becomes my American talisman. In their rock and roll way, the Eagles are wonderfully patriotic, though I assume their choice of the national bird for their name stemmed from its relationship to nature, not nationality.

Desperado is quite consciously a "concept" album. Each song relates to the others, while the first song on the first side, "Doolin'

Dalton," combined with the title song, becomes a reprise at the end. The medium is generally laid-back early seventies Los Angeles country-rock, yet the story line relates to some historic gunfighters in the Oklahoma region toward the end of the 19th century. There actually was a Bill Doolin, who got caught in the Coffeyville, Kansas, shootout in 1892. In their own hometown, trying to pull off a raid on two banks at once, the Daltons wore disguises, but neighbors recognized them anyway. The result was a bloody showdown that left four townsmen and two Daltons dead. Two Dalton henchmen were also killed, and a photo of the corpses piled up in the street is imitated on the jacket of the Eagles' album. Part of this story is related in "Doolin' Dalton." Another member of the gang who was later killed was named "Bitter Creek" Newcomb; his first name turns up as the title of another song on Desperado. The real Daltons were never lawyers, despite the Eagles' reference in "Doolin' Dalton" to laying aside one's lawbooks, but they did serve for a time as law deputies to the notorious "Hanging Judge" Parker.

Bill Doolin himself later went on to a career as a famous bandit, though he never received the national recognition accorded Billy the Kid or Jesse James. Doolin was more interested in money than fame anyhow, so his robberies were less spectacular. Even so, the man described by contemporaries as a slight, ordinary fellow from rural Arkansas had become, by 1895, the "King of Oklahoma Outlaws," and his capture at an Arkansas health spa while reading a newspaper in the warm baths made front-page news regionally.

Desperado equates the lives of these frontier outlaws of the real and mythic American West to those of latter-day rock musicians, a conceit often used by white folk singers, hard-rock groups, and country & western singers alike. But the Eagles were the first to root the equation in a real-life story from the past that carried an album from start to finish, adding an extra dimension to songs that without it might sound routine.

The Bill Doolin who joins the Dalton gang at the beginning of Desperado regards himself as a young but immortal hotshot ("Twenty One"), loses his innocence in a romantic encounter with a married woman ("Tequila Sunrise"), faces isolation in his passage to adulthood ("Saturday Night"), and confronts the emptiness of a life on the road ("Desperado"). Yet he still hones his skills ("Certain Kind of Fool") to become the best of the bunch, while at the same time he turns cynical about fame ("Bitter Creek") and eventually recognizes that life isn't what he expected it to be. Instead of a full house, it's a stacked deck (reprise), inevitably winding up in violent death.

This desperado, though, is only partly the famed Bill Doolin, King of Oklahoma Outlaws. He is also the Eagles, and every young hotshot rock-and-roller with a quick draw on his guitar. What makes *Desperado* extraordinary is that any sympathetic listener (such as myself, a woman writer rather than a male musician, or indeed anyone with the thirst for fame and adventure Americans seem prey to) can identify with the album. The concept is close to a rock version of the time-honored *bildungsroman*—a story that relates the development of character in a young person as he or she grows to adulthood.

The lyrics deal with much weightier themes than are found in most Eagles' albums, with the exception of *Hotel California*. There is the American penchant for violence, in the initial tale of the Dalton Gang's disastrous raid on Coffeyville, in the rowdy nights in frontier towns, in the ultimate showdown. There is the inevitable rebellion against one's parents, the feeling that the rebel is different from his conformist peers. This second theme is introduced in the first cut ("A man could use his back or use his brains/But some just went stir-crazy, Lord, 'cause nothing ever changed") and expands into "Outlaw Man" and "Desperado." Mixed with this psychological separatism is the craving for fame, not just adoration by faceless crowds but acceptance from one's parents of one's own way of life ("I can't wait to see the old man's face/When I win the race"). There is the impermanence of love, from the outlaw's doomed first affair, to his defiant warning to a woman who loves him in "Outlaw Man," to the bitter conclusion in the "Desperado" reprise—which buries the hope of love for good. Finally, there is the concept of honor. The rebel joins the Daltons not just for fame, money, and women but to help them avenge the deaths of their brothers. As he grows into the desperado, he still has enough honor left to express guilt when he cheats on a friend by sleeping with the friend's woman, and to show up for the last act.

The album progresses very quickly from youthful, lusty enthusiasm to regretful disillusionment. Many of these themes, especially the idea of life as a gamble, and a risky one at that, have been treated well by other rock songwriters; "The Dealer," Bob Ruzicka's song sung by Judy Collins on *True Stories*, is just one example that comes to mind. But in *Desperado*, the themes are all of a piece, more like a musical comedy/drama than a rock performance. Only the Who's *Tommy* seems to have been conceived with such close lyric connections and a coherent story line.

The unexpected density of the lyrics is complemented by a variety of musical styles within the basic L.A. country-rock framework. The Eagles have written at least four waltzes, something of a novelty in seventies rock, and "Saturday Night" is a lovely one indeed, conjuring up one of the musicale set-pieces in a John Ford western. (The other Eagles waltzes are "Hollywood Waltz," "Take It to the Limit," and "Pretty Maids All in a Row.") Hard rock ("Out of Control") blends with the more country & western sound of "Tequila Sunrise," the banjo-picking folkiness of "Twenty One," the bluegrass in the introduction to "Outlaw Man" and the piano-and-strings lushness of "Desperado." Not until *Hotel California* several years later did the Eagles once again dive head-on into such a complex mix of musical and lyrical ideas. *Hotel California*, moreover, is about modern America. *Desperado*, more interestingly, is about America both past and present.

Then there is the vocalizing. From their first hit on their first album, the Glenn Frey–Jackson Browne song "Take It Easy," the Eagles have produced some of the most pleasing close harmony in rock and roll. Neither of the leads, Frey and Don Henley (nor Bernie Leadon and Randy Meisner, who occasionally soloed on the early albums), has, individually, the most compelling male voice in West Coast rock; that title undoubtedly goes to Neil Young. One can also halve the "woo-woos" in a lot of the Eagles' music and double the pleasure. Nevertheless, taking their cue from groups of the middle and late sixties such as Buffalo Springfield, the Flying Burrito Brothers, and Crosby, Stills, Nash and Young, the Eagles' singing has a sweet hypnotic force that made not only "Take It Easy" but lesser songs such as "Lyin' Eyes," "Take It to the Limit," and "Best of My Love" huge AM hits.

On *Desperado*, the musicianship was hardly flashy. In the middle of a CSNY album, Neil Young could nail a listener to the wall with his voice and guitar work on "Southern Man," but around that song was an awful lot of blandness. Without the fleshiness of a Young, or a Joe Walsh, who joined the Eagles with *Hotel California, Desperado* still hangs tough. The guitar playing is gutsy (listen to "Bitter Creek" and "Outlaw Man"), adding just enough tartness to those sweet harmonies. The musicians have borrowed judiciously from almost every American popular music genre except rhythm & blues. (Henley's charming, scruffy tenor does owe something to black singers, while the falsettos used in so many of the songs are also of black origin.) The one quality I do miss in the album is humor.

Of course, there's a reason for choosing to spend one's life with *Desperado* rather than, say, a Randy Newman album, whose fun would probably pale quickly. Beyond its central concept of outlaw/rock star, *Desperado* presents the idea of the man or woman alone, his or her own worst enemy; there is an oddly comforting quality to the idea when one hears the album all by oneself. Sure it's sad, but also instructive. If we are all alone, then being all alone at the moment isn't so awful, is it?

In effect, I took *Desperado* to a desert island in 1975, two years after the album's release, when I moved to Colorado to be a roving newspaper correspondent covering the Rocky Mountain west. Although I loved the album before, it now became my cassette companion on many roads "where the desert meets the sky." One may argue whether the music, coming out of the L.A. rock establishment, is inauthentic in the "real" cowboy/outlaw West. That's not the point. In a four-wheel truck crossing a rutted mountain pass that led to the played-out silver mines where, in the 1890s, "Baby Doe" Tabor scandalized the country, *Desperado* was utterly appropriate on a car stereo in the 1970s. At times hardly any other music would do. The only album that came close was Willie Nelson's *Red Headed Stranger*. I had adored Stevie Wonder, the Beatles, the Rolling Stones, the early Supremes. But that was city music. I couldn't play it in my circumstances. Mick Jagger does not work in a car in Utah the way he does in a living room in New York. *Desperado* worked superbly, as did the other Eagles albums; it kept me company, through Utah, Colorado, Montana, Wyoming, Arizona, New Mexico, Nevada.

Nor was it my companion alone. By 1975, the title song was sufficiently popular among many amateur and smalltown professional musicians that one often found it in their repertory. I heard it, without requesting it, dozens of times at live shows out west. (By 1978, the song was so well known the McGarrigle sisters sang a parody of it at a New York club date.) The song seemed to follow me. One particularly eerie evening, around a campfire in Utah's Canyonlands National Park, fifty miles from the nearest paved road, 6,000 feet atop a spectacular red-rock desert plateau overlooking the Colorado River, a young woman in a cowboy hat who was cook on our camping trip began strumming the chords I knew by heart. I tried to sing along, but her pitch was too high for me and there was a lump in my throat. It was the first night of what turned out to be a magical visit to the Utah desert, where sixteen people started as strangers and seven days later became friends for life. A few days into the trip, as we hiked to see some ancient granaries used by the Anasazi (early Pueblo) Indians, I asked the cook why she had sung "Desperado" on our expedition's opening night. "It's my favorite song," she replied fervently, both of us squinting into the pure light of desert noon, a light that makes you feel as alone as a person can be, a light that makes you want to metamorphose into a lizard. "I've always felt like that song was sort of written for me," she continued. "It's as if I was just misplaced when I was born."

She was twenty-five years old, a native Californian who hated her home state and had come to the inland west in search of cowboys, desert, adventure, the myth. I was ten years her senior, a New Yorker who loved my native city and who had come to the Rockies in search of the same things. We were talking of a song, written by two young men, one from Texas, the other from Detroit, who had both quit their homes to live in California. At that moment, what we had in common was that "Desperado" spoke for us, in terms more powerful than the spoken or the written word speaks.

My love for *Desperado* occasionally had its absurd moments. Once I was driving through a desolate stretch of southwest Wyoming toward an appointment many miles ahead in the Tetons. It was early September, the rainy season. The sky was leaden. Soon it began to pour. In my rented Avis, *Desperado* was playing on my small cassette player. As I approached Jackson Hole the rolling plains of sagebrush began to give way to hillocks and then to offer glimpses of the etched mountains beyond. Almost at the exact point where Don Henley sings, "It may be raining, but there's a rainbow above you," the rainbow appeared in my smeared windshield, summoned, I was certain, by Euterpe, the musical muse. I screeched to a halt on the shoulder of the road, jumped out of the car, and stood in the stinging rain to stare at the rainbow. A minute later, a state trooper pulled up behind me.

"Anything wrong, Ma'am?"

"Uh, no, officer, nothing. I'm just looking at the rainbow," I replied, feeling drenched and foolish.

He responded with one of those she's-crazy-but-harmless nods. "Gonna get wet that way," he said with a shrug, and climbed back in his car and sped off.

I got wet, but the feeling of foolishness disappeared when he did. The Rocky Mountain west is a strip of real estate so enormous, so empty, that it makes human beings feel quite small. The very splendor of the scenery induces reflective pensiveness about one's life even as it lifts the soul with its beauty. The feeling expressed in the music of "Outlaw Man," "Out of Control," "Tequila Sunrise," and "Desperado" captured that sense of the west for me time and time again. Eventually, it seemed it was not just the west, but the general rootlessness of my then-current life that was the heart and spirit of *Desperado*.

Looked at another way, the album was the one that moved me the most among those in the subgenre of "road" music. Rock musicians, as we are reminded constantly in magazine profiles, spend part of their glamorous time moving from Holiday Inn to Holiday Inn like so many traveling salesmen. Or traveling business executives. Or traveling journalists. The difference is that in rock, life on the road has been elevated to something of an existential state, a metaphor for the anomie of the post-industrial society. Since I was one of those traveling persons, with a fondness for rock, I turned to those songs for comfort in my green shag cinderblock motel rooms the way my neighboring traveling salesmen turned to their pints of gin, the way rock musicians turned to their groupies.

My favorite road songs included Gram Parsons' "Grievous Angel," a lament about purposelessness and the need for love that is a first cousin to "Desperado"; James Taylor's "Highway Song," an ironic tribute to the lure of the road; Joni Mitchell's "Amelia," a complex homage to Earhart contrasted with the singer's own wanderings; and Carole King's "So Far Away," a sad acknowledgment that nobody these days stays in one place for long, physically or emotionally.

After I returned from the west to New York, Jackson Browne's road album, *Running on Empty*, was released to critical acclaim. Had I still been in Colorado, it undoubtedly would have joined my suitcase cassette collection immediately. But I was home. The album reached me (I especially enjoyed the multiple suggestions of the title song) yet it did not move me. Of Browne's many "road" songs I prefer "Take It Easy," less inner-directed, more adventurous (how many of us have made a stop in Winslow, Arizona, because of that song?), better sung by the Eagles than by the composer. Once I was home, L.A. country-rock, most Eagles albums included, did not have the same power over my emotions that it did when I listened to it out west. Suddenly I was more interested in Bruce Springsteen's urban "Badlands" than in Willie Nelson's rural ones. Carly Simon's urbane musings about love were once again more accessible than Emmylou Harris's countrified ones. Graham Parker's and Elvis Costello's hard-edged rock brought me closer to my rock 'n' roll teenage days than the Outlaws.

Maybe it's a question of listening to music in context. The big exception, obviously, is *Desperado*, which never loses its hold on me. I'd like to think it's a better album, overall, than *Running on Empty*. I can't make a fair judgment, nor is it necessary. *Desperado* is now part of my own history. I can no longer separate a particular riff in "Outlaw Man" from a group of creepy "Wild Bunch" gun-toting right-wingers I met in Virginia City, Montana, nor the line about freedom in the title song from the squalid Ada County Jail in which I spent a night in Idaho, nor the almost-silly raunchiness of "Out of Control" from a beer-crazed roadhouse I danced in north of Albuquerque.

The Eagles' attempts at taking a crack at the old and new wests have been noble ones, with *Desperado* the prettiest of them all. While others in the L.A. rock scene—Neil Young (who isn't truly part of it), Browne, J. D. Souther—seem to be turning psychologically inward, the Eagles continue to tell fine stories with a sociological point of view in close harmony: stories like the title song on *Hotel California*, "Life in the Fast Lane," and the less successful "Last Resort."

Not long ago, the title song of *Desperado*, my favorite rock story, was accidentally put to the test of my present tolerance level. My clock radio went off one morning as a set of songs was beginning with a new one I like a great deal, Springsteen's "Badlands." I lay there half-asleep, and the music—tough, here-and-now, street-wise, big city—segued into "Desperado." Alone, yet not any longer desperate nor western, back home at last, a street-wise big city woman, I started to sob into my pillow, not for the Springsteen song, but for the Eagles'.

LITTLE WILLIE JOHN

LITTLE WILLIE JOHN (KING 5004X)
1953–1962/1977

JOE MC EWEN

When I was young, I had a gut feeling that energy and swing could transcend even the most lingering (and banal) adolescent traumas and depressions. As a teenager, I was often morose, though the music that attracted me—"Cool Jerk," "Shotgun," "Papa's Got a Brand New Bag"—rarely ever was. I liked ballads well enough, but with few exceptions (James Brown's "Lost Someone") such songs were either overwrought or slight. Mood music, even "Tracks of My Tears," was never moody enough.

Little Willie John was a teenager when he recorded his first hit, "All Around the World," for King Records in 1955. When he faded in 1962, he was a grizzled veteran of 23. Though rock and roll singing was once the province of the young, few under-twenty singers have been able to communicate more than jittery restlessness or poignant ache. Little Willie John's records are filled with much more. The songs on *Little Willie John*, a collection of his fifteen biggest hits, are dark and mature; sometimes messy, sometimes desperate. John sounded old, but his music was also delicate and vulnerable—he wasn't afraid to show his age. But more than anything, John's songs seemed to speak for every growing pain and young adult awkwardness. His music was an expression of longing and desire beyond physical love and romance. Little Willie John understood.

Little Willie John, Sam Cooke, Jackie Wilson, and (to a lesser extent) James Brown changed the manner of black popular singing. Each was a stand-up, church-reared vocalist who had a high regard for the stock tools of the trade: technique, presentation, and flair. That alone made them different from most, though older rhythm and blues singers like Ruth Brown and Roy Brown had similar upwardly mobile concerns. But the real difference was in style, and the very manner of a Little Willie John or Sam Cooke suggested a measured cockiness and self-assured presence that was inescapably black and soulful, no matter what the song. The new music, more gospel-derived and personal than that of the forties and early fifties, also implied a new stance, for each of the singers, in his own way, mastered the art of Cool.

Cool had been a part of black popular music before: in the zany antics of Cab Calloway; in the style of Billy Eckstine, the urban Mr. B. But the jive of Calloway and the dapperness of Eckstine never left a lingering impression, maybe because emotional expression was never part of the package: Calloway had his Hep Dictionary and Eckstine made women swoon with rococo Tin Pan Alley ballads that melted, one after the other, like landscapes on the open road. The implications of Cool for Cooke, John, Wilson, and Brown went beyond the surface, combining polished talent with swagger and acumen. Cool offered the potential for self-determination, and even irresponsibility. Above all, it meant a new day for black people. Cool, for one, meant you didn't have to answer to anybody. For two, it meant you had what it takes.

Though most soul singers in the sixties aspired to the mantle of Cool, only Aretha Franklin really possessed the breadth of talent necessary to support it. Soul music itself required a kind of clumsy involvement: Solomon Burke needed a witness and raising your hand just wasn't part of Cool. There was always Motown, of course, but Motown was primarily a teenage music. And when Motown singers tangled with anything other than Motown music, the results were usually contrived and embarrassing. The Four Tops on Broadway converted few people. Besides, the choreography, which was part of Motown's flash, also helped confine its practitioners to the ghetto. A few years past its time, choreography could look awful corny. Cool knew no such restrictions, save race perhaps, in its appeal. In 1971, when the last Soul Man, Al Green, surfaced, he registered Cool's lingering influences: Cooke, Wilson, and John were ticked off as favorites.

Cool was indisputably urban, and, in a sense, Sam Cooke was its epitome. Cooke sang like an urbane, soulful crooner, projecting feeling without seeming to sweat and often giving the impression that his sad songs were only momentary dissatisfactions with the state of things. Cooke ran his own show and even had his own record label. Above all, Sam Cooke exuded class in everything he did.

For Jackie Wilson, Cool was a magnificent voice that could tackle blues, rock 'n' roll and the most unregenerate schmaltz; Cool was a hair-raising stage show that aroused audiences with splits, spins, slides, and knee-drops. Though Wilson was almost as active as James Brown on stage, he was never as intense—and besides, Wilson was much better looking. But it wasn't the sexual hysteria Wilson aroused that made him cool; Jackie Wilson overwhelming "Danny Boy" or "Night" for a black audience—that was Cool.

James Brown had much to overcome. He had a rural Georgia background; he was a fierce performer on stage. But Brown invented new dance steps and spoke the hippest slang. Like Cooke, he also ran his own operation, designed his own clothes, produced his own records, and made sure he got his money. Brown could get away with screams and grunts, and an occasional gauche outfit, simply because he was James Brown. But for real Cool, James Brown was too kinetic, too down, too black.

Jackie Wilson had more range and Sam Cooke more purity and grace, but no one had a voice like Little Willie John. While he did share a nasal, cigarette rasp with James Brown, John could punctuate even the harshest of phrases with a wild falsetto or suddenly retreat into a muffled, choked sob. John also had a fullness that Brown never possessed—a quality that gave his blues and ballads a heavy, drenching kind of melancholy. At the same time he was capable of great delicacy; his phrasing on the subdued "Let Them Talk" is meticulous and tender. At his best, John's voice simply sounded eerie. He wore snap-brim hats, smoked a pipe, and stood inches over five feet; like Sam Cooke, he could move an audience without acrobatics or show. Little Willie John had style.

Little Willie John was born in Camden, Arkansas, but moved to Detroit at an early age; R&B bandleader Johnny Otis remembers eyeing a 13-year-old John at a Detroit talent show in 1951. Otis passed the word to Syd Nathan of King Records, who ignored John and signed a group of entrants from the same show, Hank Ballard and the Royals. Through the early fifties, John made brief appearances fronting the bands of Duke Ellington and Count Basie, and toured more extensively with tenor saxophonist and R&B hitmaker Paul Williams. Little Willie John didn't lack for proper schooling. Though precious little has been written about John and his influences, those listed by Jackie Wilson (who also grew up in Detroit) serve the point well enough: Al Jolson, the Mills Brothers, the Ink Spots, Clyde McPhatter, the Dixie Hummingbirds, Louis Jordan.

When "All Around the World" was released, Little Willie John was seventeen and sounded thirty. Pop audiences didn't pay much attention. In fact, through his career, John nudged only two songs—"Talk to Me" and "Sleep"—into the Top 20. He hasn't been particularly well served by rock historians either. He receives only passing mention in both *The Rolling Stone Illustrated History of Rock & Roll* and Charlie Gillett's *The Sound of the City*, the two most comprehensive works in the field. In other, lesser treatments, John is simply ignored altogether; the only sustained reference to the singer that I know of (liner notes aside) is the two-hundred-word biography in Norm N. Nite's entertaining *Rock On.* The best tribute accorded Little Willie John came from a surprising source: James Brown, who recorded an album called *Thinking of Little Willie John and a Few Nice Things.*

But such oversights are understandable. If rock historians are drawn to anything, they're drawn to commitment, and a glance at the range of material John recorded in his career (the fifteen songs on *Little Willie John* span just seven years) reveals a noticeable lack of commitment to any form or genre. The commitment is to Making It, and a song as awkward as "Autumn Leaves" (recorded by John on *The Hot, The Sweet, The Teen-Age Beat*) was probably regarded by John as every bit as appropriate a vehicle as "Need Your Love So Bad," probably his most moving record. It was cynicism of a sort, though that attitude was more confined to record company presidents, A&R men, and producers. No doubt for John it was all just a way out.

The songs on *Little Willie John* don't quite evidence the jumbled variety of material that can be found on his oddball King LPs. He recorded everything: squeaky pop-rock, "Flamingo," blues, soul ballads, punchy funky, novelty songs, and even one funny record called "Spasms," on which he hiccups like Jerry Lee Lewis. "All Around the World" was different: a jaunty, big-band piece that sounded like any number of Joe Turner's pre–rock 'n' roll records for Atlantic. But such variety was all part of Cool, and mastering the least likely material only added to the singer's worldly luster. The Copacabana and the Apollo weren't mutually exclusive. A few years later, soul singers like Wilson Pickett and Al Green would try to mix the same oil and water, with much less success. The bottom of soul, after all, *was* commitment.

In a way, listening to a Little Willie John album is like listening to any number of post-Sun Elvis Presley records. Somewhere, amidst the show tunes and schlock, are moments of great passion and clarity. Such moments come, go, and come in bright flashes, like a dazzling move from some lazy or bored playground basketball legend. For the most part, the hits were the best of Little Willie John's work, as if to remind us that all the trendy contrivances and weird gimmicks were only so much album filler between the Real Thing. But that wasn't always so: the intensity of "Suffering with the Blues" is still a scary thing to listen to, and the gently shuffling "Home at Last" has the same doomy flavor that saturates "Need Your Love So Bad." Neither were hit 45s. On the other hand, "Sleep," a bizarre mismatch of bad orchestration and a song that had previously been associated with Fred

Waring's Pennsylvanians, became John's biggest pop hit, as if to confirm all the industry's worst instincts.

Little Willie John is an uneven album, yet it's a record that stands quite alone. It was rhythm and blues, but when inspiration struck, John (and producers Henry Glover and Ralph Bass) locked into emotions that were more complex than those in stock blues and more mature than Utopian, Boy-meets-Girl, teenage love stuff. Though his best records run a gamut of emotional expression, rarely did John ever sound happy. For a mature adult, a performance as dark and knowing as "Need Your Love So Bad" would have been an achievement worth a lifetime; for a recently turned seventeen-year-old, the song is staggering in its depth and sensitivity. "Need Your Love So Bad" is rendered as a spare blues ballad, with no accompaniment other than a light rhythm section. The tinkling triplets of the piano are simple and familiar, but what John sings is no mere recitation of words. The phrasing is deliberate, marked by fuzzy slurs and sighs, and at times it seems as if the plea is so desperate, and the singer so lonely, that he's beyond verbal expression. It's a despair that hovers near some cavernous, internal abyss.

Occasionally John was able to transfer his brooding pathos to uptempo songs, and the staccato, James Brown–inspired "Heartbreak (It's Hurtin' Me)" is a worthy successor to better-known ballad hits like "Talk to Me" and "Let Them Talk." There's one moment in "Heartbreak" when it all seems to pour out: "This morning I was happy/Tonight I got 'em bad/Heartbreak, it's killin' me."

It's hard to say what effect all this heartbreak and fever had on someone who had yet to turn twenty-two. After "Heartbreak" came "Sleep," and then a quick slide downhill. The spark that flourished in a late adolescent never quite returned after "Sleep" (released in mid-1960), and even straight-ahead ballads like "The Very Thought of You" lack the glimmer and taut emotionalism present in John's work only a year earlier. Maybe the psychic trauma of being a very young man caught up in a fantasy world of hit records and cross-country touring took its toll. Or maybe the juice was just drained dry. By the end of 1961, Little Willie

John was off the charts for good. Seven years later, after a conviction for manslaughter, he died in prison, of pneumonia, in Walla Walla, Washington, the stuff of legend.

Little Willie John is an album full of ambiguities. It doesn't define its time the way the early Sam Cooke hits did and it doesn't offer the apocalyptic drama of a James Brown song like "Please, Please, Please" or "I'll Go Crazy." It contains more mediocrity than it should (though even the mediocre songs prove to be illuminating, like the failures of all great artists), certainly more than the singer deserved in a retrospective album of this type. But the songs that move me on this record reach private emotions that I've kept sealed off since I was a teenager. When John sings "Need Your Love So Bad," I think of the lonely weekends I spent in high school wishing for a girl who not only combined a dozen mythic qualities, but who also felt the same battery of desires, fears, and depressions that haunted me. Naturally such a girl would be quite different from the rest, and "Let Them Talk" (with that wonderful phrase, "Idle gossip comes from the devil's workshop") is my bravado answer to sticking out like a sore thumb. "Fever" is surging sexual passions, and "Heartbreak (It's Hurtin' Me)"—well, that speaks for itself. Some of these emotions were simple and laughable, some poignant, and some worthy of the inarticulate rage I felt at the time. All remain as fresh and vivid as last night's dinner.

For the playground legend, the sum of the parts is always more important than the whole. And while self-sacrifice, drive, and hustle are the all-important ingredients of a successful team, there's a thrill beyond words in watching an athlete display skills that he alone owns, even if such gifts are eventually self-destructive. When thinking of Little Willie John, I'm reminded of that. When listening to *Little Willie John*, my life passes before me.

SOMETHING ELSE BY THE KINKS

THE KINKS (REPRISE 6279)
1968

JANET MASLIN

At first I thought the biggest problem would be one of acoustics, but then I thought again. No friends. No enemies. No Christmas shoppers, but no Christmas presents, either. No way to start a stamp collection. No date at the movies. Hold the phone—no movies at all! Or books! Or talk shows! Or magazines (except for one yellowing copy of *People*, with Gregg and Cher and Baby Elijah on the cover)! Or records! *No records!*

Hah. *One* record, and—this being something of a trumped-up dilemma—all the time in the world to choose it. The final selection process didn't take me anywhere near that long: *Something Else by the Kinks*, and there's no second choice. If I couldn't pack that, I'd have to make other travel plans.

If it were just a matter of setting the proper mood for a long journey, I might want to take Jackson Browne's *Running on Empty* for its all-night road songs, Bruce Springsteen's *Greetings from Asbury Park* or *Born to Run* for warding off any possible hint of drowsiness, and the Bee Gees' *Main Course* for dancing in the car. If the idea were to fall into a state of perfect relaxation once I got there, then *Abbey Road* or Arlo Guthrie's *Amigo* or *The Hollies' Greatest Hits* would be best for morning, Van Morrison's

Saint Dominic's Preview or Jimmy Webb's *El Mirage* for the late afternoon. Judy Collins's *Who Knows Where the Time Goes* would work well at that hour too, but I'd save it for later, since it's one of the best things I know for falling asleep happy.

On nights when I didn't care about sleeping and stayed awake brooding long after the fish had gone to bed, I'd want to hear Leonard Cohen's *Songs from a Room*, *Phil Ochs in Concert*, Ralph McTell's *You Well-Meaning Brought Me Here*, Elvis Costello's *My Aim Is True*, or *Warren Zevon*. Days that made me miss the city would cry out for Steely Dan's *Katy Lied*, or Laura Nyro's *Eli and the Thirteenth Confession*, or anything by Randy Newman. And balmy days, days for being merry and tan and sorry for only one thing—that I can't swim—would mean the Beach Boys, who are my favorite band during that minority of the time when the Kinks aren't. *All Summer Long? Pet Sounds? Wild Honey*. Or *The Beach Boys Love You*.

But there are certain things about this situation that make it the Kinks' cup of tea. For one thing, they'd be invaluable tour guides, having made this same journey themselves any number of times. Yes, it may have started out as something of a joke—in "I'm on an Island," on *The Kink Kontroversy*, Ray Davies sang, to a beat midway between rock and cha-cha, of being literally left high and dry because he'd lost his girl. The trip had made him nothing if not cheerfully redundant: "I'm on an island/And I've got nowhere to run/Because I'm the only one/Who's on the island."

That was in 1965. By 1967, on *Face to Face*, the Kinks were ready for a more elaborate vacation, only to discover that a "Holiday in Waikiki," spent beside billboards and high-priced souvenirs, in the company of hula dancers with New York accents, might not be the right choice. Since then, there have been the tropical exile on the *Lola* album, that flight in a "Supersonic Rocket Ship" from *Everybody's in Show Biz*, and a more ominous convalescence on *Muswell Hillbillies*' "Holiday." And those are only the literal trips. The Kinks are capable of making anything sound like a secluded retreat, whether it's a newly empty house (in "Sunny Afternoon"), or a room overlooking a busy train station (in "Waterloo Sunset"), or a café that's suddenly missing one's usual companion (in "Afternoon

Tea"). In the Kinks' scheme of things, being alone is a given even when it isn't specified.

The trip on *Lola Versus Powerman and the Moneygoround* is the closest the Kinks may ever come to smooth sailing. On side one of the album, the adventures of a would-be rock star are detailed in the most beautifully melodic song Ray Davies has thus far written ("Get Back in the Line") and one of the funniest ("Moneygoround"). The singer is down on his luck, but then he writes a hit ("Lola"— Ray really *did* write a hit, his first in four years), tastes success ("Top of the Pops") and has a devil of a time collecting his royalties. By side two, he's given up trying. On "This Time Tomorrow," a serene song full of unexpectedly tranquil harmonies, the singer is on a plane musing about making his lonely getaway.

He looks down upon "fields full of houses" with the Kinks' particularly sharp awareness that everything has its price. The many Kinks songs that set up figures in opposition—like the two sisters in the song of the same name, one a housewife and one a glamorous bachelorette, or the competing politicians in *Preservation*—aim at a notion of seesawing destinies as well as at simple dramatic conflict. They suggest that one rival is happy only when the other is miserable, that cities are built at the expense of landscapes, that the cheerful rogue in "Sunny Afternoon" is only happy because someone, somewhere, has run off crying. And yet there's something benign about all this, something very much in keeping with Ray Davies's characteristic mixture of longing and revulsion. It's quite consistent with the idea, in so many of his songs, that life is at its most vivid when seen from a distance.

The *Lola* album's runaway has a dream of winding up in the jungle, in which he maintains that the only time he's happy is when he's swinging from the trees. "Oh what a life of luxury!" he cries. When Davies writes of "luxury" he's usually sending it up, as with that stately home and yacht in "Sunny Afternoon." But the mention here is more authentic. For one of Davies's super-civilized recluses, true luxury really would mean being able to run around in a loincloth without a second thought about whether it was well-tailored. And that's one freedom this music never even hints at, except in jest. That's what would make any Kinks album at home on a desert island; it would help you celebrate being away while still reminding you—keenly, keenly—of exactly what you were missing.

And although it would be hard to leave behind *Lola* or *The Kink Kronikles*—for "Days" and "Autumn Almanac" and "Dead End Street," particularly—I'd take *Something Else,* from 1968. Of the earlier albums, the first are too raucous and uneven for me to be sure I'd want to hear them endlessly. And *Face to Face,* which I would never be without if I had a reasonable choice in the matter, is too close to a bad dream at times ("Little Miss Queen of Darkness," "Rainy Day in June") for me to be sure I could always stare it down. Much as I love the live *Everybody's in Show Biz,* I wouldn't want to be reminded of how many wonderful concerts I'd be missing. And since a lot of the *Muswell Hillbillies* material is most memorable in its live form, that would stay home, too.

So would *Preservation* and *Soap Opera,* because they need to be listened to all at one sitting (and that could be tricky, depending upon the tides); cut-by-cut, they aren't a match for more concise Kinks records. Also left behind would be *Schoolboys in Disgrace,* the only Kinks record I actively dislike. *Sleepwalker* is something I seldom listen to, and like *The Great Lost Kinks Album,* it never strikes me as being all of a piece; if I wanted a collection of unrelated songs I'd take the *Kronikles. Arthur* is still a mystery to me; I'll always hear it as the soundtrack of a British TV special I've never seen. *The Village Green Preservation Society* would have to stay home, I suppose, but it would be damp with tears. And so, I think, would be *Misfits,* although we haven't had nearly enough time to get to know each other.

Certainly *Something Else* is as exquisitely book-ended as a Kinks album could be, with "David Watts" for its beginning and "Waterloo Sunset" for a finale. There's a pure bitterness in "David Watts" that hasn't come through as bluntly in the Kinks' music before or since (although on the same album there's "Harry Rag," sung with an uncharacteristic rudeness and in much the same spirit). David Watts is the schoolboy who has everything, the one whom everyone envies, a familiar figure who takes many forms (when I knew him, he was a little girl). There are later Kinks attacks on the same fellow —he's the "Mr. Big Man" of *Sleepwalker*—but none of them are brave enough to go after the little prig without using satire as a club. "David Watts" is plain, liberating malice, not coincidentally one of the Kinks' toughest rock songs, and one of their most breathlessly economical performances. Even the first few seconds of introduction, with Ray instructing the band to make it "nice and smooth," contribute to the ferocity. They don't just begin this song; they tear its throat out.

When Ray goes machine-gunning his favorite middle-class squirrels, he's being every bit the bully that David Watts is. But "Tin Soldier Man," setting its description of a pitifully regimented workaday Johnny to a military beat, is an unusually palatable example of Kinks Overkill. If any song is going to represent that genre, this might as well be the one.

Dave Davies's songs on *Something Else* are both good enough to have established a reputation for him independent of his older brother's and enough like Ray's to dovetail gently with the rest of the record. "Death of a Clown" and "Love Me Till the Sun Shines" are probably the best known of the three (or, more properly, two-and-a-half—Ray has a co-writing credit on "Death of a Clown"). But it's "Funny Face" that remains the most intriguing: here is, all at once, a sense of murk and mystery to match Ray's on "Lazy Old Sun," a blitheness like the spirit Ray brings to singing "End of the Season," the peculiarly bland affirmation of the title ("Funny Face" is "all right" the way Dandy is "all right" or Waterloo Sunset is "fine"). And a starkly vivid physical picture: "I see you/Peering through frosted windows/Eyes don't smile/All they do is cry."

More interesting than either the prevailing fogginess of a song of such bizarre familiarity that the singer might just as easily be addressing his Uncle Phil, or the vaudeville phrasing at the end of each otherwise gloomy verse, are the abrupt swings between seemingly disjointed moods. There's a similar clash of tones on "End of the Season," with its gray opening and then more vaudeville crooning, this time from someone who describes himself as covered with mud and dreaming of flowers. Even the painfully controlled romantic overtures the singer makes in "Afternoon Tea" are at odds with that song's jaunty, lighthearted sound, as the singer cheerfully encourages his date to "Take as long as you like/'Cause I like you, girl." (By the end of the song, she has vanished; he wonders why.) In all of these songs, neither the overt attitude nor the trouble glimpsed behind it. is as compelling as the play of these various elements, the way they intensify and undermine one another. The song is that much better for being an imperfect expression of the singer's state of mind.

Some of Ray Davies's most haunting work has been written and delivered in the spirit of inaccurate expression, of subdued turmoil. Perhaps what places "Waterloo Sunset" a cut above any other Kinks song is the way it takes a perfectly forthright route yet still arrives at the old ambiguity. Whatever that "dirty old river" suggests to the singer about himself, he's long since quietly resigned himself to it; whatever he means by saying someone is "in paradise," the phrase hangs just a tiny bit closer to weariness than to hope. He sits in a room at twilight, watching the crowds of tiny figures around a railway station; he singles out one couple and, with evident arbitrariness, imagines them to be singularly blessed. Ray was once an art student and, indeed, he might as easily have painted this as set it to music. That's another argument for choosing *Something Else*, for that bonus: an imaginary picture to hang on the imaginary lean-to wall.

There's one last reason I'd settle on a Kinks record, perhaps the best reason of all: because rock doesn't often have the effect on me that it used to. Ten years ago, I wasn't quite twenty, and there was nothing to mitigate the fun of being a fan. Whatever the occasion, there was always a perfect record to make part of the moment: the right Sly or Stones or Four Tops or Creedence record to dance to, the right folk singer when things were quiet, even the right Byrds album for doing homework if there was noise in the dormitory hallway. I did a year's worth of math problems to the tune of "Mr. Tambourine Man."

I had forgotten, until lately, how much buying a record could mean to me: if I bought one, even on a whim, I felt a simple obligation to listen to it over and over, through and through. By not admitting the possibility of bad judgment, I saved myself from feeling faint-hearted.

Things have gotten easier since then, and harder too: a record that arrives in the mail doesn't have the same value as a record that's chosen, and purchased, and owned at the expense of owning something else. And listening to certain artists because you ought to makes it harder to be anyone's fan. A while ago, I'd begun giving up: most new music either saddened or bored me, and too many old records felt like relics of irretrievable moments. But I'm not fool enough to imagine my formal knowledge of rock amounts to anything, and neither am I liable to forget that hearing just the right record at just the right moment is a thrill for which there's no easy equivalent. So I quit paying attention to new records I didn't really care about—life is simply too short for me to get to know disco. And I decided to stop neglecting the records I love best; I've begun replacing the ones that have disappeared or worn out, when I can find and afford them. I'm due for a new copy of *Something Else* pretty soon, and it's long since out of print, so finding one isn't going to be easy. But it'll be a pleasure.

One grim liability of getting older is running the risk of meeting—even liking—people who aren't now and never have been rock fans. These people, I have begun to find, are likelier to take an interest in the Kinks than they are in hearing the entirety of one's Doors collection. And who would deny that having friends is nearly as important as having records?

So that's one extra selling point for *Something Else*: I'd want to have something to play for a new acquaintance, if the tides were to change and a likely-looking person swam by. After all, the wind might shift. Perhaps a shipwreck, or a stray plane, or new neighbors on the atoll next door.

Desert island? I don't *need* a desert island. *Something Else by the Kinks* is with me anyway, wherever I go.

ROCKET TO RUSSIA

THE RAMONES (SIRE 6063)
1977

TOM CARSON

In mid-summer of 1977, Sire Records released "Sheena Is a Punk Rocker," a new single by the Ramones. That summer was the high-water mark of the punk era—an era which had begun the year before, when the first wave of New York underground club bands started getting record contracts, and would end, for all practical purposes, with the breakup of the Sex Pistols in January of '78. After that, though punk survived, it was no longer a revolution. But that hadn't happened yet. At CBGB's and Max's Kansas City, the atmosphere was heady with confidence. Everyone was ready to believe that by the end of the year punk rock would have taken the Top 40 by storm, and brought the mainstream of the culture to submission in one quick and easy battle; it was the old fantasy of the American bohemian underground, of finally being accepted by the rest of the country—a dream much older than rock 'n roll itself. There was a sense that people all around you were doing fine things, in a way they might never have the chance to again. To be in New York that summer was to have some sense of what it might have been like to live in San Francisco in 1966 or '67, or in London when the Beatles and the Stones first hit.

"Sheena" caught the mood. From the shout of "Go!" that kicked off its raucous guitar attack, the chords bumping into each other in an endlessly ascending spiral, to the ethereal, soaring fadeout two minutes and forty-five seconds later, it was an unremitting frenzy of all-out exhilaration: it blew away the posturing nihilism of "Blank Generation," the only previous punk-rock anthem, in an explosion of pure, cataclysmic joy. Sheena, the girl who didn't want to go to a disco and went out looking for something better, was punk's first great convert, and there was a whole world of tension teetering in the infinitesimal pause after "Sheena is . . ." before the band broke loose into the yammering liberation of the chorus; the pride of "Well New York City really has it all" told the other half of the story. It was as casual as a throwaway—a good dance tune, no more —but it was also one of those rare songs that not only define the tempo and aura of a certain time and place, but suggest, almost compel, a whole way of life.

At that time, the Ramones had released two albums—*Ramones* and *Leave Home*—and occupied a position of almost unparalleled authority in the punk community. More than any other band, they had defined the music in its purest terms: a return to the basics which was both deliberately primitive and revisionist at the same time, a musical and lyrical bluntness of approach which concealed a wealth of complex, disengaging ironies underneath. It was zero-based rock 'n roll, and the conquest was so streamlined that the smallest shifts in nuance, when they came, had enormous implicit resonance.

At the same time, the band set the attitude: a comic resentment toward the rest of the world, a defiant pleasure in trashiness, and the tawdry excesses of urban lowlife. Punks, in the original sense of the word, were the sort of people who were such hopeless losers that they couldn't even be convincing as outlaws; far from romanticizing that status, the Ramones glorified their own inadequacy. Their leather jackets and strung-out, streetwise pose weren't so much an imitation of Brando in *The Wild One* as a very self-conscious parody—they knew how phony it was for them to take on those tough-guy trappings, and that incongruousness was exactly what made the pose so funny and true. And yet they were genuinely sexy, too; in spite of everything, they were cool. American myths are never so immediately recognizable, and irresistible, as when they're turned into a joke.

The Ramones lived out that double-edged vision in all sorts of ways. They were raised on the pop-culture religion; they believed in the Top 40 as the melting pot of the teenage American dream, where clichés and junkiness and triviality take on the epic sweep of a myth and the depth of a common unconscious. But they themselves were minority artists, working far outside the mainstream, and that, paradoxically, gave them the freedom to live out everyone's private fantasy that the Top 40 really told the truth, instead of being the shoddy compromise it always actually was; they were also sophisticated modern ironists, working with all the alienation and distance that implied. *Rocket to Russia* isn't imitation Top 40; it's a fan's vision of what the Top 40 ought to be.

What that meant, among other things, was that they could play as fast, loud, and mean as they wanted to; they could deliver on the anarchic promise hidden beneath the pieties of AM radio. And because they had no use at all for the empty fluency and virtuoso craftsmanship of most seventies rock ("'tasty licks,' and all that Traffic twaddle," as Lester Bangs once put it, being a little unfair and dead right at the same time), they could get their effects with an economy and verve. On stage, they rammed their way through their sets at the speed of a subway express slamming from station to station; Johnny and Dee Dee leaped to the rim of the stage, thrusting out their axes with the comic ferocity of Popeye tripping out on spinach, while Tommy acted smooth and unruffled and Joey just wrapped himself around the mike stand, hanging on for dear life. On *Rocket to Russia*, there's never any grandstanding, none of the careful preparation you hear in most modern rock 'n roll: there just isn't time for any of that. Even the occasional flourishes—the perfect simplicity of the four tom-tom beats that break into the last chorus of "Rockaway Beach," the faint echo on the shouts of "lo-ba-to-*may!*" that open "Teenage Lobotomy"—have a utilitarian speed. The musicians just grab for what they need, set it down, and rush on, and it all goes by in a blur.

Ramones was a tour de force of deadpan comedy; there was a furious, galvanizing wit in its reduction of rock 'n roll to the dumb, howling noise everyone always loved it for before they loved it for anything else, and in its reduction of modern urban horror to the glazed-eyed banality of a punk's "What, me worry?" shrug. It had the kick of a shared secret dragged out into the open—of a high-school dirty joke that you suddenly realize every other tenth-grader in the country knows, too. Shortly after it was released, I remember running into a redneck acquaintance of mine from Virginia, a sort of teenage derelict-in-training whom I hadn't seen in years; he wanted at once for me to tell him everything I knew of the Ramones, and later on in the evening I remember him chanting the lyrics to "Beat on the Brat" with an expression of blissful contentment on his face. It was about the only thing we had in common, but it was enough.

The sequel, *Leave Home,* necessarily didn't have quite the immediate excitement of *Ramones,* but in many ways it had more depth, lurking beneath the bombed-out surface. If there were plenty of parodic songs with titles like "You're Gonna Kill That Girl," there was also "I Remember You," with that lovely moment when the excitement in Joey's voice turns the single word "you" into pure poetry; and the wistful "What's Your Game." Most important, perhaps, in retrospect, was "Oh Oh I Love Her So," a near-perfect evocation of teenage romance in the neon-lit urban landscape which the Ramones had already claimed as their own turf: "I met her at the Burger King," Joey began, "we fell in love by the soda machine. . . ." All very funny, but genuinely evocative, too. Having completely negated the whole superstructure of received ideas which had been the bane of rock 'n roll for years, the band could now begin to approach the old clichés and stereotypes as their own discovery, and make them come alive again in this new, ironic framework.

Even so, "Sheena" was a breakthrough. Formally, the playful Beach Boys harmonies and the bouncy freedom of the riff went far beyond anything the band had done before; the lyrics, though full of teasing allusiveness, were utterly without the disengagement of irony—they drew you inside in a spirit of open celebration. Once again, the Ramones were reworking a hackneyed genre—the rock 'n roll song about rock 'n roll—and making it their own. On *Ramones,* there had been a cut called "Judy is a Punk," which was no more than another comic-horrible put-down; it's the addition of the word "rocker" that makes all the difference, and the message of "Sheena"

—like that of Lou Reed's classic "Rock & Roll" itself—is that her life was saved by rock 'n roll. For all their tongue-in-cheek humor, the Ramones, like Reed, meant it literally; in fact, it was the only kind of redemption they would admit to.

Rocket to Russia followed in late autumn. Though "Sheena" was easily the best song on it, there were still many surprises; the rest of the album took its cue from "Sheena," and took off in all sorts of new directions to affirm what "Sheena" was all about. More than anything else, it was the band's new assertiveness, their brazen pride in their own identity, that opened up the album. From the punning title—"rocket" for "rock it"—to the invocation of "Ramona" and the wonderful double entendre of "Rock, rock, Rockaway Beach," the Ramones never let you forget that this was rock 'n roll, and they had just as much of a stake in it as anyone else.

The music was manic, driving, exquisitely controlled; the songs were as barbed and funny as ever, but they also had surprising warmth. "Teenage Lobotomy" was another portrait of a modern urban zombie, but now it had turned into a gleeful, openly self-delighted boast; "I Can't Give You Anything" sounded more like a promise than a threat; "Locket Love" 's free-floating, merry-go-round rhythms belied the bitterness of its lyric. The ballad, "Here Today, Gone Tomorrow," put the disassociated bleakness of the Ramones' sound to tellingly emotional use in a painfully, comically direct account of the burnt-out end of a love affair.

Everywhere on the album, the Ramones pushed their punk ironies to the limit, and then turned around and trampled those boundaries with an infectious, all-embracing zest. Conceptually, perhaps, a song like "Rockaway Beach" is an East Coast take-off on a California surf epic—since Rockaway Beach, in Queens, is one of the few beaches in America you take a subway to get to—but it breaks the parodic mold to become a genuine celebration of the place; there's a palpable delight in the very absurdity of this artificial teenage paradise stuck in the middle of the urban concrete. Very little in seventies rock is genuinely urban; in fact, most of it doesn't have much sense of place at all—synthetic substitutes, like the Eagles' Desperado, seem to come at you out of a vacuum. The triumph of the Ramones is that they were urban, as urban and modern as Martians in their black leather jackets, and were able to find pleasure and even joy in that transient, junky, corrupt milieu.

One of the chief delights of rock 'n roll is that it's trash music for a trash culture; when Chuck Berry wrote down his version of the American dream, it wasn't any chaste pastoral grandeur he chose to mythologize, but jukeboxes and hamburgers and neon. What makes the music liberating is that it's resolutely not respectable. This is obvious enough, but it's something rock 'n roll is trying to forget—as jazz, for instance, successfully forgot: I'm sure that there are all kinds of people out there who would give a *moue* of distaste if you told them the stuff started out as whorehouse music.

When rock turned classy and "mature" in the late sixties, the move was inextricably tied up with the utopianism of the counter-culture; the possibility of revolution was the only thing that gave *Sgt. Pepper* and the flood of pretensions in its wake credibility. When the countercultural dream died, it turned all that visionary artiness into pure sludge—icing with the cake shot out from under it. The first five years of the seventies were a long tunneling out from the wreckage of the sixties, and they were among the worst years in rock 'n roll history, as smugly reactionary as the void between the apostasy of Elvis and the arrival of the Beatles; like the generation it created, the music had lost its focus. What gave a post-punk resurgence like *Some Girls* its marvelous kick was that after years of playing the seventies game, and being depressingly polite about it, the Stones were turning around and pissing on respectability, pissing on the gas-station walls again—while Mick wrote obscene put-downs of his own ex-wife in the men's room, no less!—and sounded as if they were having a great time doing it, too. They had remembered trash.

The Ramones, however, never needed to be reminded. The Edenic, anti-materialist sentimentality of an event like Woodstock would have been utterly alien to them, as alien as the glossy empti-ness that followed it; they were living out Nabokov's dictum that nothing is more exhilarating than Philistine vulgarity. They took Berry's message even further than he had, because they capitalized on the random violence and brutality that went hand-in-hand with the raw, funky charge of big-city life; it's that sense of danger—instant and enormous—that gives their music its panicky, brutalized edge. And yet the violence was so extreme, and so anonymous, that it became just another pop cartoon. If that was a depressing truth, the Ramones were cocky enough, and heretical enough, to say that it was ridiculous too; and even to say that it was not without its appeal. Their reveling in the trashy vitality of such an overwrought atmosphere was a life-affirming manifesto.

So their songs were two-minute artillery barrages of pounding rhythm without a shred of melodic soothing, and both on stage and on record they played the role of mutant Dead End kids, brain-damaged cripples, teenage fascists. Some of that was pure shock tactics; some of it was a deliberate subversion of the whole sixties peace-and-love, acid-trance sensibility, which by the time they came around had turned into the Quaalude sensibility, and which they loathed because it was false. But mostly it was just a caricatured, hence accurate, reflection of their own experience. ("The young . . . are Germans, one and all, from fifteen to twenty-one," Leslie Fiedler once wrote, in a line that rings a lot truer than almost anything the youth-consciousness pundits ever said; "We're the members of the master race," the Dictators told the teenagers of America, not too long before the Ramones came out with "Blitzkrieg Bop" and "To-day Your Love, Tomorrow the World.") The Ramones turned themselves into campy pseudo-Nazi grotesques because identity jus-tified their reality, and their rebellion, as much as Jerry Garcia's acid-fuzzed religiosity justified his.

Their best anthem before *Rocket to Russia* was a song called "Pinhead," from *Leave Home*, which was both a joke ("I don't want to be a pinhead no more/I just met a nurse that I could go for") and a call to arms: they used to finish their stage shows with its closing chant of "Gabba Gabba Hey!," with Joey holding those words aloft on a placard. "Pinhead," of course, derived from Tod Browning's 1932 underground classic *Freaks*. When it was first released, the movie—a story about the assorted cripples, geeks, and pinheads of a circus sideshow, who wreak their revenge on the nor-mality symbolized by the icily beautiful blonde trapeze artist who betrays one of them—was presented as straight horror. When it was revived in the seventies, however, the new teenage underground had no trouble identifying with the freaks' attack on the straight world. Self-proclaimed freaks themselves, they dug the misshapen outcasts on the screen as their own mythic self-image.

The Ramones brought that identification into the open, and if they instinctively treated it as black comedy, they also glorified it. By the time *Rocket to Russia* came out, those images had become familiar, and the jokes had become a great deal more than jokes: they had taken on the faceless universality of the girls in the Beatles' early rockers or the Beach Boys' California surf. "Cretin Hop," the lurching dance song that opens *Rocket to Russia*, has a crazed grandeur that goes all the way back, in its arrogant, incandescent silliness, to "Rock Around the Clock" or Little Richard's earliest assaults on human sanity. It's no accident, either, that "Teenage Lobotomy," on side two, segues immediately into the classic, sensual grace of "Do You Wanna Dance": the grotesque and the celebratory are one.

But for the Ramones there had never, really, been that much of a distinction to be made; they had inherited a sense of life as pure camp from the early sixties, from Twiggy and Warhol and movies like *Beach Blanket Bingo*. The bands which influenced them most weren't the established greats of the era, either—just to cite the most obvious example, Dylan might just as well never have been born for all the Ramones cared—but such semi-cool, semi-laughable second-echelon groups as Herman's Hermits (not only Joey's put-on Cockney accent, but a lot of his phrasing, too, derives directly from Peter Noone), the Troggs, the 1910 Fruitgum Company, the Ventures, and Paul Revere and the Raiders (what was the black-leather-and-jeans uniform, after all, but a seventies equivalent for those neat little Colonial outfits?). It was music that was close to bubblegum, and in the seventies the Ramones remained, subversively, close to bubblegum: from the cute conceit of their assumed names down to their logo—a caricature of the Great Seal with a baseball bat in the American eagle's claw and the message LOOK OUT BELOW clutched in its beak—their whole iconography came out of the cheerful travesties of sixties pop. They were like a teenybopper magazine's Dream Date gone film noir.

Rocket to Russia had all the fun of bubblegum, but it was emphatically not innocent: precisely what makes a song like "Sheena" so satisfying is that its exuberance is knowing and earned, not ingenuous. The peculiar astringency of the Ramones' style—Joey's insistence on keeping the "I" in his vocals separate from himself, and in a song like "Why Is It Always This Way" separating that "I" from everything it observes—is the result of their not being a sixties bubblegum band, but seventies revisionists fully aware of everything that's happened in between. The Rolling Stones depended instinctively on that kind of relativism from the start, which is why a cut like "Out of Time" sounds as up-to-date as ever, while the Beach Boys and a lot of the early Beatles, for all the undeniable greatness of the music, now sound, not false, maybe, but incomplete: you have to forget a little of what you know to enter into that world completely. The sixties harmonies on *Rocket to Russia* are intentionally distant echoes—they're like a half-forgotten memory floating in the background of the songs.

However, implicitly from the start, and overtly by the time *Rocket to Russia* came out, the Ramones weren't content to point up that ironic distance; if they were the children of sixties pop absurdism they never really succumbed to the pop nihilism which was its psychological nerve. For all its images of alienation and disjunction, *Rocket to Russia* is comically exultant, a conquest; the affirmation has an overwhelming power because it's wrestled out of such debased and ugly circumstances.

The attractiveness of the comic loser, the man at the end of his rope whose private victory is his own defiant pride in not letting go, is the closest thing we have to the idea of the holy fool. You can hear him in Lou Reed shrugging off the sex-and-suicide despair of *Berlin* with the hilariously tight-lipped moral, "Just goes to show how wrong you can be"; or in Gary Gilmore saying irritably to a *Playboy* interviewer, "Accidents can happen to psychopaths just as easily as anybody else, man." In most places, a line like "Hang on a little bit longer/Hang on, you're a goner" from *Rocket to Russia*'s "Locket Love," would be a baffling paradox. In America, it makes perfect sense, because failure is the national joke; failure is freedom. When, in "I Wanna Be Well," Joey follows the line "Daddy's broke" with the gee-whiz bemusement of "Holy smoke," and answers "My future's bleak" with the mocking question, "Ain't it neat?," he sounds outrageously pleased with himself.

The low appeal of turning failure into comic pride, of twisting the whole hierarchy of success and defeat around to make it say the opposite of what it seems to mean—of the subversive gesture—is most of the fun of *Rocket to Russia*, and most of its art as well. "Why Is It Always This Way" is about a suicide, but it's set to an almost frolicsome, upbeat rhythm, with a bouncy "hey, hey, hey" in the chorus; "Here Today, Gone Tomorrow" is as lovely and open a song as any the Ramones have done, but it's still played off against the up-yours kiss-off of its title; and these flippancies, far from blunting the impact of the songs, are exactly what gives them their vitality and kick. It's not graffiti transformed into art so much as it's art redeemed by the spirit of graffiti.

The Ramones are such a pure expression of American pop culture—devious, dumb, brilliant, and exhilarating—that it's an almost irresistible temptation to intellectualize about them. You can have analytical fun trying to figure out the interplay of irony and authenticity in "Teenage Lobotomy," say, or noticing the way the word "time" is used in three consecutive lines, with three different meanings, in "Here Today, Gone Tomorrow." That may not be completely irrelevant, but it somehow misses the point. The real revelations come elsewhere. They come when Johnny, for instance, plays a guitar solo on "Here Today, Gone Tomorrow" which lifts the song right off the ground, not just because the idea of Johnny playing a solo is so beautifully unexpected but because it suddenly seems so exactly right and necessary. Or when you hear the ecstatic longing in Joey's singing on "Do You Wanna Dance," struggling to stay afloat above a churning storm of heavy-metal riffing. Or in the sudden sweetness of "Ramona," a song which captures the essence of what the Ramones mean to their audience, and vice versa, in four wonderfully easy and seductive lines:

> *You're getting better and better*
> *It's getting easier than ever*
> *Hey you kids in the crowd*
> *You know you like it when the music's loud . . .*

Or in a dozen other moments one could name, when the guitar, the pumping, insistent bass, the graceful punctuation of Tommy's drumming, and Joey's back-street, punky-tough voice twisting itself around a lyric all come together with a throat-catching immediacy which has nothing to do with analysis, and everything to do with the galvanizing, primal joy of rock 'n roll itself. You could say that it's all a joke, done just for fun; but in America, simply having a good time is an elusive, tricky ideal, and even jokes have a moral significance. The achievement of *Rocket to Russia* is that it makes its own brand of fun stand for something a lot deeper and more liberating than all the heavy profundity of most of the profound and heavy albums you could name. It's the kind of deadly serious kidding that rock 'n roll, and America, couldn't live without.

THE PRETENDER

JACKSON BROWNE (ASYLUM 7E–1079)
1976

PAUL NELSON

Doing a piece with a desert-island premise is like writing a suicide note and then sticking around to cry over it. You either lapse into sentimentality ("I not only accept loss forever," Jack Kerouac once wrote, "I am made of loss") or try to Bogart your way through with some wryly stylized stoicism. Either way, you're lost.

Because, though it isn't, being here is too much like real life. On these sands, you've got plenty of past, a severely pinched present, and no future. *Everything* is an afterthought. Or, worse, all that finely honed autobiographical angst you've been saving turns inexplicably into something that's much funnier than if you'd embraced it as a joke in the first place. Even before I was marooned, I'm not at all sure I knew what was funny anymore.

So here I sit, with only my memories, my fondest quotations, a phonograph, and a copy of Jackson Browne's *The Pretender*. Back in the saddle again with *things* instead of people. You find 'em, you lose 'em, you hope to find 'em—a woman, family, friends, ideals— that's what *The Pretender*'s all about. What could be better than that?

Ross Macdonald has a wonderful line in *The Doomsters*: "Watch it, I said to myself; self-pity is the last refuge of little minds and aging professional hardnoses." Gatsby, the *real* Pretender, had it down cold: he both mourned *and* sought that last, lost golden mote of summer in the second act of his very American life. Probably because Americans make the poorest nihilists, he never quit. Neil Young summed it up best: "It has often been my dream/To live with one who wasn't there." Mine, too.

Two of the truest songs I know—i.e., songs that hit me straight in the heart—are Bob Dylan's randy and exhilarating "Spanish Harlem Incident" and Jackson Browne's passionate hymn to romanticism, "Farther On." Though vastly dissimilar (youthful sexual gunfire versus a remembrance of things past), both numbers are built on the bias of hope and an ability to be consumed and transformed by emotion and thought. But if the former exemplifies the jangling pulsebeat of a chance meeting with a pretty girl on the street, then the latter might well refine, reflect upon, and ratify equally volcanic circumstances to represent a (possibly) more mature overall philosophy concerned with the occurrences of a lifetime. "Farther On," like the majority of Jackson's work, has its eye firmly fixed on long distances.

> *But the angels are older*
> *They can see that the sun's setting fast*
> *They look over my shoulder*
> *At the vision of paradise contained in the*
> *   light of the past*
> *And they lay down behind me*
> *To sleep beside the road till the morning*
> *   has come*
> *Where they know they will find me*
> *With my maps and my faith in the distance*
> *Moving farther on*

Back in New York City, I was aware of the profundities in Jean Renoir's credo: "You see, in this world there is one awful thing, and that is that everyone has his reasons." Stranded now on another island, I've got time to think about the specific reasons. While the previously quoted final verse of "Farther On" is the one I'll undoubtedly end my days with, the song's initial stanza once and for all pins to the wall the cosmic haze of growing up. When I first heard it, I was absolutely unable to put any space between myself and someone else's childhood.

In my early years I hid my tears
And passed my days alone
Adrift on an ocean of loneliness
My dreams like nets were thrown
To catch the love that I'd heard of
In books and films and songs
Now there's a world of illusion and fantasy
In the place where the real world belongs

As an adult on this peculiar island, still I look for the beauty in songs. As the sun beats down, I'm reminded that memories are as warm as the climate here, and the loved ones who haunt those memories are warmer still. Though these sands and songs bear traces of mother and father, long-lost wife and child, friends, enemies, lovers, their presences exist once again as works of art—nice to think about, pleasant to listen to, but it gets very cold at night. In a college of soft knocks, some professional pessimist once told me that all of existence could be reduced to a cycle in which false expectations, harsh education, and darkest despair went round and round until it was simply too painful for anyone to make the swing from despair back to expectations again. These days, a lot of optimists would probably relate the same fable, adding only that it's too late to stop now. The reason I picked *The Pretender* was that it seemed to pick me.

If there were people who sold sleep for a living, they'd never make more than a few cents off Jackson Browne. From late October 1975 through February 1976, he worked in Los Angeles producing his friend Warren Zevon's first LP for Asylum, taking only a few weeks off to marry Phyllis Major, the woman with whom he'd been living for over three years. Jackson, Phyllis, and their three-year-old son

Ethan spent most of December in Hawaii. *Warren Zevon* was completed on February 29. On March 1, Jackson began recording *The Pretender*, his fourth and perhaps finest album. Early in the morning of March 25, Phyllis Major Browne committed suicide by taking an overdose of sleeping pills. All work on the record was suspended until May 6. In May, June, and July, Jackson was in the studio five days a week. Throughout most of August and September—except for a camping trip with his son—he worked on the LP every waking hour, weekends included. Mastering was finished on September 27.

About ten days later, on an all-night bus ride from Binghamton, New York, to Manhattan, Jackson (just starting a forty-five-city tour) and I are talking about *The Pretender*. For a week now, I've been avoiding an essential question, and I know I'm finally going to ask it. For the first time, I feel like the journalist-as-ghoul. "This album is going to be widely taken as the story of you and Phyllis," I say. "Is it?"

Jackson looks out the window for a minute. But he refuses to be as melodramatic as certain writers. "Yeah," he says. "It was like looking at a photograph coming up in a solution. When I started to see these songs coming up and I began to see the image, it sort of scared me for a while. It scares me but, in the final analysis, it doesn't bother me. It's all right. *The Pretender* depicts the last couple years of my life. It picks right up with *Late for the Sky*. However, its coming together was a rather sudden thing. All of these things were sort of like half songs and half ideas—and then, at certain moments, there was really nothing to do but sit down and put them all together.

"You've raised a fundamental question, though. I'm not sure how worthwhile my describing such a personal tale is—as a matter of fact, I think it would be more worthwhile if it weren't that way —but it's something I simply accept about myself. The nature of my music has to do with dealing with very fundamental things by depicting my own experience. That's the way it is, and I guess it's okay. I mean, the truly personal and private things are not in there— there's nothing that isn't pretty fundamental, you know."

Jackson Browne's art works in a wide arc—and never more so than on *The Pretender*, a record of life and death, love and the lack of it, staying or leaving, birth and rebirth. One mood is almost always balanced by another, and the emotions in the songs tend to flow into each other. It is always darkest ("Your Bright Baby Blues," "Linda Paloma," "Here Come Those Tears Again," "Sleep's Dark and Silent Gate," "The Pretender") just before the dawn ("The Fuse," "The Only Child," "Daddy's Tune"). And, of course, vice versa.

"The Fuse" is the first—and probably the last—song in the circle: it sounds very different once the rest of the story is told. If any piece of music can offer forewarnings about both life and death—and make each seem equally ominous and triumphant—then I guess this composition can. The singer hears something in the desert and is reborn, but what he's probably heard is the LP's introductory progression of formal, funereal bass notes that portend nothing but disaster. Invocations to eternity abound, and God is called upon (as He often will be throughout *The Pretender*). Though we've got maps and—sometimes despite the palpable proof of doom right in front of our eyes—an inherent faith in the distance, somehow that fabled "farther on" always appears to backfire on us. The postman never stops ringing.

In "The Fuse," Jackson manages a fusion of youthful learning/yearning and ageless wisdom: the start of an odyssey, the conclusions of one. What's set up is an effective Arthurian California myth —the young man on a quest. His journey takes him through such darkness that romanticism can't possibly be the same again.

"The Fuse" begins with some apparently hard-earned apocalyptic complexities and then seems to regress into a sixties-style simplicity that ends with the image of children laughing. Though the artist acknowledges loneliness, uncertainty, and "years that I spent lost in the mystery," his viewpoint becomes passionately, almost naively positive. By song's end, Jackson sings out with affirmation (questions like "Oh Lord/Are there really people starving still?" are answered by the unrefined reformer's buoyant claim: "I want to say right now I'm going to be around/. . . I will tune my spirit to the gentle sound") after proffering advice that strongly suggests that destiny is anything but fatalistic ("Forget what life used to be/You are what you choose to be").

But that's just the there's-a-better-world-a-comin' portion of "The Fuse." The other, perhaps more important, more mature part ignites the whole of *The Pretender* ("Through every dead and living thing/ Time runs like a fuse/And the fuse is burning") and illuminates the writer's thematic strategy: he hits more archetypes than anyone else because they're what he's aiming at.

In "Your Bright Baby Blues," burned-out boy meets mixed-up girl, and the LP's on-again, off-again love story begins. Years seem to have gone by since the optimistic last verse of "The Fuse"—rather than thinking about what he can do for mankind, Jackson is now desperately hoping that a woman can do something for him—though the tone and some of the deliberately unsophisticated early imagery of "Your Bright Baby Blues" still suggests the late sixties and early seventies.

The song starts small, with a blues image—the singer "sitting down by the highway," wanting to go home, feeling completely useless, and watching what he perceives as a purposeful world go by—and then slowly blossoms into a remarkably full picture of not one but two lost souls. The man is seeking nothing less than salvation and wants badly to escape from himself and into another person. He meets her. "Baby you can free me," he says, "I can see it in your eyes." Then he adds, rather chillingly, "You've got those bright baby blues," and we realize that he's talking about a lot more than his lover's eyes here. He's talking about his own problem—i.e., *bright-baby* blues—as well as hers (and probably yours and mine). These are two smart, too-smart people who can't help but question the hell (or, more likely, the heaven) out of everything. When Jackson sings

> You don't see what you've got to gain
> But you don't like to lose
> You watch yourself from the sidelines
> Like your life is a game you don't mind playing
> To keep yourself amused
> I don't mean to be cruel baby
> But you're looking confused

he's indicting himself, the woman he loves, and a whole generation who saw only the positive side of Bob Dylan's "Like a Rolling Stone."

Because mere independence can never carry the day. In addition, there are drugs and the problems they cause (in a conversational aside, the singer tells this story on himself: "I thought I was flying like a bird/So far above my sorrow/But when I looked down/I was standing on my knees") to go along with the pure panic. In the end, Jackson merges dope and dependence, hope and helplessness, love and sex, an awareness of character flaws and an *Alice in Wonderland* fantasy into a single image: "Take my hand and lead me/To the hole in your garden wall/And pull me through."

"Linda Paloma" is the cruelest cut of all. The girl's gone. Grown up—or not grown up—and left. Romance and romanticism weren't enough. In "Your Bright Baby Blues," Jackson, under the influence, mistakenly thought he was a bird; here, it's his lover who sees him as "the endless sky" and herself as his Mexican dove. Older now, the singer has become something of a realist ("I know all about these things"). The couple look at each other across the table in a Mexican restaurant. She's disappointed in him, and he feels he exists primarily as an idealization in her eyes.

While the woman, "looking through tears," equates music to love, the man who wrote songs about her now equates love to dreaming. He thinks it could all work out "If tears could release the heart/From the shadows preferred by the mind." Love dies in a remarkably subtle verse that can't help but remind one of these lines from "The Fuse": "It's coming from so far away/It's hard to say for sure/Whether what I hear is music or the wind/Through an open door." There, though uncertain, the singer felt that something good was on its way. Now, as he looks at the sleeping face of the woman he loves, he's obsessed with death. There is both symbolic and real death here (the "Love will fill your eyes" line is particularly terrifying in this context), with not a word wasted.

> *Like a wind that comes up in the night*
> *Caressing your face while you sleep*
> *Love will fill your eyes with the sight*
> *Of a world you can't hope to keep*
> *Dreaming on after that moment's gone*
> *The light in your lover's eyes*
> *Disappears in the light of the dawn*

Jackson on "Linda Paloma": "Let me tell you a personal thing. One of my wife's and my favorite songs is this Mexican song called 'Cu Cu Ru Cu Cu Paloma.' When my wife and I first met, we used to hear it quite often because we'd go to this certain restaurant and a certain couple of mariachis would always sing it to us.

"So I sort of set out to rip off this song in 'Linda Paloma.' I think I came closer to ripping off Ry Cooder's version of 'Maria Elena' instead, though. I love Mexican music and wondered how close I could come to sounding authentico. It's a genre I felt comfortable with to write about a particular subject—the classical, ah, *goodbye*. I mean, I don't know whether you focus on whether or not the girl is leaving and whether that is important to you, or whether or not what seems to be wrong is that a person has illusions about what love should be rather than who people are.

"It was a comfortable place to go with an idea which began with the opening image: 'At the moment the *music* began/And you heard the guitar player starting to sing/You were filled with the beauty that ran/Through what you were imagining.' Now I was singing about Phyllis. It's funny but every time I sang that for her, she never heard 'You were filled with the beauty that ran/Through what you were imagining.' She heard me singing: 'You were filled with the beauty *of the man*/That you were imagining.'

"At some point, I really feel that I'm going to have to write in some more classical genre because the parts I could write are endless—they occur to me forever. In 'Linda Paloma,' I could have written an entire Mexican song, sung in Spanish, where the mariachis in the background are singing these rather cynical and funny lines describing this moony couple at the table with their little problems of love. I hope I got at least some of that *feeling* on the record. In the end, when I sing 'Fly away/Linda Paloma,' the Mexicans in the restaurant were going to say, 'That's right, man, throw the little ones back. Forget it. *Forget it*, man. Let her *go*.' "

"Here Come Those Tears Again," unlike "Linda Paloma," finds the man crying over the woman. Years have gone by, and during that time, there's been a lot of staying and leaving; the "open door" of "The Fuse" has now become the door through which Jackson's lover often departs. This song has its own vicious circle, and the singer, hurt and closing himself off fast, finds he simply can't handle the reconciliations anymore. So he makes what may be a negative promise ("I'm going back inside and turning out the light/And I'll be in the dark but you'll be out of sight"), yet one that previews the allegedly positive promises in "The Pretender." If the man succumbs to symbolic death here ("I'll be in the dark"), the woman actually dies somewhere after the final notes of side one.

Side two begins with two songs about families. Tied to "The Fuse," both compositions are concerned with either a boy (Jackson's son, Ethan, in "The Only Child") or a young man (Jackson himself in "Daddy's Tune") just starting out. In the former, the saddened singer offers all the comfort and advice he can to a boy whose mother has just died, and who, as the years go by, will think back on his tragedy:

> But take good care of your mother
> And remember to be kind
> When the pain of another will serve you
>   to remind
> That there are those who feel themselves
>   exiled
> On whom the fortune never smiled
> And upon whose lives the heartache has
>   been piled
> They're just looking for another
> Lonely child

During his 1976 tour, Jackson refused to play "Ready or Not," a courtship composition manifestly about Phyllis. When someone yelled out a request for it in Toronto, the performer spun around, grabbed the microphone, and snapped: "I don't *do* that song anymore. I *know* it but I don't *do* it. What I do instead is that other song, 'The Only Child,' about my son."

Thinking about his son's future, the singer remembers the estranged father in his own past. "Daddy's Tune" recalls the time of "The Fuse" and "Your Bright Baby Blues"—in fact, its first few lines are practically a combination of the beginnings of both early songs, though the "wind" from "The Fuse" is "dirty" now. In "Daddy's Tune," after a "Your Bright Baby Blues"–like call for help, Jackson ties the "sound of the drum/Like a part of me" reference from "The Fuse" right to his jazz-musician father in a wonderful, Woody Guthrie–style passage about growing up and hitting the road in America:

> No sooner had I hit the streets
> When I met the fools that a young fool meets
> All in search of truth and bound for glory
> And listening to our own heart beats
> We stood around the drum
> Though it's fainter now
> The older I become

By song's end, a familial reconciliation has taken place, as, to soaring Dixieland music, Jackson realizes:

> But Daddy I want to let you know somehow
> The things you said are so much clearer now
> And I would turn the pages back
> But time will not allow . . .
> Somewhere something went wrong
> Or maybe we forgot the song
> Make room for my forty-fives
> Along beside your seventy-eights
> Nothing survives—
> But the way we live our lives

A lot is happening here (and, in a way, those last two lines serve as the album's message and happy ending). Jackson's reconciliation with his father is meant to perform symbolic and emotional double duty: the singer looks back into the past to try to come to terms with the dead wife (who was every bit "The Only Child" that Jackson and Ethan are), while looking ahead toward a future in which Ethan may well be singing "Daddy's Tune" to *his* father.

But happy endings are rare—remember, *The Pretender* isn't over yet. "Sleep's Dark and Silent Gate" paints a stark picture of the full impact of a death in the family. The woman's dead—nothing can change that—and the finality of it is overwhelming. The man can do nothing but think back about the missed chances, good times and bad times, when and why. While the song's similarities to "Linda Paloma" and "Here Come Those Tears Again" are obvious (all three numbers equate death and departure to nighttime), it's really the last chapter of "Your Bright Baby Blues." Compare the chorus ("Sitting down by the highway/Looking down the road/Waiting for a ride/I don't know where I've been") to the first verse of the earlier tune.

In "Sleep's Dark and Silent Gate," the singer is lost, hurt, confused. As he tries to understand what's happened—

> *Never should have had to try so hard*
> *To make a love work out, I guess*
> *I don't know what love has got to do with*
> *   happiness*
> *But the times when we were happy*
> *Were the times we never tried*

—his voice cracks ("Oh God this is some shape I'm in") and so do we when, for a brief moment, he reunites husband, wife, and child at the close of the chorus: "When the only thing that makes me cry/Is the kindness in my baby's eye." Small wonder that the composition ends with the feeling that *everything* is finished.

Thus, "The Pretender": one of Jackson Browne's "big" songs (e.g., "Rock Me on the Water," "For Everyman," "Before the Deluge," "The Fuse," "The Load-Out"/"Stay") and one of his finest. Ostensibly a series of promises or vows—

> *I'm going to rent myself a house*
> *In the shade of the freeway*
> *I'm going to pack my lunch in the morning*
> *And go to work each day . . .*

I'm going to find myself a girl
Who can show me what laughter means . . .

I'm going to be a happy idiot
And struggle for the legal tender—
And believe in whatever may lie
In those things that money can buy
Thought true love could have been a contender

—from a man who's experienced marital tragedy and now desires nothing so much as an utterly conventional, safe, suburban-commuter life, the title track (not unexpectedly) turns out to be about a lot more than that. Between the hero's mundane, everyday promises, he's still a haunted man who wants some real answers ("I want to know what became of the changes/We waited for love to bring/Were they only the fitful dreams/Of some greater awakening") and who can neither forget nor escape from the romance—and romanticism—of his past.

When Jackson sings, "Out into the cool of the evening/Strolls the pretender/He knows that all his hopes and dreams/Begin and end there," the listener feels the chill of death and realizes that this "pretender"/"contender" may never again be whole. Looking out into the night, the man sees and remembers, in the LP's most heartbreaking message:

Ah the laughter of the lovers
As they run through the night
Leaving nothing for the others
But to choose off and fight
And tear at the world with all their might
While the ships bearing their dreams
Sail out of sight

Yet the natural urge to try again prevails. One can pretend that it doesn't, choose commerce over compassion, ask God, "Are you there?/Say a prayer—For the pretender/Who started out so young

and strong/Only to surrender." But, soon enough, these lines from
"The Fuse" roll around again:

> Though the years give way to uncertainty
> And the fear of living for nothing strangles
>   the will
> There's a part of me
> That speaks to the heart of me
> Though sometimes it's hard to see
> It's never far from me
> Alive in eternity
> That nothing can kill

I once asked Jackson how "The Pretender" could possibly be
autobiographical.

"It is—it's completely about me," he insisted. "But what I'm saying is that it's not *merely* about me, it's about a lot of people. After
the sixties, people began to decide that they would just work in a
bookstore or be a plumber or drive a truck—and that would be cosmic, you know. Or—hey, Bob Dylan saying all he wants is a cabin
in Utah and a couple of kids who call him Pa. What an amazing
thing for him to say after having been the most rebellious and surly
and unhappy and blindingly sarcastic and satirical person. Everything was based on that fundamental attitude he had, you know,
and for him to capitulate was wonderful—it was very warming and
startling and sad, too.

"Then you come up with this little hope that you're going to
find this girl. And right away, you're talking about fulfilling each
other's most predictable and mapped-out ideas. It's utterly humor-
ous. It's funny. It's black. 'I'm going to find myself a girl/Who can
show me what laughter means'? I could have written that when I
was eight—and meant an entirely different thing.

"What is romance? Romance isn't necessarily positive, is it? 'And
then we'll put our dark glasses on' is a cynical thing to say because
putting your dark glasses on is basically hiding yourself. 'And we'll
fill in the missing colors/In each other's paint by number dreams'?
Remember those little squares with the numbers on them? *This* is

supposed to be blue, *this* afternoon is supposed to be lovely, *this* is a picnic. It's prefab, you know. I'd be very unhappy if the 'paint by number' line were misread. I mean, I think that's the most cynical thing I've ever said—that your dreams are rather prescribed and determined.

"But you can't escape thinking of life as beautiful. It's the natural thing to do—the one thing we'll *always* do—and *that's* what's positive about 'The Pretender,' not all those vows he makes. That you can actually just laugh at yourself and say, Well, here I am, I'm dreaming about this girl again. She's going to be all these things, we're going to do all these things. And in the middle of that realization, you go, Yeah, well, the truth is that you keep your fucking dark glasses on, you wear your cheaters. We'll probably just keep our shades on and fuck in front of the TV. If you weren't like that, you'd probably just check out. A lot of people do, you know.

"So 'The Fuse' not only comes before 'The Pretender,' it's a refutation of 'The Pretender.' The overall message at the end of 'The Pretender' is that he's pretending—*he* knows it and *you* know it. He's going to pretend that all he gives a shit about is getting his paycheck, but even then he's saying, 'Say a prayer for the pretender.'"

Every time I hear *The Pretender*, it makes me feel that it just might be possible to get out of this place.

NEW YORK DOLLS

THE NEW YORK DOLLS (MERCURY/UK 1234)
1973 AND 1974/1977

ROBERT CHRISTGAU

Although an American re-release has long been rumored, the two
New York Dolls albums—*New York Dolls,* produced by Todd
Rundgren in 1973, and *New York Dolls in Too Much Too
Soon,* produced by Shadow Morton in 1974—are currently available only as a two-LP reissue on English Mercury. A living
memorial it is. Out of catalogue and then raised from the dead
3000 miles away, all within three years of release—that's what you
call a legend in its own time. Of course, the legend seems rather
more heroic in England—where the Dolls inspired the most
interesting music (whatever else, punk is/was undeniably *interesting*) to hit the U.K. since the Beatles—than in the city that
spawned them, where the details of their suicide are too well-
remembered. And elsewhere in the universe their story is cherished
primarily by fanzine readers and other big-beat aesthetes. Still, a
legend is what it is.

There are people who love the Ramones or the Sex Pistols yet
continue to find the Dolls deficient in melody or power or punch.
"I guess you had to be there," they say, at once paying their
respects to history and implying that those of us who actually
were there are no more fit to judge the resulting phonograph record

than fans of *Frampton Comes Alive!* It must be admitted, though, that seeing the Dolls on stage helped you understand their music. They didn't play any better than on record, and—despite the theatrical reputation of "glitter rock," a reputation based on the attraction of photographers to unusual clothing and of David Bowie to mime—they didn't "put on a show" in the Alice Cooper or Bruce Springsteen sense. But they certainly tried to look like something special, and they succeeded.

Just as the impressionable listener was often deafened psychologically by the sheer rapid fire of the Dolls' music, so the impressionable onlooker was often blinded by the sexual ambiguity of their roles. It ought to be established, therefore, that the only time the Dolls ever affected vampy eyes, bowed red lips, and pancake makeup was on the cover of their first album. Ordinarily, their gender-fuck was a lot subtler. It did capitalize on a slight natural effeminacy in the speech patterns and body language of leader David Johansen and bassist Arthur Kane, but at its core was Johansen's amazing flair for trashy clothes. The man was a thrift-shop genius. So Arthur, who was tall and ungainly even without his platform shoes, would squeeze his torso into a child's dress or put on a crotch-length hockey jersey over white tights; David would wear a shorty nightgown instead of a shirt, with fishnet stockings showing through the rips in his jeans; Syl would turn into Liza Minnelli doing a Charlie Chaplin impression.

Partly because it coincided with Bowie's publicly gay phase, this stuff seemed very significant at the time, and symbolically it was. But in retrospect it's clear that the rather sweet street-tough alienation projected by guitarists Johnny Thunders and Syl Sylvain and drummer Jerry Nolan was where the collective sexuality of the band was really at. These were boys who liked girls; they shared the traditional rock and roll machismo, which is adolescent and vulnerable. What made them different was that their sweetness and toughness and alienation knew no inhibitions, so that where love was concerned they were ready for anything. By their camping they announced to the world that hippie mindblowing was a lot more conventional than it pretended to be, that human possibility was infinite. Of course, between Arthur's instinctive awkwardness and Syl's clowning and David's pursuit of the funny move, they suggested in addition that human possibility was hilarious. And the band's overall air of droogy desperation implied as well that human possibility was doomed.

All this was conveyed from the stage without props or bits or any but the most elementary business—David and Johnny share mike, Arthur steps forward for falsetto phrase, like that. But in another way it was the real living theater. To be a Doll was to appear twenty-four hours a day in an improvised psychodrama, half showbiz and half acting out, that merely got wilder in front of the microphones. Arthur played the beloved weirdo and Syl the puckish jack-in-the-box; Jerry was the all-American dynamo who kept the machinery juiced. But the big parts went to David, whose mobile face and body accentuated the humor, smarts, and purpose not just of the lyrics but of everything the band was, and Johnny, who threatened constantly to detonate David's volatile handiwork. David was a benevolent ringleader; his exaggerated moves and gestures made fun of the whole crazy project even as they sharpened its meaning and established his authority. But Johnny was forever testing the flexibility of David's conception. He was a j.d. with a bomb sticking out of his pocket, careening from microphone to amplifier to beplatformed fellow Doll without ever (almost ever) knocking any of them down or ceasing to wrench noises from his guitar. He was Chaos personified, put on display virtually untamed for our pleasure and edification.

Of such stuff are legends made—and from such stuff does all this I-guess-you-had-to-be-there stuff proceed. The Dolls prove how easy it is to dismiss a legend as nothing more than that, especially when it's crude and raucous and flashy. That their music was consciously primitive was obvious; what wasn't so obvious was that it was also difficult. Even people who loved their records found those records hard to listen to—not because the concept (or legend) was greater than the music, but because the music wasn't merely fun. The Coasters and the Beach Boys and even the Rolling Stones were each in their own way avatars of fun-filled if alienated affluence. But the joy in the Dolls' rock and roll was literally painful; it had to be earned. The Dolls carried to its illogical conclusion the egalitarian communalism that was one logical response of fun-filled affluence to alienation: they refused to pay their dues. So we had to pay instead. These weren't Woodstock brethren—skilled, friendly musical specialists plying their craft in organic harmony, eager to help the energy go down. They were lonely planet everyboys, ambitious kids who'd drifted in from the outer boroughs of Communications Central and devised new ways to cope with information overload. Although they were addicted to the city, they knew damn well that "Somethin' musta happened/Over Manhattan." And they wanted their music to sound like whatever it was.

Especially after a siege of pent-up urban frustration—although the Dolls could also provide welcome relief from pastoral o.d.—I found no rock and roll anywhere that delivered comparable satisfaction. It articulated the noisy, brutal excitement the city offered its populace as nothing else ever had, and so offered a kind of control over it. The Dolls were at once lumpenkids overwhelmed by post-hippie New York and wise guys on top of it. They lived in the interstices of the Big Apple war zone on their wit and will, their music at once a survival tactic and a kind of victory. They never whined because it was fun making do, and they rarely complained about their powerlessness because they were too busy taking advantage of what ordinary power the city provided its citizen denizens—mobility and electricity especially. That's why it seems completely appropriate to me that their music evokes nothing so much as the screech of a subway train.

I'm not talking about lyrics here—the lyrics were wonderful, and they do convey comparable messages, but not so unequivocally. It's the music that makes the Dolls hard to listen to, and the music that satisfies. Since neither album affords the kind of pristine sound quality that distinguishes cleanly between garage-band guitarists, it's impossible to be sure, but as I hear it Syl is the only Doll who doesn't add something unique to a sound that pits the competent-plus musicianship of David and Jerry against the rude thrashing of Johnny and Arthur. And it is the playing of Johnny and Arthur—one a primitive genius, the other a primitive klutz—that is the Dolls' contribution to musical history.

Johnny's offering was buzzsaw guitar charismatic enough to vie with heavy-metal fuzz in the hearts of rock and rollers everywhere. Ron Asheton of the Stooges and Wayne Kramer and Fred "Sonic" Smith of the MC5 were the fathers of the style, going back to Pete Townshend's rhythm chords with the Who as opposed to Eric Clapton's lead licks with the Yardbirds, to the Link Wray of "Rumble" rather than the Duane Eddy of "Rebel-'Rouser," to create a drone-prone guitar countertradition that was not only loud but tumultuous. It was Johnny, however, who made buzzsaw definitively young, fast, and unscientific, undercutting the elephantine beat that had deadened hard rock since the early days of Led Zeppelin and the only days of Blue Cheer.

Despite heavy metal's ill-mannered pretensions, its guitar move was always (relatively) discreet because it was (relatively) discrete, often simply responding to the call of the vocal line with a neat, standardized electroshock phrase that incorporated both factory-approved sound effects and natural feedback. Not that there was no galvanic spillover—amplifiers were molested until they screamed in conspicuously unpredictable revolt. But for Asheton and Kramer and Smith spillover was the be-all and end-all. Exploiting their own continuous, imprecise finger action a lot more than the fuzz box, they threw together an environment of electric noise with which everything else had to contend, replacing the deracinated call-and-response of heavy metal with music that was pure white riot. Without violating the primordial totality of this environment—if anything, the Dolls intensified buzzsaw's drone—Thunders made it speak, gave it shape and idiosyncrasy and a sense of humor.

To be fair, Johnny couldn't possibly have made all that noise himself. Syl pitched in with a will and a wink, laying a bottom for Johnny's jerrybuilt ideas; you can hear his essential racket in its pristine state, a little bluesier than one might expect, on the first guitar break preceding "It's Too Late." But while a lot of guys could have done Syl's work for him, Johnny made up his own job, varying the tasks to suit his eternally teenaged sense of what was and wasn't boring. Often he created the impression of perpetual motion with intermittent music, as with the scalar figure that turns into a solo on "Jet Boy" or the fills of sheer sonic matter that surround Syl on "Looking for a Kiss" or the squawking licks that decorate his own "Chatterbox." The bursts of ersatz slide that he explodes at regular intervals through "Babylon" add up to a drone, while on "Subway Train" he breaks a whole drone into components, playing each half of a primal background riff for a full measure instead of alternating the two four times a measure as in workaday buzzsaw. And even when he provided a straight drone, he was too loose (or too sloppy) to leave it at that, and that was his gift. The crude variation on Bill Doggett's "Honky Tonk" that opens "Human Being" soon devolves into something more general, yet though it never quite regains its shape it never stops gathering force either; "Pills" thrusts forward on the almost tuneless phrase that Johnny repeats throughout the track. In both cases, the charge of the music is equivalent to the severely delimited (Johnny was obviously no technician and didn't improvise in the usual sense) yet unmistakable (boom) expressiveness of his playing. You get the sense that even though Johnny's lines could probably be notated, he was too restless (and too lazy) to master them absolutely. His mistakes are indistinguishable from his inspirations. Each of his solos and comments and background noises on these albums is a point in an infinite series of magically marginal differentiations.

If Johnny's contribution was the fruit of irrepressible individuality, Arthur's was a by-product of individuality repressed by incompetence. Johnny's untutored spirit found voice in technique, but Arthur (playing the instrument fellow bumpkin Ringo Starr declared "too hard") never got that far. You can hear how much bass he's learned in between the two records, but it's not nearly enough to play around with. If he doesn't sink a blues line under Johnny's force field on (Bo Diddley's) "Pills" on the first album, it's only because he doesn't know one that fits; by the time of (Sonny Boy Williamson's) "Don't Start Me Talkin'" on the second he is double-timing an utterly conventional Willie Dixon part as Johnny sows discord all around him. In general, on the first LP he either echoes the rhythm guitar or just thumps along on a minimum of notes, sometimes difficult to distinguish from the bass drum. By *In Too Much Too Soon* his playing has definitely acquired a lilt, funky on "Bad Detective" and bluesy-tuneful on "Stranded in the Jungle," echoing the melody after a showpiece walk on "It's Too Late." But when he really wants to generate excitement, as on the climactic "Human Being," he resorts to the old thunderthud.

Arthur was the key to the Dolls' unyielding and all but undanceable rhythms. Harmonically, he could have been a far more sophisticated technician without doing the band anything but good —tricky melodic hooks helped make their music lovable. But although the Dolls would have been tastelessly aggressive and urban even without Arthur, his inability to come up with a catchy counter-rhythm, to supply the kind of syncopation that sets the body swaying, left them no room to be anything else. His style was anticipated to some extent by various protopunk pioneers, notably John Cale, and he shared more than Thunders did with the purveyors of heavy metal. But Arthur Kane is the definitive punk bassist, the source not only of Dee Dee Ramone's wall of rhythm but of Paul Simonon's military intricacies. As for Sid Vicious, well, it sounds as if he studied with Arthur—Sid was the more confident player only because he didn't have to prove it could be done.

Admittedly, there's reason to wonder just how much Arthur was capable of proving: nobody else ever carried the Dolls' anyone-can-do-it gospel so far. Even among the English punks, only X-Ray Spex aimed for self-transcendence with such passionate inaccuracy. The responsibility of compensating fell to Syl. Syl's guitar was the band's fulcrum. By mediating between rhythm and melody, a bassman's work, he picked up some of Arthur's slack. And while it's really true that he had nothing unique to add to the Dolls' sound, he wasn't an ordinary circa-1971 hard rock guitarist either. If he had been, the band might well have sunk under his weight, but Syl was a Doll because he was in love with speed, and he knew enough to counteract Arthur's inertia by keeping his touch unusually light. There's even a sense in which his ordinariness—the very fact that he had nothing unique to bring to the sound— provided a modicum of conceptual stability, a common ground where the band's primitives could meet the musicians.*

* Thanks to Lenny Kaye for helping me think about Syl Sylvain.

But for all his love of speed Syl didn't have the drive to power the band himself, and if the forward motion had been left to Arthur, the Dolls might never have gotten anywhere at all. He just followed along, defining the beat in his own peculiar fashion, as Jerry Nolan provided the propulsion. Insofar as the Dolls believed in music *cum* music—in the power of rock and roll alone and unaided to provide salvation—Jerry embodied that belief. He was an ordinary rock and roll madman at heart—schooled in 1-2-1-2, with the jumbo-size panoply of rolls, cymbal accents, and crossbeats at his disposal. He led the band in chops, but like so many punk drummers he never showed any conceptual commitment to the forced rhythms that are punk's mainspring. Not that this is surprising in a style whose innovators on the instrument—Maureen Tucker, who rejected the backbeat, and Tommy Ramone, who went so minimal he made Charlie Watts sound like Elvin Jones— had never struck a tom-tom in earnest when they first tried out for their jobs. Ignorance can be the mother of invention too—it guarantees an uncluttered mind.

As it happens, though, drummers aren't required to use their minds much, not in rock and roll—they're just supposed to follow the right instincts (or the right orders) and play the right stuff. This Jerry certainly did. However traditional his conceptual commitments, he played with obligingly modernist steadiness; although drawn to the backbeat, he submerged it, never funking around the way, for instance, Frankie LaRocka of David Johansen's current band likes to. This was essential discipline in what was supposed to be a definitively white style. The effects and rhythm changes were there when needed—he provided more dramatic support for David than anyone else in the group—but for the most part held in check. There was no bombardiering or gratuitous noisemaking. In short, Jerry never showed off. As explosive as his sound seemed, it turned out to be surprisingly even in the moment-to-moment execution. His only self-indulgence was to play unceasingly, on every beat. The faster the tempo the happier he was.

Nolan was not an original Doll—he succeeded Billy Murcia, a cofounder of the group with Thunders and Kane who died of a drug overdose during the Dolls' first tour of England in 1972—and he always seemed a little simpler than the others. Syl, for instance, acted no less happy-go-lucky, yet at the same time projected a dirty old man's sagacity. But Jerry was street-smart without being street-cynical, so unfailingly eager that later, after he'd dyed his hair bright blond and helped compose a classic song about heroin for the Heartbreakers, he still seemed a naif clumsily astray in the rock and roll demimonde. He was the band's link to what people smugly consider normal emotions, and his musicianship did the same job—like any drummer who does his or her work well, he provided roots.

David Johansen was Jerry's converse in all this, both as a public figure and as the band's other practical technician. The most worldly of the Dolls, the group's lyricist and concept-master, David took an undisguised pleasure in the ironic persona play that is the privilege and/or responsibility of rock's leading men, although his style of humor was a lot more generous than Dylan's or Jagger's—he was as dedicated to the principle of fun as any great rocker since the Beatles themselves. But it seemed that this group might require more musicianly skills from its leader. With such a defiantly amateurish concept, wouldn't the concept-master have to do more than strike poses and think a lot if the music was to survive the force of its own forward rush? After all, without decoration and identifying detail it would turn into instant blur.

A great vocalist like Little Richard could sing right over this endemic rock and roll problem, but more often it has been solved by means of hooks. These are usually tuneful little snatches of provisional significance that are composed into a song or added by some clever musician or producer, but in a pinch almost anything memorable will do. And because David's specialties were striking poses and thinking a lot, he was compelled to fashion more hooks out of less melody than a tone-deaf Eskimo. He did it, though—in constant consultation with his boys—and as a result the Dolls' music ranks not only with the hardest and fastest ever made, but also with the wittiest and most charming. A few touches on the Dolls' LPs must have been donated by Todd Rundgren (e.g., the two-tone double-track at the end of "Personality Crisis," not to mention the piano playing) and Shadow Morton (e.g., the soul girls on "Stranded in the Jungle"). But most of them were part of the Dolls' music long before it got inside a studio, offshoots of

David's acting (as opposed to singing) ability and of his encyclo-pedic fondness for rock and roll trivia. If Jerry's craftsmanship provided roots, David's bestowed spirit. He struck poses, he thought a lot, and he came up with what the group needed.

Even by modernistic standards, Johansen was not a great vocalist. He was competent-plus in the post-Dylan manner—he had presence and rhythm and a teasing knack for enunciating just enough to whet your word hunger—but Little Richard he wasn't. His range was quite narrow and his timbre rather dry, and with the Dolls his singing was neither deeply expressive (that came later, when he went solo) nor acutely phrased. Yet his histrionic flair saved him, and not just live, where his rubber mug and felicitous gesticulations tended to overshadow his equally deft (and broad) vocal role-playing. His shifts of character and caricature on these records are an ongoing delight. "Personality Crisis," directed at a schizy imagemonger, pauses dramatically before David roars back with: "And you're a prima ballerina on a spring afternoon/Changed on into the wolfman howling at the moon." Shape up, that's cer-tainly his warning—but disapproval doesn't prevent him from whistling a birdie-type tune (and doing a plié, although the rustle of tulle gets lost in the mix) after the first line, or awhooing joyously after the second. It is on the great novelty covers of *In Too Much Too Soon* that David really indulges his taste for this kind of impersonation—the 14th Street high stepper of "Showdown," "Bad Detective" 's all-too-scrutable Charlie Chan, and (most exorbitantly) the alternating Amos 'n' Andy reject and lover's-lane ass man of "Stranded in the Jungle." But on occasion he would momentarily change the gears of his basic vocal transmission, which filters a drawling pout through a tough, loud New York accent—as in the adolescent-reverting-to-childhood dudgeon of "you better tell me" on "Who Are the Mystery Girls?" or the maidenly "oh—all right" that closes "Private World." And every one of these personality crises helps to decorate and identify the song.

But David's tricks didn't stop there. He stole mnemonic devices from everywhere and made up a few of his own, and his desire to work with Shadow Morton, rock and roll's greatest sound effects man, was not a casual one. A cut might begin with a gong, a harmonica, sighs, some sloppy power chords, monkey chatter, hand-claps, a whistle, a spoken intro, a shouted "One-two-three-four," a pouted "Oh . . . break-down," or the greatest of all the Dolls' credos: "Aah-ooh/Yeah yeah yeah/No no no no no no no." It might end with a gong, a harmonica, a sigh, a saxophone coda, a big fat kiss, a drum roll, a rifle shot, some climactic feedback, a shouted "Whatcha gonna do?," a pouted "oh—all right," or the greatest of all the Dolls' metaphysical questions: "Do you think that/You could make it/With Frankenstein?" The Dolls also loved to quote obscure classics—the Edsels' "Rama Lama Ding Dong," Del Shannon's "Runaway," the Shangri-Las' "Give Him a Great Big Kiss," Mickey & Sylvia's "Love Is Strange"—and would refer more allusively to anything from Jan & Dean to Chinese movie music to "I've Been Working on the Railroad." This kind of fooling around had a recontextualizing effect, of course—"Love Is Strange," for instance, pins down the meaning of "Trash"—but it also provided additional hooks, and time-proven ones at that. No wonder the group believed that if you were smart enough you didn't have to practice.

Since there are still people who label this kind of craft "gim-micky," as if that were a devastating insult, it ought to be em-phasized that David's gifts as a practical technician went beyond what I've been describing. He knew how to use his voice (in the post-Dylan manner) and he knew how to put a song together (his basic compositions—which on the two albums comprise three written solos plus eight collaborations with Johnny, three with Syl, and one with Arthur—are moderately catchy in a primitive way). As if to prove his competence-plus, he suddenly became a "better singer" who wrote "better melodies" when the more conventional concept of his solo career demanded it. Admittedly, I could have the order wrong—maybe increased competence is what David, whose father is an opera buff, would have preferred all along. But that wouldn't mean he was right. His melodies and his singing with the Dolls weren't merely adequate to the artistic venture— they were brilliantly appropriate to it. The most charmingly tune-ful Dolls song, "Lonely Planet Boy," is also the most anomalous, and was written solo by David before he joined the band.

Finally, David offered one additional accoutrement—lyrics every bit as apposite as his music, lyrics that focused and aimed the band's thrust. His father may have been an opera buff, but his mother was a college librarian, and like the good rebel he was he betrayed and fulfilled both birthrights simultaneously. Of course, in an era of pop surrealism, the bedlam of the Dolls' music had fewer precedents than the elusive logic of their words. But David's lyrics distinguished themselves from the post-Dylan norm by one simple expedient—they never sounded at all like poetry. It was to be expected that sometimes they wouldn't even sound like words— indecipherability was a rock and roll tradition, one David respected with a passion that passed all understanding. But the avoidance of imagery that declared itself to be imagery was a mark of sophistication that he shared with very few contemporaries, espe- cially in America. Even a master of the colloquial like Jaime Robbie Robertson, that fervent opponent of "glitter rock," was capable of something as "poetically" obscure on the face of it as "The Weight."

The Dolls' obscurities were at once deeper and less considered. Often the inexactness of their words, like that of their music, seems unintentional, so that the opacities of "Subway Train," for instance, bespeak careless workmanship more than anything else. But David clearly regards ambiguity as a significant mode. How else to explain "Trash," in which "Please don't you ask me if I love you" is followed first by "If you don't know what I do," then by "'Cause I don't know why I do," then by "'Cause I don't know if I do," and the "life" in "Don't take my life away" changes at various times to "knife," "night," and "lights"? Yet so fetching was the hook—"Trash! Pick it up! Don't take my life (knife) (night) (lights) away!"—that you could hear the song dozens of times without ever puzzling over such quiddities. Especially as David performed them, all the lyrics offered some turn that earned a chortle of recognition, and the tendency was to leave it at that.

Since the phrases that stood out often signaled "decadence" and/or "camp," this tendency reinforced the impression that the Dolls were purely (and exploitatively) decadent and campy. Even when it was quite explicit, for instance, that David was looking for "a kiss not a fix," the song's shooting-gallery ambience (not to mention the way David used to tie off with the mike cord and jab himself in the bicep as he sang) wasn't calculated to imprint this on one's mind. And in "It's Too Late," which posits lessons from trivia history against the latest nostalgic fads, the name of camp heroine Diana Dors has far more initial impact than the speed-kills putdown she's featured in. On the verbal surface, this is a band of kitsch-addicted, pill-popping teen Frankensteins on the subway train from Babylon to nowhere. Not only do they consort with bad girls, mystery girls, and other trash, they aren't even sure whether that jet boy up there wants to steal their baby or *be* their baby.

Like the Dolls' musical surface, this verbal surface offended many, but although the band certainly wasn't above sensationalism, their intent wasn't merely sensationalistic. Once again they were trying to create an environment that jibed with their experience. Just as it was dumb to write sensitive melodies that went unchallenged by anything else in the music, it was dumb to moralize in a benign, namby-pamby universe. This was the modern world the Dolls sang about—one nuclear bomb could blow it all away. Pills and personality crises weren't evils—easy, necessary, or whatever. They were strategies and tropisms and positive pleasures, and David wasn't so sure that those who disapproved even deserved to be called human beings: "Well if you don't like it go ahead and/ Find yourself a saint/Find yourself a boy who's/Gonna be what I ain't/And what you need is/A plastic doll with a/Fresh coat of paint/Who's gonna sit through the madness/And always act so quaint/Baby yeah yeah yeah."

Well, nobody ever called him humble. But his arrogance is moral arrogance as opposed to the arrogance of power, and it's moral arrogance of the best sort, infused with comedy and a feeling for human limits. His basic theme is authenticity—sometimes as an explicit subject, as in "Personality Crisis" and "Puss in Boots," sometimes in tales of lost "kidz" like "Babylon" and "Subway Train" —in the midst of massage parlors, Vietnamese babies, and other seventies exposés, and his solution (counsel?) (message to the world?) is a little surprising only because it is so traditional. Johansen is a kind of cartoon prophet—a prophet posing as a bitchy scold. Don't you start him talking, he'll tell everything he knows. And what he knows is love l-u-v.

The only reason this denouement qualifies as any kind of big deal is the context, and David does go out of his way to avoid making a big deal of it himself. It's almost as if love enters his music by accident, because it happens to be the classic rock and roll subject. In "Bad Girl," when he tells the waitress who makes his heart hurt that he's "gotta get some lovin' 'fore the planet is gone," he reduces his world view to a way to get laid; in "Trash," when he wonders whether his "lover's leap" will land him in "fairyland," he belittles his own proud (if ambiguous) pansexuality. But on the other hand, maybe the reason David is attracted to rock and roll is that it's always been a way to connect the cold cruel world with love l-u-v. Pills and personality may be okay up to a point, but they're obviously not going to get anyone past that point. In fact, the mood and message of these songs is not only expressly anti-phony (Dolls, not plastic dolls) but also expressly anti-drug (just like Bo Diddley); what David tells that Diana Dors freak is: "You invite us up to that speed trip/Well that's nothing new on me/That reminds me of Buck Rogers/Back in 1933."

For the Dolls, the old answers can't be revived—the only conventional I-love-you songs here are Johnny's jokey, roughly affectionate "Chatterbox" and David's "Lonely Planet Boy." But the old answers can be adapted to the dangerous world where the Dolls' music finds its life, just as rock and roll itself can be reinterpreted to get rid of most of its sexy backbeat and twenty years of acquired polish. By the seventies, the love-suffering of "Lonely Planet Boy" was a hoary pop cliché and the love-nastiness of "It's Too Late" a virulent one. But the sardonically optimistic, quadruple-edged contingency evoked by songs like "Looking for a Kiss" and "Trash" and "Bad Girl"—so far from the self-serving transience of the rocky-road mythmongers and the fashionable equivocation of the sensitive singer-songwriters—was always unique to this band. In "Frankenstein" and "Vietnamese Baby" Johansen even moved from eros to agape, an agape that negated the universalist mush of the music-as-brotherhood sermoneers because it was rooted in horror.

This was tough stuff in every way, and if the Dolls' record company couldn't put it to use, neither could the Dolls. The arrogance of power wasn't in their karma—they didn't lust after it enough to trouble themselves with the discipline it required. It took them much too long to learn that getting your name in the papers was not equivalent to world conquest, and in the end they didn't even win over the city that taught them everything they knew. After it became obvious that Mercury wasn't going to break them, they did some touring and gigged sporadically for their sizable local cult, even hooking up briefly with Malcolm McLaren, who later devised the Sex Pistols. But their failure had put a damper on the New York rock scene, and before the punk audience had redefined itself at CBGB the Dolls were down to David and Syl. The first album sold perhaps 100,000, the second rather less.

As far as their legend goes, it's just as well that they were never forced to translate permanent insurrection into success. But the split meant the end of all their most invigorating tensions: between feeling and alienation, love and escape, craft and anarchy. Arthur, who'd fallen away well before the final breakup, surfaced looking very ravaged, first in a disturbingly Nazoid outfit called the Corpse Grinders and later behind Sid Vicious, of all people. David wrote deeply felt conventional I-love-you songs with an unconventional come-on-boys spirit and was joined by Syl in a band to match. And Johnny and Jerry became the soul of the Heartbreakers, who somehow managed to make junkiedom sound like laughs and fast times. It was on the Heartbreakers' *L.A.M.F.*, rather than *David Johansen*, that the old gestalt came through most emphatically. After all, what made the Dolls the Dolls was the way they energized negatives.

For me, even that is a side benefit, because for me, the Dolls perfect—in a properly inexact way—a new aesthetic. Camp or no camp, theirs was not a cause of "a seriousness that fails," of this-is-so-bad-it's-good. On the contrary, the Dolls were the ultimate instance of the miracle of pop, using their honest passion, sharp wits, and attention to form to transmute the ordinary into the extraordinary. Like the greatest folk artists, they plugged into an enormously expressive (and accessible) cultural given and then animated it with their own essence. But this was not a folk process—not orally transmitted, naive, somehow "natural." It was consciously aesthetic, rooted in bookish ideas about art that were alive in the downtown boho air. Their music synthesizes folk art's communion and ingenuousness with the exploded forms, historical acuity, and obsessive self-consciousness of modernism. As culture, it is radically democratic and definitively urban; as art, it is crude and sophisticated at the same time. It epitomizes why rock and roll began and why it will last.

HUEY "PIANO" SMITH'S ROCK & ROLL REVIVAL!

HUEY "PIANO" SMITH (ACE 2021)
1957–1959/1975

JAY COCKS

"You got me rocking when I ought to be rolling"
—"Don't You Just Know It"

Rock was the tough part, the part that made you holler. The fun was all in the roll, and in the beginning, down in New Orleans, they rolled the finest.

Leave the fury to the rockabillies, with their middle-finger salutes in rhythm and their eight-bar assaults on hit parade gentility. In New Orelans they found the groove, made music that, like the gulf town it sprang from, devoted itself to easeful enjoyment and antic meditations on absolute insignificance.

Elvis and Jerry Lee found the angry edge, used it to hack even when it wasn't full sharp enough to cut. Chuck Berry wrote deft short stories, tunes that defined the backseat horniness of rock with the lecherous, lyric precision of a prancing Pan who played guitar, not pipes, and could do a mean jump-split into the bargain. The black rockers of New Orleans voiced those themes in a different way. Whether raw and rambunctious, like Professor Longhair; unruffled, ever truthful of heart, like Fats Domino; whether bereft, like Ernie K-Doe, or burned and jumping, like Chris Kenner; or even berserk, like Little Richard—all these New Orleans cats always seemed cool at the core, ever bemused. Or wise-assed, like Huey "Piano" Smith. My man.

Huey Smith can stand as a fitting example of the hilarious, careening excesses of rock, New Orleans–style. Now, he's usually been considered a first figure of the second rank, shadowed by Professor Longhair, who influenced him, and Fats Domino, who outsold him, then bypassed by Allen Toussaint, who learned a few lessons from him before moving along. But to me, Huey Smith's always been the town's premier roller.

Today Huey has embraced a different faith. He's a Witness now, a roller no longer, and can be found around town on occasion distributing copies of the *Watchtower* to the benighted. He hasn't made a record under his own name in a decade, although it is possible—one must rely on rumors—that he has contributed his inimitable piano to some obscure gospel recordings. There, presumably, his rollicking style has been somewhat subdued, his insinuating left-hand rhythms dressed, for the occasion, in Sunday-go-to-meeting.

This Smith style, which knotted chords and made heavy-handedness into a paradoxical marvel of dexterity, can be caught, at its height, on any oldies anthology that includes "Sea Cruise." It can also be heard, in all its goofy glory, on an Ace retrospective collection called *Huey "Piano" Smith's Rock & Roll Revival!* For sheer velocity, for its typical but very special kind of innocent hedonism, for its sense of unstrung celebration and never-ending play, I'd match it against any record I know.

Huey Smith's great strengths are also his severest limitations. The beat gets repetitious, the lyrics are nonsense. The songs are often without a subject and usually without a point. None of that ever bothered Huey, of course. Good times was good enough for him, and of what he wanted, and what he chose, he provided an abundance.

Those who rank Smith as a minor figure take his limitations too much into account, don't hold thoroughly to heart Smith's humor, the feeling all his music passed along of having been made by a touring medicine show in the throes of a never-ending party. His considerable keyboard skills have been diminished, it seems, by Smith's own deprecating, even sardonic attitude toward his gifts as expressed in the full-throttle whimsies of his music, and as well by musicologists and critics who see this attitude as a statement, not a posture.

In fact, Smith was one of the best sessionmen around New Orleans; you can hear him rolling true in the intro to Smiley Lewis's "I Hear You Knocking." He even laid in some piano behind the eruptions of Little Richard. Richard denies this—heatedly—but it is inarguable that Smith was working out his style while Richard was still singing Dinah Washington tunes, and it was that very style—no matter who supplied it on records—that Richard steam-heated and mutated into his own.

Press a little and you could say that Huey's romps along the 88s were not only an extension of the prevailing piano style around town, but a loving parody of it. Professor Longhair, probably New Orleans's most redoubtable R&B legend, gets the historical credit for putting this style together out of the hot sounds in the air. Years before, Jelly Roll Morton had done much the same thing by deflecting some of the Caribbean rhythms off the docks and into the whorehouse jazz he was knocking out nightly. There's a distinct Caribbean undertow in Professor Longhair's music—in "Tipitina," "Bald Head" and, most especially, in "Mardi Gras in New Orleans"—but his approach was bluesier, closer to country roads than Rampart Street. The second line lays snug beneath his music, but so does the sardonic growl of the blues, raw but tipped over into something a little more casual. A shrug, maybe, instead of a snarl.

Huey Smith built on this approach, then cut it up and knocked it over. He was a joker. His group was called the Clowns, and, like a lot of wise guys, Huey stowed a lot of wild aggression behind his easy smile. On some of his early sides—a couple are included on Savoy's The Roots of Rock & Roll—he plays pretty straight-ahead R&B, prancing on the keys where, a few years later, he'd commence to pounding. This older music is adept, if not altogether distinguished. It would take the giddiness, even the inconsequence, of mainline rock to turn Huey into a demolition expert.

Huey started training for the call early. He was fifteen when he hit the road in 1949, with Guitar Slim and a drummer named Willie Nettles, to embark on what Slim later called "a nationally-known tour." In the early fifties, Huey settled into session work, mostly for Specialty, playing dates behind Lloyd Price and Smiley Lewis. According to John Broven's *Walking to New Orleans* (a book you can't do without, and the source for many of the facts I've used here), Huey also toured with Shirley and Lee besides backing Richard on those Specialty sessions. It's worth noting that work—Richard's first for Specialty—resulted in some solid, down-the-middle R&B, and one raver, "Tutti Frutti." Richard took over piano on that one. The song was an afterthought, a goof, and Bumps Blackwell, Richard's manager-producer, had only fifteen minutes of studio time left to cut it, hardly enough to teach Huey the arrangement. So Little Richard sat down on the bench and let fly. Sure sounds like Huey, though, which may not be all that surprising when you figure that Richard had been listening to Huey take his turns on every other tune.

There's little question that Huey was a far more adept player than Richard. Dave Bartholomew, the great band leader who wrote and arranged a lot of Fats Domino's best material, once tipped Huey that his playing was too perfect—technically, that is—and suggested he bang out a few wrong notes "like Little Richard." What put Richard over was his delirium tremens vocalizing; he used the piano to batter and bash himself along. Now, this approach could not have been entirely lost on Huey. He may not have taken Bartholomew straight at his word, but Huey's first hit, "Rocking Pneumonia and the Boogie Woogie Flu," released in the summer of 1957, a year and a half after "Tutti Frutti," had much of Richard's anarchy. Smith played fine bust-a-blood-vessel piano—no wrong notes, either—but, ever shy of singing, enlisted the Clowns to handle the vocals. Along with James Black and a gent named "Scarface" John Williams, the original Clowns featured Bobby Marchan, whose voice could rip and shriek like a pair of nylons being torn by a fingernail.

During his time with the Clowns, and later, gone solo, Marchan paced Little Richard in dementia and, some say, for a time almost outdistanced him. Marchan was partial to makeup and leapt into falsetto vocals that dared the upper register to crack. He kicks off Huey's "High Blood Pressure" by revealing his symptoms—"I get high blood pressure when you call my name"—with the pride of an inveterate cruiser showing up for mandatory inspection at the VD clinic. On the flip side, "Don't You Just Know It," Marchan and the rest of the Clowns set down the call-and-response theme ("Ah ha ha ha, hey-ey you, gooba gooba gooba") like a gang of twisted Masons shouting a password. It was Huey's fleet piano, though, that anchored both songs; on "High Blood Pressure" he rolled right into the middle break with the same riff he'd used twice before, on "I Hear You Knocking" and a wonderful Earl King tune, "Those Lonely, Lonely Nights." "People started to complain when I had done it three times," is the way Huey defends himself in Broven's book. "But it was such a damn good piano solo."

Marchan's singing with the Clowns pushed Huey and his gang over the edge of eccentricity into free-fall. Their sound could have been low-down sinister, but the sense of what they sang was safe and serene as only nonsense can be. "I want to holler, but the joint's too small"—if that's in fact what's being sung at the beginning of "Rocking Pneumonia"; it's hard to say exactly—sounds scruffy enough, a fearful dilemma, part of the parcel of troubles that goes with this particular affliction. As much as Marchan might camp it up, he was at rock-bottom a blues belter, so the silliness was never thorough, just—like Richard's—a gesture of caricature sensuality and grand defiance.

Huey's own vocalizing, which is short on fine shading but does have a fair share of gruff gumption, can be heard on occasion, fighting for life against the roundhouse force of his piano. On *Rock & Roll Revival*, Greg Shaw, who compiled the record, included an alternate version of "Sea Cruise," minus the bells and foghorns and white singer Frankie Ford. Huey sang, with the excellent Gerri Hall (a member of the Clowns by that time) setting down a sprightly track which apparently sounded a little saw-toothed to Johnny Vincent, who ran Ace Records. He scrubbed it up with Frankie Ford, presided over the laying in of the maritime effects, and put out one of the great singles in rock & roll history.

Today Frankie Ford is underrated and still looking for his due, probably because of what many consider his ofay incursions. But his *Let's Take a Sea Cruise* album on Ace is a snug, near-masterful collaboration with Huey Smith, who played on the record and provided most of the material. Huey sounds bushy-tailed as ever all over the set, and Frankie Ford was too good to be slick. He just smoothed the music out, made it go down a touch easier. The best thing about the official version of "Sea Cruise" is still the rhythm track, and nobody messed with that. "Sea Cruise" has a fine melody, but to get an idea of how thoroughly the record is Huey Smith's, how it craves his piano, listen to any remake—say, John Fogerty's. It's game, but it drags. It's got bells and horns and a little lapping water, too, but it doesn't have the dazzle. Fogerty plays piano on the cut, and that's what trips everything up. Huey had such ease on the keyboard he made it all sound a cinch.

Huey could get a little unhinged. He never strayed from the groove, but he pressed its limits once in a while. His one original album—the others were mostly made up of recycled singles—is likely the wildest record he ever made: *'Twas the Night Before Christmas*, copies of which can still be found occasionally in oldies stores, priced forbiddingly. It was a collection of seasonal tunes—a standard or two like "Jingle Bells" and "Silent Night" were given the New Orleans treatment and laid down to rest beside such originals as "'Twas the Night Before Christmas" (a song featuring "Boogie woogie Santa Claus, comin' down the chimney makin' lots of noise"). The record is flush with holiday spirit, made on a whim, it would seem, and performed as a goof. It could have been recorded in a rumpus room; each successive cut sounds looser than the last. The only thing missing at the end of side one is the sound of bottles being emptied and next-door neighbors bellowing for quiet.

The record isn't so much a celebration of Christmas as a definition of the essential spirit of New Orleans rock & roll, so free it can never shake down. Huey played better elsewhere—pressures of the revels may have finally foxed him into making a few of those Little Richard mistakes—and the Clowns' horseplay had certainly been sharper. The material would challenge no one. But the humor that prevails, the good-natured cool and untroubled technique are definitive. Phil Spector's grander Christmas album has the same enterprise, but misses the irreverence. The only place I've ever heard traces of this same giddy, gleeful spirit is in the commercially unreleased version of "Santa Claus Is Coming to Town" that Bruce Springsteen and the E Street Band put on the radio in 1977. They may have gotten the idea from Spector, but the momentum's all toward Huey Smith.

The unstrung core of New Orleans music comes out of a casual professionalism common to musicians of the fifties. Even when Huey lets things unravel, as on the Christmas album or "Beatnik Blues," a fiercely silly single, there's a certain border of discipline he never crosses, a barrier of pride and skill. Certain of those few who followed along after him—like Dr. John—weren't so particular, an attitude that could sap the music of spirit, turn it toward unchecked indulgence. The Dr. John of *The Last Waltz*, laying down his lazy, sexy "Such a Night," is the best Dr. John, the true Mac Rebennack; the Night Tripper was for the tourist trade. Rebennack has the skill, and he can show the fire. He did an album in homage to New Orleans, *Gumbo*, and included a Huey Smith medley that was respectful and sassy in rightful measure. His hoodoo masquerade was always jive, though, part of his cynical side, even though it could be argued that the backwater decadence of the Night Tripper was just another extension of the time-honored New Orleans playfulness which Huey had raised to such a pitch of raggedy perfection. After Dr. John latched onto it, coated it in gris-gris and set it loose to pass for some sort of bayou psychedelia, the good times turned synthetic. When Little Richard or Bobby Marchan strutted their stuff, they keyed their energies too high for pure camp. It took the Doctor to write that particular prescription. Huey always had a taste of shuck in his music, but again—even at its silliest—he held fast to his craft. It was his particular pleasure to make light of his skill, as well as his music. Fats Domino did the same, in a homier, fond-uncle sort of way; so did Professor Longhair, and Allen Toussaint, who dazzled only in his music and arranging, using shyness and modesty—reclusiveness, even—to mask his pride just as Huey hid behind his humor. Toussaint never caught a terminal case of the rocking pneumonia, as Huey did. Like all bold experimenters, Huey infected himself with the disease before he could diagnose its symptoms. Judging from his example, the terminal stages of the disease do not impair any vital functions or talents. They only bring on a fit of the giggles.

Such home truths can only take you so far; the same problems come up every direction you take, and the thought is inescapable that Huey took his music the furthest he could on a very short path. Styles changed, sure, and R&B slid into soul. Regional music, which in the fifties had a toehold in Top 40 radio, began to lose ground in the sixties: when business got bigger, record companies enlarged, and smaller regional labels—like Ace, Instant, Minit—had to bust ass harder than ever to get proper distribution. It wasn't only commerce that made the music change, though. It was taste, the particular fickle nature of the pop audience, then the coming of the British groups. That combination of circumstance and commerce contrived to move rock & roll in directions that were barely on the compass. Huey, of course, tried to follow along.

When the changes first consolidated and started to hit, in 1962, Huey was enjoying his first chart single in over three years, a novelty dance number called "Pop-Eye." It was his last score. Treading water during the deluge that followed, Huey tried to get a fix on high ground. He started tuning up his social conscience, released a couple of sides like "Ballad of a Blackman" and "Epitaph of Uncle Tom" that invoked Martin Luther King, Booker T. Washington and other luminaries. Huey's intentions were all of the best—a little desperate, maybe, though still sincere —but he couldn't shake his old antic disposition. Even preaching and paying due homage to black pride, Huey sounded like he was cutting up. Messages didn't sit easy with such a good-time fella. Moving into the late sixties, Huey started his own label, Pity-Pat, and recorded a variety of soul acts like the Pitter-Pats (for whom he played piano) and the Soulshakers. He even had a small local hit in 1968 off a tune called "Coo Coo Over You" which must have sounded, in that stormy year, comfortingly quaint, a little memento of innocence. A while after that, Huey took up the Bible.

The question remains—will always remain, with no hope of sure solution—how much longer the whole New Orleans sound could have continued before it fizzled into redundancy. By and large the stuff that sounds best today—Huey's, Fats's, Smiley Lewis's and Chris Kenner's and Ernie K-Doe's—is the music made during the prime years that stayed true to form. Subsequent attempts to retool and adopt the sound, as the Meters have done, come out bottom-heavy and a little contorted. Allen Toussaint, the great guiding spirit of New Orleans in the seventies, is a musician in whom all traditions are replenished, and from whom flow all kinds of marvels. His work with Lee Dorsey marries funk, soul, and a little dab of disco to the high, sweet spirit of days gone by. The music is intricate, full of cunning tricks, and Dorsey is not just the best singer now working out of New Orleans, he's one of the most enduring and gifted R&B singers of the seventies. Still, the Toussaint/Dorsey collaborations don't have the deep colors of the older material. Maybe those come with time and distance; maybe it's the perspective that makes them more vibrant—that, and sentiment, too.

In other quarters, R&B had a more diabolical edge or could sustain a greater social urgency. In New Orleans, the good times set the limits of the music. There was just so far you could go and so much you dared say without souring the party. After all the other arguments and considerations have been cut away, it is this prevailing attitude that finally fences the music in. It doesn't date it. Music doesn't need to freight a major message in order to survive. But it does need to be powerful enough, all on its own, to transport us to its time and place without auxiliary power: special interest, scholarship, nostalgia. New Orleans R&B can do that; Huey Smith can sure do that. All the music's glory is right in that. Its weakness is that this is a place to revel in, but then to pass through.

The music's special, particular, and persistent value, its rough-house joy, is not only inseparable from this weakness, it almost depends on it, thrives on impermanence. I'd take an over-the-shoulder guess that Huey Smith thought no further than the charts, and hoped no higher than a gold record, every time he went into the studio. There is no deliberation behind his music, little calculation beyond a kind of instinctive reliance on commercial novelty. Thoughts of history, concerns about the staying power of the music, would have been considered presumptuous at best, notions puffed up past any recognizable or manageable size. It was immediate impact folks thought about then, not resonance. Once you hear an echo, it means the music is already fading away.

That it's lasted this long is a simple wonder. That it will endure, age, but never turn antique, seems a safe augury. The joy of Huey Smith's records is retroactive and regenerative, self-perpetuating past any arbitrary limits. That spirit travels well, too, because, like Huey's keyboard skill, it seems so spontaneous and effortless, so true. This gift of joy is so generous, not only to have but to spread around, that it should never be a matter of just settling for it, and missing all you may be sacrificing. Transitory though it may be, joy like this is substantial enough, and its own reward.

So rock has always told us, anyhow. But this is dangerous territory, vulnerable to scrupulous reasoning. You need a kind of innocent hedonism—just what Huey delivers—to live here in harmony, and you must accept, as a precondition, that you will always be prey to assaults of rationality that beat at you like a bad conscience. You know, at these times, that you've come too far, gone through too much, grown too old, to still believe that pleasure is where it all starts and stops. As much as you know that, though, as hard as you hold to it, Huey Smith and that piano can sucker you every time.

If you want to reflect, and experience has warned you away from exploring the social implications or pop-myth infrastructures of the work of Huey P. Smith, if you want to ruminate a minute, and not dance, and not feel guilty, either—then, as Huey takes his souped-up jitney races across the keyboard, you might think on the role of the piano in rock & roll. You might think, as I have, that the piano is the keystone rock instrument. You might realize that the guitar sends out the flash, but the piano carries the weight.

You might even reckon that though a record heavy on guitar might be just right for a time capsule, it's an album of rock piano you'd want tucked under your arm if eternity was giving you the eye.

When Huey lets loose—or Professor Longhair, for that matter, or Fats, or Toussaint—the very prankish agility of his gifts can make you banish all the other instruments to the rear of the stage. That has in part to do with the particular vibrancy of the performer, certainly. But the fact that the piano is often back-seated in rock has something to do with the paucity of good practitioners, and even more with the very practical matter of portability. Try kicking out the jams on a Steinway.

All Huey's musical hi-jinks notwithstanding, he was, by all reports, a fairly contained stage performer. Huey and the Clowns may have romped, but they romped in place. Same with the Professor. Little Richard used the piano kind of like a launching pad, from which he would surge forth on his unlikely trajectories. (Elton John's been trying to get into this same orbit for years.) The original piano stomper himself, Jerry Lee Lewis, used his instrument as the object of both affection and aggression, and took things about as far as they can go, even once setting fire to his instrument on stage at the Apollo. Jerry Lee could stand, knock the bench aside with the back of his knees and start pounding. He could stomp the keyboard with the stacked heel of his lizard-skin boot, and get a great sound all the while, too. But he couldn't compete with the guitar as a talisman, and no matter what he tried, he couldn't beat the final damn dignity out of the piano.

No way to best the figurative as well as literal electricity of the guitar, and no way either that you can do the same sort of stunt flying with any other instrument. You can stand still and play great, like Ry Cooder or Dave Edmunds or Eric Clapton. But you can also jump around and rave up and play great into the bargain, like Chuck Berry or Pete Townshend. With a piano, you just play. Showboating's such an integral part of rock—sheer physical movement, as well as musical momentum—that the very presence of a piano seems to promise inflexibility, no matter what kind of sound comes out of it.

There is another, even stronger preconception at work here. Since the early fifties, guitar has been the symbolic instrument of rebellion. The piano is what your parents wanted you to play. Not even clown anarchists like Huey Smith could completely dispel hovering shades of relentless piano teachers and pitiless metronomes. You learned guitar from your friends, or—better—off records, in your room, by yourself. Guitars traditionally have been a poor man's instrument, for the field and front porch, and pianos graced proper gatherings of the gentlefolk. But less obviously, pianos have a saving dark side: they were the instrument of choice in the cathouse parlor. It's a comfort to keep that in mind.

Huey Smith can help you remember. In all his music, even the giddiest rock, there is fond remembrance of the rolling syncopation that comes straight from the back streets. It wasn't only Caribbean inflections that Huey and everyone else heard in Jelly Roll Morton, and it wasn't just calypso that Professor Longhair busted up in a compound fracture and reassembled along his keyboard. It was the below-the-belt rhythm of jazz. This proudly dishonorable piano tradition doesn't—and likely can't—go far enough to dispel all the received notions and stubborn ghosts that bedevil the instrument. Huey Smith suffers fallout from those prejudices; so does most other New Orleans rock. It's piano-moored and horn-based. It's hard to think of a hot guitar player from the Crescent City.

So the action moved elsewhere, and hasn't returned. While younger musicians hungry for material and tradition have ransacked most every other territory from rockabilly scruff to the Wagnerian summits of Phil Spector, New Orleans has remained pretty much untouched and untraveled. In the early seventies, Dave Edmunds had a hit off a loving revival of "I Hear You Knocking." Smack in the middle of the tune, right in the instrumental break, Edmunds shouted the names of the New Orleans pantheon with all the fervor of the last true believer: "Smiley Lewis! Fats Domino! Huey Smith! Dave Bartholomew!"

Because there are so few keeping the faith, the speculation has arisen that the New Orleans sound has died. Apparently this news has not reached Louisiana. Allen Toussaint writes, makes his own records, produces others. The Meters, the Neville Brothers, the aptly named Wild Tchoupitoulas, are still productive. According to the eternally enthusiastic owner of the town's largest oldies store, even Huey is thinking on the possibility of settling into some secular music again.

Most important, though, is that New Orleans continues to honor these musicians as generative figures, not waxworks to respect, then dismiss. Their music hasn't been stashed away in the archives. In New Orleans, it's never a question of music being outdated, or out of style. This is a town where tradition is the style.

The weekend that Muhammad Ali danced his championship away from Leon Spinks, the city was alive with music. Clarence "Frogman" Henry was holding down his regular gig on Bourbon Street. The wonderful Irma Thomas was serenading the tourists on a moonlight cruise aboard a paddlewheel steamer. And her name was carved, fresh and bold—SWEET IRMA THOMAS—into the timber of a club where Professor Longhair was holding forth. SWEET IRMA THOMAS: the inscription of a fan for whom there is no past history, only persistent good times.

And the Professor played on, about as sassy as ever before an audience that did a whole lot more than just cherish him. The club was called Tipitina's in his honor, but the people who came weren't there to pay solemn tribute or to hunker down for some serious ethno-musical history. It was Saturday night, and they were there to party. The Professor blistered through his repertoire, paying no mind to time, not wanting to stop, and the people responded as they should, as they were meant to, all dancing to the music.

PRECIOUS LORD:
NEW RECORDINGS OF THE
GREAT GOSPEL SONGS OF
THOMAS A. DORSEY

(COLUMBIA KG 32151)
1973

TOM SMUCKER

When black slaves sang, "I looked over Jordan and what did I see, Coming for to carry me home," they were looking over the Ohio River. "Steal away" meant to sneak into the wood for a secret slave meeting, and "Follow the Drinking Gourd" meant following the Great Dipper to the Ohio River and freedom. But . . . not all black slaves could hope to make it to Africa, Canada, or even to the northern section of the United States. . . . And blacks also began to realize that the North was not so significantly different from the South as they had envisioned, particularly in view of the Fugitive Slave act of 1850 and the Dred Scott Decision of 1858. . . . Thus they found it necessary to develop a style of freedom that included but did not depend on historical possibilities.

—James H. Cone,
The Spirituals and the Blues:
An Interpretation

Some mysteries.

I'm a little boy, and I'm playing an old 78 by Arthur Godfrey, "For Me and My Gal," on the old phonograph that's been demoted to the breezeway. To my astonishment, I find I can play this one record over and over and over again without getting tired of it.

My older brother's old enough to be a teenager and an Elvis Presley fan. We're visiting grandparents in Kansas City and he buys two early EPs: one with "Shake, Rattle and Roll," "I Love You Because," "Lawdy Miss Clawdy," and "Blue Moon," and one, oddly enough, that's all religious, with "I Believe," "It Is No Secret," "Precious Lord," and "Peace in the Valley."

I'm too young to be a juvenile delinquent and too frightened of the sex and rebellion to try when I'm older anyway. Pat Boone's my man—clean, Christian, smart, and popular; but it's "Blue Moon" by Elvis that I keep coming back to. And I can't figure out how someone so sleazy can sound so involved with religion on his "other" record. It's more than a ploy to confuse parents (or younger brothers) who want to disapprove. In fact, by comparison, Pat's devotional fervor sounds suspicious.

"I Believe" and "It Is No Secret" are at least familiar to me, although not with Presley's heavy emoting and hillbilly embellishments, but "Precious Lord" is a shock. "Take *my hand*" sung by Swivel Hips, the man whose TV appearance inspires my brother to threaten to wear *blue jeans to church*? It's too physical, too personal, too self-affirming for me to grasp, while "Peace in the Valley," lacking the disturbing sensuality of "Precious Lord," is worse for being perfect in its balance of despair and hope. My young mind reels—this has got to be my favorite religious song, if not the best song ever. It's also a big hit for Elvis. What is going on?

I've escaped an unhappy adolescence in the suburbs and folk music is my bag. The FM side of my radio, which is folk and classical, is broken, so I'm listening to big hits on the AM. The Beach Boys come on singing I don't remember what anymore and I realize that this is *me*. I accept the revelation, but I wish it was about something bigger than pop music and better than the Beach Boys.

Months later I'm living in a black neighborhood in Detroit, spending the kind of collegiate interracial Christian summer I doubt still exists. This is long ago, before the riot, before Motown Records leaves Motown for L.A. Detroit has great AM radio (still does, they tell me), and "Satisfaction," "Like a Rolling Stone," "Tracks of My Tears," and "Since I Lost My Baby" are the hits. Who needs FM? The words to "Since I Lost My Baby" are written on a wall in the neighborhood. A guy I meet knew the Supremes in high school. At the black church we attend the singing gets so enthusiastic people faint, and I'm surprised to find I like some of the songs as much as the ones I'm listening to on the radio. Three little sisters who live down the block sing great gospel music together and one of them asks me why all of the songs that I sing when I play my banjo are about freedom. The teenager downstairs, who practices Bach for her piano lessons, can accompany the sisters on gospel piano, evidently without trying.

At the settlement house where I help out, the Summer Bible School is changed to a Freedom School and we point out to the kids that they should use a brown or black crayon to color in the faces of Ralph Bunche and Frederick Douglass in their coloring books, instead of using the Flesh-Color crayon. A black minister, Rev. Cleage, who's running in the city elections, preaches that Jesus was black.

After spending the next summer getting stoned and listening to the Beatles and Bob Dylan I buy the Beach Boys' *Pet Sounds* in the fall, just out of curiosity. I'm shocked to find that the more I listen to it, the better I like it. On acid my suspicions are confirmed—a great record.

Most of my acquaintances, however, prefer the Rolling Stones, Dylan, Aretha, and Otis Redding. One song that Otis sings, "A Change Is Gonna Come," overwhelms me—it seems more political and spiritual than his other stuff—and I have a secret obsessive desire to be able to sing it. But Otis sounds so black and I'm so white. For some reason I resolve the problem by deciding that if I did sing the song, I would sing it like Pete Seeger would if he sang it.

The next year I move to New York, hoping to become a hippie or a radical. Events are transpiring, particularly in Viet Nam, that make the second possibility easier and easier. But, while crashing the New Left in time to witness its collapse, I also find myself—for the first time—with a full-time job and, as they say, some discretionary income. I indulge my obsession with the Beach Boys, who are between their early sixties and late seventies popularity. Record stores are clearing out their Beach Boys stock at bargain prices and I buy everything and find, oddly, that I like it all. I get paid to write an article about the Beach Boys that is never published, but which nonetheless justifies my extravagant purchases.

Time goes by and I find that if you write about rock and roll, record companies will send you free records, most of which aren't any good. If you only write infrequently, as I do, only some record companies send you records. In 1973 I am temporarily on Columbia Records' freebie list and get a record called *Precious Lord*. It doesn't look like something I'd want to listen to, but it looks like something I should own. It's two LPs, it's got a classy cover, and it's gospel music, which maybe I should learn a little about. I file it away.

(Two footnotes. Somewhere along the way I find out that country & western star Red Foley, who is Pat Boone's father-in-law, had a hit with "Peace in the Valley" before Elvis, and I mistakenly decide that Foley wrote the song. Also, one day while examining my Otis Redding records I notice that Sam Cooke, someone I'd never thought much about, wrote "A Change Is Gonna Come" along with some other Otis trademarks. I'd always taken Cooke for a black pop singer the Stones improved upon, but now I wonder.)

A couple of years later, I actually play the *Precious Lord* collection of Thomas A. Dorsey songs and of course, I'm surprised that I want to play it again, that it's not just interesting but enjoyable, that I haven't noticed any duds, and that it bounces around an amazing variety of styles. One day, listening a little more closely, I notice that both of my old Elvis bugaboos—"Precious Lord" and "Peace in the Valley"—are on the record, that they were both written by Dorsey, and that "Peace in the Valley" is sung by a guy named R. H. Harris who impossibly enough outstrips Elvis's fervor with his urgency, commitment, and desperation. The notes mention that Harris was in the Soul Stirrers gospel group before

Sam Cooke, that he taught Cooke his style, that Cooke replaced him and continued to acknowledge his debt to Harris after he went pop.

And I fall through a hole, listening to this record, back to my childhood puzzling over Elvis, back to that summer in Detroit, back to being Christian, being white, being a radical. Toward a place where mysteries are explained.

I found that Elvis had frightened me with a little black gospel music, which he may have gotten via Red Foley—his version of "Peace in the Valley" is a hipper, more emotional reworking of Foley's basic structure—but which came originally from Thomas A. Dorsey. Born in 1899 and still living, Dorsey—inspired in 1939 by thoughts of the war in Europe—wrote what sounded like a hillbilly pastoral infused with the feeling of the blues. His past reflects the complexity of his music. Before he began writing gospel about 1930, Dorsey was a well-known blues musician who called himself Georgia Tom, particularly famous in the late twenties for his suggestive, double-entendre lyrics; he took credit for the introduction of the blues moan into black religious music, and for the invention of modern gospel music itself.

Ten years after "Shake, Rattle and Roll" it was common to consider Elvis some sort of original, primordial hippie-yippie, and to point to his introduction of black blues into white culture as a prefiguration of the explosions of the sixties. But Elvis also utilized the reverential (more as time went on) and apocalyptic (less as time went on) qualities of evangelical southern Christianity. And what I heard, and what confused me with its sensuality, despair, and hope, were two songs by a black bluesman, adept at 1920s pop, who turned to gospel without turning his back on anything he'd done before. Buried under the obedient sound of Red Foley's hit were liberating feelings. Elvis discovered this, and I spotted his discovery with some alarm.

This is also what I heard that summer in Detroit in church, and what shocked me with its closeness to what I was listening to on the radio. Both kinds of music were coming from the same source, even if I didn't know it—because while for a white group like the Rolling Stones the debt to black blues was direct, the debt to black gospel was indirect, through transitional figures like

Sam Cooke. "A Change Is Gonna Come" was Sam Cooke's reworking of gospel despair and hope in a pop context—no wonder I wanted to sing it. And no wonder, though it seemed odd at the time, that I resolved to sing it like Pete Seeger. Seeger's brand of American left-wing folk song had often used black religious music with secularized lyrics to promote its secular message of despair and hope—from Paul Robeson to "We Shall Overcome." The spirit that I felt in the frenzy of those Sunday mornings, that inspired the frightening feelings buried in those Elvis records, and that flowed through Sam Cooke and Pete Seeger, was the same spirit that rose up and laid the bus boycott on Martin Luther King when he was a young minister in Montgomery, Alabama, in the 1950s. But King not only came out of and identified with this culture—"Precious Lord" was the last song he requested before he was assassinated—he understood its political potential. When the spirit of the black church confronted him in historical specifics in Montgomery he knew what was going on, and he was able to carry that spirit, at least temporarily, from Alabama to a nationwide explosion, even while much of the black church as an *organization* remained relatively cautious.

Thomas A. Dorsey has been writing gospel music for forty years, in every style from show-biz to blues (Mahalia Jackson called him "our Irving Berlin"); *Precious Lord*, among other things, is pure pop product. Dorsey's songs are performed here by seven different venerable gospel groups and soloists who stretch pretty far across the black gospel, and therefore pop music, spectrum. The production's great. The whole record's shot through with the feeling of classic expression and fresh improvisation. It's as if the artists are driven by their all-star surroundings to do their best recorded work.

But more important, as the best and most varied collection of black gospel that I've heard, this record is *interesting* for me to listen to, think about, and use to define myself. And it sounds like it will continue to interest me for a long, long time. It speaks to some of my unanswered questions. It solves some mysteries, and points to others.

Originally I thought of my potential island shipwreck as a

metaphor for my worst left-wing paranoid fears. What would I be like if the fascists (or Stalinists, Maoists, S.L.A., or Third World terrorists) tortured and imprisoned me? What would I be like if I were the Rosenbergs? (Or Solzhenitsyn?) But life as a castaway felt so much less social, less logical, less comprehensible, more catastrophic and ultimate. I'm all for throwing anything at all against the void of Existential Despair. But what kind of parody of political obsession would it be to spend out my days, and die alone, contemplating the class struggle, the ERA, or the elections in my union back in New York City? So when I contemplated an abandoned existence I thought, "Hmm. A good time to catch up on my religious thinking."

But luxuriating in the ultimate, while listening to this record in preparation for my long, solitary sojourn, I was constantly reminded of the here and now. The familiar religious themes were stated, but stated with a desperation and ecstasy I wasn't used to. Of course, ecstasy can become a "trick" of gospel music, as surely as an exhausted rock star on tour sometimes fakes his interest in a guitar solo. But I began to wonder why ecstasy and desperation were the central themes of *Precious Lord*, rather than just embellishments. And my thinking went back to that black church, and then back to rock music in the sixties.

The hostile analysis of this religious frenzy contends that it's a safety valve for letting off steam that is more rightfully directed as revolutionary anger, or at least directed toward concrete conditions. And of course this is partially true: I remember, along with the frenzy of Sunday mornings, how run-down the church building in Detroit was, and the new wood paneling in the preacher's private office. But the positive analysis, which I *feel* to be true, and think is more historically accurate, argues that experiencing the Holy Ghost is a way of having one's human worth and eventual liberation confirmed, even if it's not possible in that historical time. "Every day will be Sunday by and by," Dorothy Love Coates sings, meaning to me that somehow, in *some* time, everyone will feel the freedom and self-confirmation they get on Sunday on *every day*. When R. H. Harris pleads an eerie "Send Your spirit, now and then," or Marion Williams demands of her Precious Lord,

"Here's what I want You to do for me" and then begs, "Please Sir, please Sir," experiencing the Holy Ghost begins to sound *crucial*, rather than like a pay-off for being good, as it's often conceived of in white Christianity.

Revolutions are caused by changes in expectations, not changes in circumstances. But how can you have the expectation of freedom in an unfree world unless you're in touch with a freedom that judges history, but is independent of it? Seen in this way, my catastrophic shipwreck isn't apolitical if I can have a vision of myself that surpasses the constrictions of my circumstances, social and personal, including my isolation and death. The trick is just in understanding how to invite the spirit into the reality of each situation.

But what right do white people have ripping off black Christianity for their own personal use? No right at all, of course, and no interest either, for this Beach Boys fan. Except that through social movements, and through rock and roll from Thomas A. Dorsey to R. H. Harris, to Sam Cooke, to Otis Redding, Aretha Franklin, Elvis, Janis Joplin, and the Rolling Stones, these ideas have been transmitted to me anyway. So long as I'm thinking about them, why not refer back to the source?

Listening to Janis Joplin's imitations of blackness now, she sometimes sounds pathetic to me. She sounds so transparent. Yet it's only accurate to describe her attempt to appropriate black music and its spirit as, yes, liberating. And maybe she's pathetic because she risked so much. The independent-of-history ecstasy we white fans of Janis Joplin felt with her music convinced us of the possibility of our own kind of historical liberation. Ask any feminist. If Janis (or Thomas A. Dorsey, even, maybe) didn't have a clear political line, she had a political effect. Her creation was larger than politics, but not directed against it.

But in a way, didn't the chaotic disintegration of rock and roll culture, of the New Left, and Janis's own death convince us that maybe the ecstasy wasn't worth fooling with? That the domestic caution of maybe Carole King was more conducive to survival? Yes, but.

What can be seen as the potential radicalism (many of Dorsey's songs can be transformed into "Civil Rights" anthems just by changing the social context of their performance) but actual conservatism of black religious music can also be seen as an accurate assessment of the power of the experiences involved. Divine revelation can convince us of realities beyond our human limitations, but it can also chew us little humans to shreds unless prudently applied. As all the burned-out hippies who lusted after ecstasy ten years ago have shown.

Elvis and Janis discovered something, and discovered how to transmit it as white people to white people. But they couldn't figure out how to hold onto it. Elvis let it go. Who knows what Janis would have done. Sam Cooke died before he could work out a similar problem: you can hear him trying on "Good Times" and "A Change Is Gonna Come." But R. H. Harris can frighten me singing "Peace in the Valley" when he's in his fifties, as I'm sure he could have thirty years ago.

White people have an annoying habit of approving of everything black people produce except what they are producing in the present. Or finding in black culture an archetypal model for bohemianism or radicalism, and disapproving of everything that's black that doesn't fit into that model. Sometimes I think that white fans of black blues who find soul or disco too watered-down are speaking to their own fears of assimilation and lack of roots, and that the classic era of gospel that Dorsey represents is ripe for such an odd appreciation, if only it will slip safely into the past.

Perhaps I'm only tripping out on my own doubts and insecurities by focusing on a scene that I can never get inside of. But listening to black gospel music reawakened my desires for certain things related to, but beyond, the blues-based needs for reality and self-affirmation. I felt how much we all need community and hope. Recast in a way that's true to this white boy's experiences. But recast to withstand, as Dorsey's music does, the paranoia of personal (i.e., social) betrayal and the ultimate bummer of one's own death.

I keep wondering about that little girl in Detroit who asked me why all my songs were about freedom, meaning, Why was the name of Jesus changed to freedom in every song? The answer may have been that there are times when freedom should be expressed in terms of its historical possibilities, and that summer felt like such a time. But there might be situations when freedom should be invoked independently of the historical circumstances, and right now might be such a time, or a desert island might be such a place. Maybe, if this is true, Thomas A. Dorsey and R. H. Harris have something to offer me; maybe this is something Sam Cooke was trying to work out; maybe Al Green is working this out right now. Who knows?

Ever since my encounter with Arthur Godfrey I've been developing a mode of social- and self-contemplation connected with listening to records, a mode confirmed by my Beach Boys revelation, nurtured in the AM summer of Detroit, brought to flower that pothead summer with the Beatles, and unleashed when I found I could make money off it. Or at least as much money off it as I spent on it, thus staying even.

If I'm going to be on an island without a working phonograph, or with one I can count on only until the batteries run down, then I'd like to be marooned with my beloved *Pet Sounds* by the Beach Boys, preferably in the original mono version with the pictures from their Japanese tour on the back. Gazing at it, I could recall every cut, I've listened to it so often. Just having it near, I would be reassured. This is the record that defines me; it's a symbol of my own self-acceptance.

It would be a kind of rock and roll fan's hell to be stuck with only one record no matter what it was, to have to listen to that record forever: a version of those Japanese soldiers who continued to fight World War II in isolation twenty years after it was over. ROCK CRITIC EMERGES FROM DESERT ISLAND IN 1990s AFTER ANALYZING "BLONDE ON BLONDE" FOR THIRTY YEARS. Being a rock and roll fan is an identity forged in the consumer culture—it's dependent on new product.

But if I can have only one record, and a phonograph that works, give me *Precious Lord*. With it I could make a stab at the eternal, and think about the possibilities for liberation that include but aren't dependent on history. With it, I would try to prepare both for my death in isolation and for my return to the American culture and politics that I love and depend on so much.

DECADE

NEIL YOUNG (REPRISE 2257)
1966–1976/1977

KIT RACHLIS

It's the voice that gets you. A high, wobbly voice, so thin it's a wonder it supports as many words as it does. It comes out of nowhere—certainly not rock tradition or R&B or country. Oh, you probably could argue that it belongs to the lonesome whistle and far-away whine of old time Appalachian singers, and you wouldn't be wrong. But those are the voices of upright men trying to maintain dignity and order in a world that offers little of either. If it's the years of varnish that those singers are showing off, what interests us now are the cracks in their voices. Neil Young understands that. His voice is all cracks and no varnish. If this makes him an archetypal Appalachian singer, it somehow misses the point, for there is nothing upright or dignified about his singing. Or rather, dignity and righteousness are questions that Young has given up on. His voice is that of a child—messy, vulnerable, insistent, halting, so transparent that everything, every catch, howl, and yammer, is on the surface. It's a voice that points rather than explains, that can hold two or three different impulses without sorting them out, a voice so ambivalent that its jerky grate and listing falsetto are rhetorical devices, not sexual ones. And it's in that gap between implication and explanation, between simile and surface that Young's voice finds its riches. I prefer to think that it belongs to the night—

fit company for an insomniac's pacing and a child's plea. That it has risen out of some gaseous swamp, to frighten and reassure us—and never let go.

"What am I doing here?" Young cries out about three-quarters of the way through "Love in Mind," wrenching the song back into focus. He repeats the question two more times, his voice tighter and more strained, the tremor more apparent each time he comes down on "here." There's nothing in the song that leads logically to that question—we don't even know where "here" is. Two minutes long, the verses three lines each, "Love in Mind" is exactly that—an interior dialogue about love lost and love found that veers wildly from adulthood to adolescence, from bedroom to backseat. "What am I doing here?" bursts across the song like an act of will, yanking Young out of his early morning reverie, stretching his voice across the jagged ruins of his piano chords. It's not a story-teller's flourish, a magician's wave of the cape—but a cold slap across the face that resolves nothing, just breaks the dreamer's spell.

Young's songs often come down to a single moment, a gesture that crystallizes and then breaks the tension, because they depend so much on the vagaries of mood. This undoubtedly is one of the things that Young has found so attractive about folk—the sense it often conveys of being a found music, with tone and atmosphere almost everything. A song could be whipped up on the spot, like a talking blues, and what mattered was not the proper convergence of theme and metaphor, but comic timing. If you were good, the process of making up the song—how long you paused to fit the right word into the rhyme—was as important as the completed song itself. A half-finished verse, a redundant refrain, was valued if it hit the moment. Young has always loved those kinds of throwaways; long after they became passé even in folk circles, he has persisted in dotting his albums with such songs as "Love in Mind," "Till the Morning Comes," and "Crippled Creek Ferry," one- to two-minute fragments that end in ellipsis.

Their open-endedness is the source of their power. The repetition of "till the morning comes" takes on the obsessive double-edge of a domestic quarrel: the impatient threat and the imploring request of a lover who has drawn the line, but secretly wants to see it crossed. The sudden fadeout of "Crippled Creek Ferry" (it's over before the credits roll) leaves us hanging—which is exactly its point. Young doesn't put much stock in resolutions. He has said that in making his first album he learned that "everything is temporary." By themselves, those words are clunky; they drip with supermarket mysticism, but I think that Young means them to be taken at face value: that his albums are about the passage of time. They're like journals—brutal, detailed, ingenuous, trivial, spilling out with all the art and artlessness of day-to-day life. Young has the megalomaniacal belief—and the diarist's faith—that everything he says is important. Which, of course, isn't true. He has never made a perfect album— one that has the conceptual unity of *Sgt. Pepper* or the spiritual unity of *Astral Weeks*. The closest he has come is *Zuma*, and even that is marred by the gauzy nostalgia of its conclusion—Crosby, Stills, and Nash harmonizing on "Through my Sails." But you don't expect perfection from journals, even if they are meant for public consumption—by definition they are raw, immediate, and incomplete.

Because his honesty is often confused with intimacy, Young creates the illusion that no gap exists between public appearance and private truth. This trick—what F. Scott Fitzgerald once called "a trick of the heart"—is necessary to confessional songwriters and is probably Young's deepest inheritance from the folk movement of the sixties (which of course denied that it was a trick at all). In its blanket repudiation of pop (everything from Jerry Lee Lewis to the Ronettes), the folk movement championed the unadorned performer. Electric guitars and drums, perfectly calibrated hooks and neatly hinged lyrics, dance steps and matching suits—these things, according to the folk pieties of the day, spoke of slick-talking salesmanship and money-grubbing ambition; sincerity, casualness, authenticity were the values that folk clung to its breast. Like Dylan, Young sidestepped folk rhetoric and used its strategy for his own ends. He lays himself open in order to shut you out. His songs, like those of all confessional songwriters, invite you into his house, but when he opens the door all you see at first is a goddamn mess. Sentences are strewn around like forgotten laundry, images are piled up like last week's dishes. Lyrics end like the half-opened magazine on the bathroom floor. The disorder seems overwhelming, the piles of books and records arbitrary. What does Richard Nixon's soul have to do with the night Young's fictional lover wept or, for that matter, with "roads that stretch out like healthy veins" ("Campaigner")? If Young is oblivious to your discomfort—since *Time Fades Away* he has rejected the demands of his record company and his fans—it's because he knows where to find everything, and what the hell, he's probably going to change it all around next week anyway. Truth in Young's hands—and that means not having pop music's maid clean house for him—is a way of keeping everyone at bay.

Like all of us, Young is caught between memory and desire, private acts and public events. "The Loner" who announced himself so boldly on the first cut of his first solo album is the same person who warns us in "Star of Bethlehem" that all our dreams and lovers won't protect us. It's Young's refusal to give himself any outs that gives his work its moral edge. I don't mean the easy generalities of "Southern Man" or "Alabama," but the leap of imagination that allows him to envision himself as both Montezuma *and* Cortez ("Zuma"), that can suggest that Nixon's got soul. When Young picks up his guitar in "Like a Hurricane," he's not offering protection —he's like an Ahab maniacally and crudely lashing the chords to the mast. When he seeks refuge in the slow white heat of the guitar's upper register it's no different than the uneasy peace he finds in his falsetto. But it is the uneasy peace he has settled for and the only one he's holding out. If Young's fatalism allows him to identify with Cortez or Nixon or Ahab—convinces him that he will ruin whatever he touches—the rest of him recoils at the idea. "I know all things pass/Let's make this last," Young says in "Hey Babe," but he is rarely that assertive. When he tells his lover in "I Believe in You" that he comes to her at night and feels all his doubts, he means it quite literally; most of his love songs ("When You Dance," "Journey Through the Past," "Harvest") are structured around questions. And the music shows it, even—no, especially—at its most violent. With Crazy Horse, those questions emerge from massive blocks of chords for Young's guitar to hack its way through, turbulent rhythms for him to find his sea legs. With Nashville sessionmen the questions are in the ornamentation—a piano that's a little more aggressive than intended, a steel-guitar lick that arcs too high. "Out of pitch but still in tune," is how Young describes "Tired Eyes," but he could be talking about any of his songs. With Young the pitch is almost always strained—it's the overreaching of a performer still in the midst of discovering what he wants to say and how he wants to say it, and not afraid to let the process show.

That process is what holds together *Decade*, Young's three-record "selected works," which was released at the end of 1977. Collections are invariably frustrating, and your first response to *Decade* is to throw half of it away and rearrange the whole thing. It places too much emphasis on Young's early career, overlooks *Time Fades Away* and includes only five songs from *On the Beach, Tonight's the Night*, and *Zuma*; in short, the four albums that contain Young's most barbed and eccentric work are given the least attention. But it would be a mistake to view *Decade* as another haphazardly compiled "Greatest Hits" package. It is as carefully assembled as "Ambulance Blues" or "Don't Be Denied"—Young's earliest attempts to sum up cultural history and his place in it. Neither song is on *Decade*, but they can be heard rattling down its halls, anticipating every turn. Like *Decade*, they deliberately try to conjure up the past, try to put a lid on it, only to discover that is has slipped their hold.

"An ambulance can only go so fast," Young says and the one he's driving in "Ambulance Blues" is going about as fast as a hearse—picking up bodies on the back streets and broad avenues of what once passed for the counter-culture, the years that *Decade* encompasses. Chasing down names without faces, dates without events, Young has got Richard Nixon, Patty Hearst, and several burnt-out hippies strapped down in the back. "It's hard to know the meaning of this song," he says at one point, but Doug Kershaw's fiddle, which intermittently stabs the air, gives the lie to that line. "Ambulance Blues" is a dirge for a past that promised more than it gave, and Young's punch-drunk harmonica and staggering guitar is leading the way. If Young's not sure whether to take his detritus to the hospital or the morgue, it's because he prefers his memories neither revived nor dead, as removed and persistent as his own ghostly voice.

"Don't Be Denied" is the flip side of "Ambulance Blues," as explicit and celebratory as Young gets. On the surface, it's the stuff of press releases, a rocker's tale of victory over adversity—parents' divorce at three, sudden move to new town, fights in the school yard, playing music all night, hitting it big—and "don't be denied" is its rallying call. But the crack in Young's voice, the nervous kick in the drums, the rush of the final verses, gives the game away: "He's a millionaire through a businessman's eyes." It's not a matter of corroded dreams; Young is escaping his adolescence all right, but the song cuts because he's still inside those dreams, can still remember the white bucks he wore, because he still thinks that rock and roll promises more than innocence and corruption—that it's possible to play for the highest bid and not sell yourself short.

To be a rock and roll star, especially a confessional songwriter whose stock-in-trade is personal rapport, is to discover that a lot of people you've never met consider you their best friend. It is, of course, a relationship that works both ways. To have a great number of people see their lives in your own is pretty heady stuff. One's natural response (certainly the initial one) is to encourage it, sharpen the stories, get the tone down, which is what Young did with *After the Goldrush* and *Harvest*. But to play father confessor is also an enormous responsibility, and you begin to resent the next time the phone rings, the next time the crowd roars. If you resent it enough, you begin to withdraw or lash out—or not to be there when they expect you to. In his notes for *Decade* Young says that he found the middle of the road a bore and headed for the ditch; he turned the seventies notion of the confessional songwriter on its head. His songs went beyond the personal and entered his own fantasy-morality world; the "I" of his early songs became a ghost, a figment of his own psyche that hovered over but did not dominate his songs. The wide-open spaces of *After the Gold Rush* and *Harvest* gave way to the compression chambers of *Tonight's the Night* and *Zuma*.

Tonight's the Night is Young's most roughshod and freewheeling album and not coincidentally the one he considers his best. Inspired (if that's the right word) by the drug overdoses of Crazy Horse guitarist Danny Whitten and roadie Bruce Berry, it's Young's semi-documentary (with Young as director and star) about dope and death, the scarred remains of the counter-culture and the bloody brotherhood of rock and roll. The film is grainy and the camera wobbly. On *Decade* Young reduces the tale to a triptych—"The Needle and the Damage Done" (from *Harvest*), "Tonight's the Night," and "Tired Eyes." They are the closest Young has ever come to the blues: the slow recitation of description, the broken voice tearing through the dispassion of fact, the lethargy of defeat and deceit. Tonight's the night for what? To mainline, to die, to exorcise it all? Close whose tired eyes? Young is as vague as the violence—not because he doesn't want to tell, but because he doesn't know.

"It's better to burn out than to fade away," Young says in "My My, Hey Hey (Out of the Blue)." *Decade* is about not burning out *or* fading away. By closing with "Long May You Run" the album comes full circle. Young writes that the song is about "his first car and last lady." Don't let him kid you. It's his benediction on the album and his career. With the notes falling perfectly into place with the inevitability of the future, it's his hymn to friendship, things coming to an end and things continuing. It's the only song on *Decade* that doesn't have a moment of dread, which makes it suspicious.

ASTRAL WEEKS

VAN MORRISON (WARNER BROS.–SEVEN ARTS WS 1768)
1968

LESTER BANGS

Van Morrison's *Astral Weeks* was released ten years, almost to the day, before this was written. It was particularly important to me because the fall of 1968 was such a terrible time: I was a physical and mental wreck, nerves shredded and ghosts and spiders looming and squatting across the mind. My social contacts had dwindled almost to none; the presence of other people made me nervous and paranoid. I spent endless days and nights sunk in an armchair in my bedroom, reading magazines, watching TV, listening to records, staring into space. I had no idea how to improve the situation, and probably wouldn't have done anything about it if I had.

Astral Weeks would be the subject of this piece—i.e., the rock record with the most significance in my life so far—no matter how I'd been feeling when it came out. But in the condition I was in, it assumed at the time the quality of a beacon, a light on the far shores of the murk; what's more, it was proof that there was something left to express artistically besides nihilism and destruction. (My other big record of the day was *White Light/White Heat*.) It sounded like the man who made *Astral Weeks* was in terrible pain, pain most of Van Morrison's previous work had only suggested; but like the later albums by the Velvet Underground, there was a redemptive element in the blackness, ultimate compassion for the suffering of others, and a swath of pure beauty and mystical awe that cut right through the heart of the work.

I don't really know how significant it might be that many others have reported variants on my initial encounter with *Astral Weeks*. I don't think there's anything guiding it to people enduring dark periods. It did come out at a time when a lot of things that a lot of people cared about passionately were beginning to disintegrate, and when the self-destructive undertow that always accompanied the great sixties party had an awful lot of ankles firmly in its maw and was pulling straight down. So, as timeless as it finally is, perhaps *Astral Weeks* was also the product of an era. Better think that than ask just what sort of Irish churchwebbed haints Van Morrison might be product of.

Three television shows:
A 1970 NET broadcast of a big all-star multiple bill at the Fillmore East. The Byrds, Sha Na Na, and Elvin Bishop have all done their respective things. Now we get to see three or four songs from a set by Van Morrison. He climaxes, as he always did in those days, with "Cyprus Avenue" from *Astral Weeks*. After going through all the verses, he drives the song, the band, and himself to a finish which has since become one of his trademarks and one of the all-time classic rock 'n' roll set-closers. With consummate dynamics that allow him to snap from indescribably eccentric throwaway phrasing to sheer passion in the very next breath, he brings the music surging up through crescendo after crescendo, stopping and starting and stopping and starting the song again and again, imposing long maniacal silences like giant question marks between the stops and starts and ruling the room through sheer tension, building to a shout of "It's too late to stop now!," and just when you think it's all going to surge over the top, he cuts it off stone cold dead, the hollow of a murdered explosion, throws the microphone down and stalks off the stage. It is truly one of the most perverse things I have ever seen a performer do in my life. And, of course, it's sensational: our guts are knotted up, we're crazed and clawing for more, but we damn well know we've seen and felt something final.

1974, a late night network TV rock concert: Van and his band come out, strike a few shimmering chords, and for about ten minutes he lingers over the words "Way over yonder in the clear blue sky/Where flamingos fly." No other lyrics. I don't think any instrumental solos. Just those words, repeated slowly again and again, distended, permutated, turned into scat, suspended in space and then scattered to the winds, muttered like a mantra till they turn into nonsense syllables, then back into the same soaring image as time seems to stop entirely. He stands there with eyes closed, singing, transported, while the band poises quivering over great open-tuned deep blue gulfs of their own.

1977, spring-summer, same kind of show: he sings "Cold Wind in August," a song off his recently released album *A Period of Transition*, which also contains a considerably altered version of the flamingos song. "Cold Wind in August" is a ballad, and Van gives it a fine, standard reading. The only trouble is that the whole time he's singing it he paces back and forth in a line on the stage, his eyes tightly shut, his little fireplug body kicking its way upstream against what must be a purgatorial nervousness that perhaps is being transferred to the cameraman.

What this is about is a whole set of verbal tics—although many are bodily as well—which are there for reason enough to go a long way toward defining his style. They're all over *Astral Weeks*: four rushed repeats of the phrases "you breathe in, you breathe out" and "you turn around" in "Beside You;" in "Cyprus Avenue," twelve "way up on" s, "baby" sung out thirteen times in a row sounding like someone running ecstatically downhill toward one's love, and the heartbreaking way he stretches "one by one" in the third verse; most of all in "Madame George," where he sings the word "dry" and then "your eye" twenty times in a twirling melodic arc so beautiful it steals your own breath, and then this occurs: "And the love that loves the love that loves the love that loves the love that loves to love the love that loves to love the love that loves."

Van Morrison is interested, *obsessed* with how much musical or verbal information he can compress into a small space, and, almost conversely, how far he can spread one note, word, sound, or picture. To capture one moment, be it a caress or a twitch. He repeats certain phrases to extremes that from anybody else would seem ridiculous because he's waiting for a vision to unfold, trying as unobtrusively as possible to nudge it along. Sometimes he gives it to you through silence, by choking off the song in midflight: "It's too late to stop now!"

It's the great search, fueled by the belief that through these musical and mental processes illumination is attainable. Or may at least be glimpsed.

When he tries for this he usually gets it more in the feeling than the Revealed Word—perhaps much of the feeling comes from the reaching—but there is also, always, the sense of WHAT if he DID apprehend that Word; there are times when the Word seems to hover very near. And then there are times when we realize the Word was right next to us, when the most mundane overused phrases are transformed: I give you "love," from "Madame George." Out of relative silence, the Word: "Snow in San Anselmo." "That's where it's at," Van will say, and he means it (aren't his interviews *fascinating?*). What he doesn't say is that he is *inside* the snowflake, isolated by the song: "And it's almost Independence Day."

You're probably wondering when I'm going to get around to telling you about *Astral Weeks*. As a matter of fact, there's a whole lot of *Astral Weeks* I don't even want to tell you about. Both because whether you've heard it or not it wouldn't be fair for me to impose my interpretation of such lapidarily subjective imagery on you, and because in many cases I don't really know what he's talking about. He doesn't either: "I'm not surprised that people get different meanings out of my songs," he told a *Rolling Stone* interviewer. "But I don't wanna give the impression that I know what everything means 'cause I don't. . . . There are times when I'm mystified. I look at some of the stuff that comes out, y'know. And like, there it is and it feels right, but I can't say for sure what it means."

> *There you go*
> *Starin' with a look of avarice*
> *Talkin' to Huddie Ledbetter*
> *Showin' pictures on the walls*
> *And whisperin' in the halls*
> *And pointin' a finger at me*

I haven't got the slightest idea what that "means," though on one level I'd like to approach it in a manner as indirect and evocative as the lyrics themselves. Because you're in trouble anyway when you sit yourself down to explicate just exactly what a mystical document, which is exactly what *Astral Weeks* is, *means*. For one thing, what it means is Richard Davis's bass playing, which complements the songs and singing all the way with a lyricism that's something more than just great musicianship: there is something about it that's more than inspired, something that has been touched, that's in the realm of the miraculous. The whole ensemble—Larry Fallon's string section, Jay Berliner's guitar (he played on Mingus's *Black Saint and the Sinner Lady*), Connie Kay's drumming—is like that: they and Van sound like they're not just reading but *dwelling inside of* each other's minds. The facts may be far different. John Cale was making an album of his own in an adjacent studio at the time, and he has said that "Morrison couldn't work with anybody, so finally they just shut him in the studio by himself. He did all the songs with just an acoustic guitar, and later they overdubbed the rest of it around his tapes."

Cale's story might or might not be true—but facts are not going to be of much use here in any case. Fact: Van Morrison was twenty-two—or twenty-three—years old when he made this record. He sounds ageless. Certainly it is not a young man's record; there are lifetimes behind it. What *Astral Weeks* deals in are not facts but truths. *Astral Weeks*, insofar as it can be pinned down, is a record about people stunned by life, completely overwhelmed, stalled in their skins, their ages, and selves, paralyzed by the enormity of what in one moment of vision they can comprehend. It is a precious and terrible gift, born of a terrible truth, because what they see is both infinitely beautiful and terminally horrifying: the unlimited human ability to create or destroy, according to whim. It's no Eastern mystic or psychedelic vision of the emerald beyond, nor is it some Baudelairean perception of the beauty of sleaze and grotesquerie. Maybe what it boils down to is one moment's knowledge of the miracle of life, with its inevitable concomitant, a vertiginous glimpse of the capacity to be hurt, and the capacity to inflict that hurt.

Transfixed between rapture and anguish. Wondering if they may not be the same thing, or at least possessed of an intimate relationship. In "T.B. Sheets," his last extended narrative before making this record, Van Morrison watched a girl he loved die of tuberculosis. The song was claustrophobic, suffocating, monstrously powerful: "innuendos, inadequacies, foreign bodies." A lot of people couldn't take it; the editor of this book has said that it's garbage, but I think it made him squeamish. Anyway, the point is that certain parts of Astral Weeks—"Madame George," "Cyprus Avenue" —take the pain in "T.B. Sheets" and root the world in it. Because the pain of watching a loved one die of however dread a disease may be awful, but it is at least something known, in a way understood, in a way measurable and even leading somewhere, because there is a process: sickness, decay, death, mourning, some emotional recovery. But the beautiful horror of "Madame George" and "Cyprus Avenue" is precisely that the people in these songs are not dying: we are looking at life, in its fullest, and what these people are suffering from is not disease but nature, unless nature is a disease.

A man sits in a car on a treelined street, watching a 14-year-old girl walking home from school, hopelessly in love with her. I've almost come to blows with friends because of my insistence that much of Van Morrison's early work had an obsessively reiterated theme of pedophilia, but here is something that at once may be taken as that and something far beyond it. He *loves* her. Because of that, he is helpless. Shaking. Paralyzed. Maddened. Hopeless. Nature mocks him. As only nature can mock nature. Or is love natural in the first place? No matter. By the end of the song he has entered a kind of hallucinatory ecstasy; the music aches and yearns as it rolls on out. This is one supreme pain, that of being imprisoned a spectator. And perhaps not so very far from "T.B. Sheets," except that it must be far more romantically easy to sit and watch someone you love die than to watch them in the bloom of youth and health and know that you can never, ever have them, can never even speak to them.

"Madame George" is the album's whirlpool. Possibly one of the most compassionate pieces of music ever made, it asks us, no, *arranges* that we see the plight of what I'll be brutal and call a lovelorn drag queen with such intense empathy that when the singer hurts him, we do too. (Morrison has said in at least one interview that the song has nothing to do with any kind of transvestite—at least as far as *he* knows, he is quick to add—but that's bullshit.) The beauty, sensitivity, *holiness* of the song is that there's nothing at all sensationalistic, exploitative, or tawdry about it; in a way Van is right when he insists it's not about a drag queen, as my friends were right and I was wrong about the "pedophilia"—it's about a *person*, like all the best songs, all the greatest literature.

The setting is the same as that of the previous song—Cyprus Avenue, apparently a place where people drift, impelled by desire, into moments of flesh-wracking, sight-curdling confrontation with their destinies. It's an elemental place of pitiless judgment—wind and rain figure in both songs—and, interestingly enough, it's a place of the even crueler judgment of adults by *children*, in both cases love objects absolutely indifferent to their would-be adult lovers. Madame George's little boys are downright contemptuous—like the street urchins who end up cannibalizing the homosexual cousin in Tennessee Williams's *Suddenly Last Summer*, they're only too happy to come around as long as there's music, party times, free drinks and smokes, and only too gleefully spit on George's affections when all the other stuff runs out, the entombing winter settling in with not only wind and rain but hail, sleet, and snow.

What might seem strangest of all but really isn't is that it's exactly those characteristics which supposedly should make George most pathetic—age, drunkenness, the way the boys take his money and trash his love—that awaken something for George in the heart of the kid whose song this is. Obviously the kid hasn't simply "fallen in love with love," or something like that, but rather—what? Why, just exactly that only sunk in the foulest perversions could one human being love another for anything *other* than their humanness: love him for his weakness, his flaws, finally perhaps his decay. Decay is human—that's one of the ultimate messages here, and I don't by any stretch of the lexicon mean decadence. I mean that in this song or whatever inspired it Van Morrison saw the absolute possibility of loving human beings at the farthest extreme of wretchedness, and that the implications of that are terrible indeed, far more terrible than the mere sight of bodies made ugly by age or the seeming absurdity of a man devoting his life to the wobbly artifice of trying to look like a woman.

You can say to love the questions you have to love the answers which quicken the end of love that's loved to love the awful inequality of human experience that loves to say we tower over these the lost that love to love the love that freedom could have been, the train to freedom, but we never get on, we'd rather wave generously walking away from those who are victims of themselves. But who is to say that someone who victimizes him- or herself is not as worthy of total compassion as the most down and out Third World orphan in a *New Yorker* magazine ad? Nah, better to step over the bodies, at least that gives them the respect they might have once deserved. Where I live, in New York (not to make it more than it is, which is hard), everyone I know often steps over bodies which might well be dead or dying as a matter of course, without pain. And I wonder in what scheme it was originally conceived that such action is showing human refuse the ultimate respect it deserves.

There is of course a rationale—what else are you going to do—but it holds no more than our fear of our own helplessness in the face of the plain of life as it truly is: a plain which extends into an infinity beyond the horizons we have only invented. Come on, die it. As I write this, I can read in the *Village Voice* the blurbs of people opening heterosexual S&M clubs in Manhattan, saying things like, "S&M is just another equally valid form of love. Why people can't accept that we'll never know." Makes you want to jump out a fifth floor window rather than even read about it, but it's hardly the end of the world; it's not nearly as bad as the hurts that go on everywhere everyday that are taken so casually by all of us as facts of life. Maybe it boils down to how much you actually want to subject yourself to. If you accept for even a moment the idea that each human life is as precious and delicate as a snowflake and then you look at a wino in a doorway, you've got to hurt until you feel like a sponge for all those other assholes' problems, until you feel like an asshole yourself, so you draw all the appropriate lines. You stop feeling. But you know that then you begin to die. So you tussle with yourself. How much of this horror can I actually allow myself to think about? Perhaps the numbest mannikin is wiser than somebody who only allows their sensitivity to drive them to destroy everything they touch—but then again, to tilt Madame George's hat a hair, just to recognize that that person exists, just to touch his cheek and then probably expire because the realization that you must share the world with him is ultimately unbearable is to go only the first mile. The realization of living is just about that low and that exalted and that unbearable and that sought-after. Please come back and leave me alone. But when we're alone together we can talk all we want about the universality of this abyss: it doesn't make any difference, the highest only meets the lowest for some lying succor, UNICEF to relatives, so you scratch and spit and curse in violent resignation at the strict fact that there is absolutely nothing you can do but finally reject anyone in greater pain than you. At such a moment, another breath is treason. That's why you leave your liberal causes, leave suffering humanity to die in worse squalor than they knew before you happened along. You got their hopes up. Which makes you viler than the most scrofulous carrion. Viler than the ignorant boys who would take Madame George for a couple of cigarettes. Because you have committed the crime of knowledge, and thereby not only walked past or over someone you knew to be suffering, but also violated their privacy, the last possession of the dispossessed.

Such knowledge is possibly the worst thing that can happen to a person (a *lucky* person), so it's no wonder that Morrison's protagonist turned away from Madame George, fled to the train station, trying to run as far away from what he'd seen as a lifetime could get him. And no wonder, too, that Van Morrison never came this close to looking life square in the face again, no wonder he turned to *Tupelo Honey* and even *Hard Nose the Highway* with its entire side of songs about falling leaves. In *Astral Weeks* and "T.B. Sheets" he confronted enough for any man's lifetime. Of course, having been offered this immeasurably stirring and equally frightening gift from Morrison, one can hardly be blamed for not caring terribly much about Old, Old Woodstock and little homilies like "You've Got to Make It Through This World on Your Own" and "Take It Where You Find It."

On the other hand, it might also be pointed out that desolation, hurt, and anguish are hardly the only things in life, or in *Astral Weeks*. They're just the things, perhaps, that we can most easily grasp and explicate, which I suppose shows about what level our souls have evolved to. I said I wouldn't reduce the other songs on this album by trying to explain them, and I won't. But that doesn't mean that, all things considered, a juxtaposition of poets might not be in order.

> *If I ventured in the slipstream*
> *Between the viaducts of your dreams*
> *Where the mobile steel rims crack*
> *And the ditch and the backroads stop*
> *Could you find me*
> *Would you kiss my eyes*
> *And lay me down*
> *In silence easy*
> *To be born again*

—Van Morrison

> *My heart of silk*
> *is filled with lights,*
> *with lost bells,*
> *with lilies and bees.*
> *I will go very far,*
> *farther than those hills,*
> *farther than the seas,*
> *close to the stars,*
> *to beg Christ the Lord*
> *to give back the soul I had*
> *of old, when I was a child,*
> *ripened with legends,*
> *with a feathered cap*
> *and a wooden sword.*

—Federico García Lorca

LIVING IN THE U.S.A.

LINDA RONSTADT (ASYLUM 6E–155)
1978

JOHN ROCKWELL

What I'm going to write here is a piece of passionate advocacy, and one doesn't normally introduce advocacy defensively. My defensiveness, such as it is, derives from the nature of my intended audience. Linda Ronstadt hardly needs defenders in the world at large. She is the most popular woman singer of the 1970s, and perhaps ever, as measured by record sales; in 1977 she had the most commercially successful album by *any* solo artist, with *Simple Dreams*.

But with popular music the relationship between popularity and critical approbation is an especially complex one. Rock critics are by definition populists, yet simultaneously they must trust their own instincts with the same elitist ferocity as any high-art connoisseur. In rock criticism, commercial success doesn't so much attest to quality as corroborate it; if you like something the millions like, their general enthusiasm adds resonance to your private enthusiasm, certifying its universality.

In Ronstadt's case, her reputation among rock critics is not very grand. In Britain especially, she is widely regarded as a mindless puppet in the hands of her producer, Peter Asher—which must be an odd irony for Asher, who was a British pop star once. A typical passing crack about Ronstadt in the British rock press comes from a recent *Melody Maker*, in which Michael Oldfield grumbles that "it's ridiculous that the most successful female rock singer is Linda Ronstadt, whose voice is nothing special, but who has made it through ruining other people's songs." And the British attitude, or at least something approaching it, is shared by many of the best-known American rock critics; Ronstadt didn't even make the *index* of *The Rolling Stone Illustrated History of Rock & Roll*, which was a compendium by exactly the writers I'm talking about—many of the same people who have contributed to this book.

The problem is further complicated by the fact that several of those writers are my friends, and so is Linda. My love for her music long antedated my friendship with her, and that friendship has remained the exception rather than the rule in my dealings with the people I write about. But knowing her both adds to my knowledge of her music and reinforces my desire to champion her work with my peers. As you will see below, I am by no means blandly uncritical about Ronstadt's accomplishments. But ultimately I love both the accomplishments and the accomplisher, and it frustrates me that more people whose sensibilities I respect don't get as much pleasure as I do from this wonderfully pleasurable music. My friend Dave Marsh thinks I'm the ringleader of a media plot to win Ronstadt some critical respect, and he's right.

Before I launch into my advocacy, I should say something about why I've chosen her latest album, *Living in the U.S.A.*, as my ostensible subject. I was originally going to write about *Heart Like a Wheel*, which came out in late 1974 and by early 1975 had made her a superstar after nearly a decade of cult success. This was her first album produced entirely by Asher, and it inaugurated a string of discs that have defined both her commercial dominance and her mature artistry; even the weakest of her Asher-produced albums, *Prisoner in Disguise* of 1975, is superior to any LP she'd done without him. *Heart Like a Wheel* is also the album least disliked (most liked?) by critics who generally find Ronstadt uninteresting, although at this writing *Living in the U.S.A.* has just been released, so its critical reception has yet to be determined.

Heart Like a Wheel remains a fine album. I can remember put-

ting it on my turntable for the first time and being instantly thrilled
by the new authority and assertiveness of the singing on the first
track, "You're No Good," which eventually became the first of the
album's two number one singles. For all the diversity of its personnel, the album boasts a convincing focus and a solid consistency;
there are no obviously weak or misguided selections here, even if
"It Doesn't Matter Any More" and "You Can Close Your Eyes"
don't seem really memorable. But there are both specific and theoretical reasons for picking *Living in the U.S.A.* One, quite simply,
is that although I haven't lived with it as long as the others, it's the
one I'm fired up about right now. That means I am still in the
process of thinking it through, which may lend the whole enterprise of writing once again about Ronstadt a certain spontaneity.
Another is that after ten or fifteen listenings it seems about as strong
an album as she's done. And as her most recent, it is more characteristic of her evolution in the past five years than *Heart Like a
Wheel*, whose arrangements sound more pop and less rock than her
recent work. Quite apart from her growing intelligence and range as
an interpreter, there's been a steady shift since 1974 from innocence
and vulnerability to sophistication and aggression, and that's a shift
worth considering.

In any case, I planned all along to devote as much space to Linda
and her work in general as to whichever specific album I finally
chose. Partly that's because any selection of a "best" or a "favorite"
is a distortion. All of Ronstadt's records have things on them I'd
want on a desert island, and nearly all of them have what I consider
"mistakes"—songs that she might better not have sung. Beyond that,
for all my love for Linda, I would not seriously suggest that she was
the most important single artist in the history of rock music. But
she *is* the one I've been the biggest fan of, the one whose music has
meant the most to me over the longest time. Pop music has always
been about emotional release, about passionate responses to artists
who might not rank at the very top of our rational hierarchies. There
are those of us who like to think about *why* that happens, and this
book offers us at last the chance to explore our compulsions in depth.
What follows is for those who could be moved by Ronstadt, by one
who has been.

. . .

Any consideration of Linda Ronstadt has to start with her voice. Objectivity may be a myth in art, but it's hard to avoid the flat statement that Ronstadt has the strongest, most clearly focused, flexible, and simply beautiful voice in popular music. As a physical instrument, it is capable of authoritative usage in almost any kind of pop music, and with a bit of technical work, could encompass most any classical style, as well. Many of the great voices of the past have been "natural"; subsequent technical work has served only to refine an already extant gift. Most pop voices are defined by a certain huskiness, which is generally the result of a vestigially developed voice or one that has been driven to a near-hoarseness by strain. At its best, such huskiness can serve as a metaphor for passion or warmth; one need only think of Rod Stewart. But at its worst the huskiness leads to nodes or nodules on the vocal cords that can so reduce a singer to whispery silence that an operation becomes necessary, and sometimes that operation can radically alter a voice (occasionally for the better, as in the case of Bonnie Tyler) or end a career. With Linda the only huskiness is that which she consciously applies to specific syllables as coloration. Her voice has a strength, size, and basic technical security that enable her to sing with force, yet without the sort of strain that leads to its rapid degeneration. And it has a focus or "edge" that helps lend it that ultimately undefinable character that constitutes her essential "sound." Throughout her career that sound has been there, and apart from the natural shifts of aural color and the slight lowering of basic range that comes with age, it will probably serve her well for decades to come.

Ronstadt is a soprano, although she never worked to develop the ringing upper extension that constitutes the climactic top octave or more for an operatic soprano. She can in fact sing in an overtly "operatic" way, plummy and full of a marked vibrato, and by so doing can reach higher notes than she normally attains. But that method of vocal production doesn't sound stylistically appropriate to her for the music she sings. By choosing not to deploy that register of her voice, she has constricted her range from what it could be. What's left is not really wide in operatic terms, as anyone who heard her bull her way through "The Star-Spangled Banner" during the 1977 World Series can attest. Her effective range is from around G below middle C to the C above it, with a few notes beyond that in falsetto.

Compared to the average pop singer, however, that range is relatively wide. Singers with multi-octave voices, operatic or otherwise, attain their breadth through the more or less smooth knitting together of several distinct registers, from a booming chest voice through the middle and up to various head-voice or falsetto top extensions; operatic training consists largely of the cultivation of those registers and of evening them out—of engineering transitions between them that don't sound too inadvertently disjunct. For all practical purposes Ronstadt's great natural instrument, her wide-ranging and near-perfectly focused middle register, has never been subjected to any vocal training (which is different, of course, from a steady improvement in her musicianship and her command of various musical styles). She lacks a chest register, at least in the sense of an operatic contralto. She thinks of the lower notes of her range as her "chest voice," and feels them resonate in a different, deeper part of her body than her top notes. But at the very bottom of her voice, the sound could hardly be heard at all in concert without amplification. It is defined mostly by its characteristic vibrato— the rapid pulsations that nearly all singers have and most modern instrumentalists affect to excess. Too much vibrato can sound mawkish and, at its extreme, can be a sign of near-terminal vocal strain. Too little vibrato sounds plain and churchy, and makes the attainment of proper pitch needlessly difficult.

As she moves up the scale into her middle and upper-middle range, which she calls her "pharyngeal voice," the body of her soprano fills out. This is the typical Ronstadt sound, loud or soft, and most of her singing is done here. As she ascends in pitch, toward the C above middle C, her limitations at the top become apparent: the vibrato thins out and the voice can sound like a hard, nasal yell. That can have its expressive virtues, especially in hard rock (cf. the end of her live version of "Tumbling Dice," in the *FM* soundtrack album). But at the very top it's neither a very grateful nor a very controlled sound, and when she's not singing at her best in concert, the voice can crack at that altitude; eventually, one suspects, it will become increasingly difficult for her to hit such notes consistently, and she may have to pitch some of her standards down a half or a whole step. Even now on records, in material that courts operatic comparisons like Sigmund Romberg's "When I Grow Too Old to Dream" from 1935 (unless otherwise specified, all Ronstadt songs mentioned henceforth are on *Living in the U.S.A.*), it's possible to wish for just a bit more operatic control, tone color, and flexibility; on the other hand, there's a folkish naturalness to Ronstadt's sound that an operatic fullness and upper extension would preclude.

Above the "natural" top of her middle register comes her falsetto, which she has been employing more and more in recent years. This is really a delicate version, thin and tenuously supported, of the operatic head voice she *could* develop if she so chose. She uses it partly for expressive purposes, and sometimes it works very nicely, as at the end of "Alison" or throughout "Ooh Baby Baby." In that song she makes the shifts between mid-volume full voice and falsetto smoothly, but on the whole her falsetto remains undeveloped in comparison to the confident power of her full middle voice, and too often (e.g., at the very end of "Blue Bayou" on *Simple Dreams*) it sounds simply as if she had no other way to reach a high note.

Now, this is all semi-technical description, and it quite completely avoids the issue of one's gut response to the sound. There is nothing inherently superior, aesthetically, to a well-produced voice ("produced" in vocal terminology, that is, rather than in the recording-studio sense). But the actual sound of a voice is indeed an aesthetic consideration, perhaps the prime one for a singer. And a voice with a solid technique (natural and/or acquired) not only secures the vocal quality over time, but ensures a wider and more varied use of that quality. In Ronstadt's case the sheer joy and physicality of her singing has always been instantly communicable to me, and the specific coloration has seemed intensely moving. To take just one example—and we're still speaking here of sound alone, not the interpretive uses to which it is put—consider Linda's version of "Just One Look." Doris Troy, who had a hit with the song in 1963 (her version is on Vol. 6 of Atlantic's *History of Rhythm*

& *Blues* series), sang it with a good deal of gusto, and the Ronstadt arrangement and phrasing emulate her record in every respect but one. Troy essentially fades out on the phrase "just one look" after the last chorus; I say "essentially" because she raises the note values slightly on the last two repetitions. Ronstadt constructs an entire coda that's not in Troy's version at all, full of exhilarating "come on babys" and other shouting manifestations of lust. She can do this because her voice has all the authority and strength of Troy's in the lower-middle range, but can extend upward to climactic upper-middle notes in a way that Troy's simply cannot. For a direct comparison, listen to both women's treatment of the word "wrong" in the second line of the bridge; next to Ronstadt's joyous vocal authority, Troy sounds hard and pressed. And of course it's ultimately impossible to separate technical and interpretive issues entirely. The sort of buoyant strength Ronstadt flaunts in her "Just One Look" makes an aesthetic and emotional statement all by itself; when she sings the line "without you, I'm nothing," you don't believe her for a minute.

People who can't respond to the sheer power of Ronstadt's voice sometimes complain about her "belting" style: they don't find the sort of vocal musculature that epitomizes her sound at its loudest either very attractive or very appropriate to much of the music she sings. Partly this is a question of the husky sound-color that characterizes most popular-music voices, forming the model against which many pop critics compare Ronstadt. In my own case, after an early fascination with pre-rock pop and mid-fifties rock and roll, I became immersed in classical music, and only came back to pop in the 1960s after my tastes in vocal music had been crucially influenced by opera. Today I can love all sorts of vocal sound, but my longtime attraction to Ronstadt's voice, dating back to the late 1960s, was clearly reinforced by my instant appreciation of its operatic qualities.

The most provocative theorist of classical and popular vocal singing has been Henry Pleasants, in his book, *The Great American Popular Singers*. To compress his argument brutally, Pleasants suggests that the original Italian notion of *bel canto* some four hundred years ago was an intimate, highly flexible vocalism, built around declamation. Over the course of centuries, under the pressure of man's innate tendencies toward virtuosic and rhetorical display and the growing size of opera houses (itself a result of the democratization and popularization of opera), opera evolved (or devolved) into a more brilliant, less expressive excuse for clarion vocal athleticism. The introduction of the microphone and electronic amplification after 1925 has meant that singers like Bing Crosby and Frank Sinatra could be freed from the need to sacrifice expressivity on the altar of volume and could revert to the traditional virtues of *bel canto*. Thus, one could conclude with a straight face, Frank Sinatra was a better *bel canto* singer than Jussi Bjoerling.

Pleasants himself has never paid much attention to rock; generationally it's beyond him. He tends to regard rock singers as brutes who bellow into the microphone even when they don't have to. Quite apart from the blues-rock shouters, there is indeed a whole school of semi-operatic rock emoters, epitomized by Bruce Springsteen. But of course a great deal of contemporary popular culture corresponds exactly to the models Pleasants himself has posited for pre-rock pop, particularly the folk style that underlies both modern-day country music and the folk-rocking singer-songwriters. Next to them, Ronstadt can sound like an anachronistic reversion to the semi-operatic emoting of Al Jolson and back to the days of the American vaudeville stage. For me, though, that aspect of her vocal style can be very appealing, since it both echoes the operatic singing I love and evokes a whole image of nineteenth-century America. It's not just a matter of vocal style, either; Linda's way of pronouncing the English language is very much of this country. In fact, of contemporary women popular singers, only Bonnie Koloc, with her wonderfully direct mid-American declamation, surpasses Ronstadt for the sheer Americanness of her singing—in that respect, the otherwise somewhat spurious "American" theme of *Living in the U.S.A.* makes perfect sense. Anyhow, "belting" isn't all Ronstadt can do; her soft singing combines the purity of an operatic voice with the simple plaintiveness of folk-singing, and her clarity of focus and security of pitch makes her harmony-singing a special joy.

When one says "American," one means white America. Until the advent of jazz, blues and soul-singing in this century, white culture *was* American culture; blacks made their influence felt on the mainstream, but usually in such white translations as Stephen Foster. No doubt John David Souther meant something deeper and broader by the phrase "white rhythm and blues" in his song on *Living in the U.S.A.*, but it seems to me that it suggests something important about Ronstadt's singing style. Even when singing black songs she remains an inescapably white singer. This could be—and has been—taken as a condemnation, a proof that she has no business assaying such songs. Her critics complain that some of her cover versions of black hits have sounded uncomfortably close to the bland reductions that Pat Boone used to inflict on Little Richard (e.g., her version of "Heat Wave" on *Prisoner in Disguise*). But at her best, it seems to me, she has developed a most convincing solution to her black material, with a style that simultaneously evokes the original interpreters yet remains honorably white.

But terms like "black" and "white" are both vague and possibly racist, and in any case we should realize that by this point we have moved into a discussion of Ronstadt's interpretive abilities, as opposed to her voice. Blacks have represented the principal symbols and agents of passion, spontaneity, and rebellion in recent white American culture, and most of the best white rock singers have not only built their music on black foundations, but assumed similar attitudes. Linda's singing has been criticized interpretively on a number of grounds, but all of those grounds have a common theme. As the most popular woman singer of the 1970s and a quintessential Southern Californian, she epitomizes for her critics all that is soft, safe, and retrogressive about this decade. Her singing has been called stiff and hopelessly uptight, with that uptightness carried over into her stage shows, which rarely approach the mass celebratory rapture of great rock events. Her records, and in particular Peter Asher's production, have been branded as too coldly, clinically "perfect," a studied formalization of songs meant to be sung with loose, improvisatory fervor. Her song selection has been dismissed as formulaic (mechanically trying to recreate the pattern that made *Heart Like a Wheel* such a hit) and misguided, in her frequent selection not only of black songs, but material by such as Randy Newman and Warren Zevon that supposedly suggests subtle, ironic, or abstract connotations that she's too dumb either to understand or to project.

And her overall image of love and sexuality has been called both manipulative and reactionary.

There is a bit of truth to every one of these charges, especially in years past, although I would argue that some of the criticism of Ronstadt on feminist grounds is itself just a bit sexist: it's unconsciously suspected that someone who is small and pretty and who admits openly to emotional vulnerability can't simultaneously contribute creatively to her own music and image, and that to the extent that she does so, she is a manipulator.

Before we consider the charges point by point, however, three other issues need to be raised. Linda Ronstadt is an interpretive singer, even if she collaborated on two songs from her 1976 album, *Hasten Down the Wind*, and may one day compose more (according to her collaborators, she played the determinant role in both songs). Composers as executants of their own music have by no means always been the rule, in either classical or popular music. In the Tin Pan Alley days—think of Crosby or Sinatra—singers generally sang others' songs. But with the advent of rock, the two functions have tended to merge. This has led to an unparalleled intensity of personal expression in the music, even if the composers weren't always particularly fluent singers. But critics used to the singer-songwriter (or his rock equivalent, stripped of that term's folkish connotations) generally prefer the composer's original, no matter how roughly executed, to another's interpretation; it's somehow assumed that a "mere" interpreter will lack the insight of the creator. Furthermore, the very roughness of a singer-songwriter's voice somehow symbolizes an honesty that a more polished interpretation supposedly must lack.

Now, in my own hierarchy of musical values, a composer may indeed rank higher than an interpreter; clearly Bob Dylan and Neil Young are more important to the history of rock music than Linda Ronstadt. Yet such a bias need hardly consign all interpreters to the slag heap. And insofar as interpretive singers can project a focused, interesting image through the music of others, welding disparate materials into a new unity, they can make their own cohesive artistic statement. Besides, not all composers are great singers, even within the terms of a singer-songwriter aesthetic; it's no accident that Linda has enjoyed some of her greatest successes with the work of Zevon, Souther, and Eric Kaz. And not having to come up with an ever-better collection of ten tunes every year enables interpretive singers to develop more steadily and surely than many composers; if Karla Bonoff, for example, fails to match the quality of songs of her previous album, it won't make much difference how well she sings.

There's another basic bias to consider before we go on. It isn't just that contemporary rock critics prefer husky, untrained voices over more polished varieties, or that they tend sometimes unthinkingly to doubt that any interpretation can conceivably equal the composer's original. There is a widespread prejudice against beauty per se in present-day popular music. People are so appalled by our culture's tendencies toward slickness and surface packaging that they seize hold of almost any rougher alternative. Pretty voices, pretty faces, pretty songs all become suspect to such a sensibility. Yet surely we have to allow for that part of life if the rebellious alternatives are to have meaning.

Or at least we do if we tend toward an attitude that in some crucial sense accepts things as they are. For better or for worse, I have always been the kind of person that tries to keep things in balance. I may be drawn to extremes in art and behavior, but I find them most desirable when contained within the sum total of human experience. And with my longtime fascination for German art and thought, I ultimately conceive of extremes in terms of the dialectical tension between them.

This runs counter to the extremist positions about art, politics, and life that shaped the ideology of today's active rock critics, people who grew up in the 1960s. I spent most of that decade in Berkeley, and in my parents' eyes I was a hopeless hippie. But I never really rejected them or their values, however much I may want to see changes effected in the way society works. Most serious rock critics think in more radical terms, whatever their day-to-day lives may be. For them the greatest rock serves as an explicit or implicit call to battle. For me it can well do that, but it can also echo the softer sides of life. They think of the polarities between rock's extremes—or between the extremes and the middle ground—as combatants in which only one side can be victorious. For me, there may be slow movement of the whole societal and artistic organism in a progressive or retrogressive direction, but all positions along the scale from radicalism to conservatism have at least some potential for validity. Those three speculative considerations aside, however, a rational defense of Ronstadt's interpretive style and public image has to begin with the admission that she has been and still can be a constrained performer. She herself has often worried in interviews (especially in years past) about being considered a "lame" singer, particularly by the circle of musicians and songwriters who are her closest collaborators. And even during the making of *Living in the U.S.A.*, one song was ultimately left off the album because, as Linda put it, "I sang it like a librarian." Related to that constraint is her stiffness in public performance. Ronstadt has never been one to whip up her audiences to rock frenzy; if your standard of comparison is Bruce Springsteen, then she is certainly a failure.

But of course Springsteen can't be the standard, since what he is doing and what she is doing are so different. Admittedly, Ronstadt's stiffness could be relaxed to her own advantage, and it has been over the past few years, especially in the matter of her singing. But as I've already indicated, that stiffness can have its own validity and charm, as an echo of a particular kind of white, churchish gentility. Her performing manner can be effective on its own terms, too. Often the simple sight of her standing there with her blend of beauty and shyness can be intensely touching, and serve as a fine foil for her sassier rock numbers. And when she's singing well, the sheer *sound* of that voice absolutely aceing a song can be just as thrilling as the most frenzied rock celebration.

There's also some validity to the charge of the "cold perfection" of Peter Asher's production, even if some of those qualities derive from Linda's own fears and perfectionism. In any case, one man's clinical coldness can be another's jewel-like beauty. Much of the best rock has striven for spontaneous passion above all else, with technical correctness far down on the scale of virtues: Bob Dylan's deliberately helter-skelter recording technique is the epitome of this tendency. Asher is trying for something different, something approaching the formal clarity and abstraction of classical music, that holds up under repeated listenings in a manner akin to precisely structured Western art music. At its best—and perhaps especially for those of us with a strong background in classical music—the sheer taste and *rightness* of his work has a real conviction of its own.

But to what extent it's *his* work and to what extent it's that of Ronstadt and her other collaborators is an extremely difficult matter to judge, even for them. Which in turn makes the assumption by some critics that Ronstadt is a mindless puppet a misapprehension. The one thing Asher does indisputably in both the recording studio and on the road is organize details like a computer. But the arrangements are a joint matter between Linda, the band, and Asher, with Linda's role far more crucial than her detractors might think. And a simple consideration of her last few albums indicates that her closest collaborators in the band have had an influence that rivals Asher's, and that shifts in personnel become a key way to vitalize and extend her sound. In particular, the change from Andrew Gold to Waddy Wachtel as unofficial band-leader was a significant one. Gold has a sensibility that is very close to the McCartneyesque British-pop cleverness that underlies Asher's style, and the two of them together pushed Ronstadt's work a bit too close to the ornate and brittle. That phase reached its peak on the last Gold album, *Hasten Down the Wind*, in 1976; the arrangements are often supportive and always ingenious, but Linda herself had grown uncomfortable with the distance that the sound had traveled from the harder and/or more folkish roots of the music she loved best. Thus the next album had a tougher, sparer sound that reflected not only her own inclinations but the more rock-oriented spirit of Wachtel; its title, *Simple Dreams*, referred in part to the arrangements.

As an interpretive singer, Ronstadt needs collaborators even more than singer-songwriters, and thus her interaction with her musical co-workers is a complex and delicate one. She has to cultivate songwriters and performing musicians both, and she has to develop relationships with them that work to her advantage yet aren't either domineering (which would be self-defeating) or unduly submissive. Her success in this regard (for all her periodic insecurities) is a quite remarkable one. Linda stands at the center of a number of overlapping musical worlds. She is the queen of the so-called L.A. school of rock—a "school" that these days seems stylistically ever more the anachronistic invention of some rock critics, given the distance some of its members have traveled from the old country-rock clichés. But it remains a viable grouping in a social sense, as a network of friends who share songs, appear on one another's records, and support one another in various ways. Ronstadt is also the leader of the burgeoning crop of women singers that has helped define one crucial aspect of 1970s rock. She is not only the best-known and most commercial of the lot, but she has gone out of her way in numerous specific cases (Karla Bonoff, Nicolette Larson, the Roche sisters, Annie McLoone, etc., etc.) to help younger singers get recognition and record contracts. In that sense, the long brooded-over trio album with Emmylou Harris and Dolly Parton would be not only a joy to hear, but a fitting symbol of the cooperative, loving spirit of this musical community in general and its women in particular.

In light of all this, the charge of supposedly "formalistic" song selection and sequencing on Ronstadt's albums since 1974 seems silly. As an interpretive singer and a leading member of a musical community, she naturally works with the best songwriters she can find. And since many of those songwriters are her friends and since good songwriters generally write more than one good song, she often goes back to the same people. There has perhaps been a tendency to choose well-known hits of the past over more obscure songs that would free her from invidious comparison, and a slightly recurrent pattern in her selection of oldies composers. But there's been greater variety than repetition; each album finds new names entering the lists, with new themes—or fresh variants on the old themes—underlying the song-by-song selection. Thus whereas earlier albums produced by Asher relied on people like the Eagles, Lowell George, and James Taylor, she later moved through close identification with the music of Kaz, Bonoff, Zevon, and Mick Jagger; Souther remained a constant throughout. In no case has she broken with any of these songwriters, but as circumstances shift (e.g., Bonoff needing all her new material for her own albums) the search for songs and songwriters moves on. And songs don't of course always come directly from songwriters. Linda relates as intensely to people as she does to music itself, and hence her wide network of friends has been a continual source of suggestions for oldies and promising contemporary songs.

Some of these relationships are romantic; others are friendships. It would be absurd, in the light of her own past interviews, to deny that Linda has been romantically involved with many of her collaborators. For her, consciously or unconsciously, sex is a way of getting what she wants. I don't mean it is just a device for her, that she is a cold manipulator; vivacity, warmth, and honesty define her nature. But she is an overtly sexual person, and she likes to relate to men on that level (or, with her many women friends, on a nonsexual but deeply emotional level) and is often ready to fall back on flirtation when she feels insecure about dealing with men in an intellectual or musical way.

Many of the troubles that some rock critics have with Ronstadt as a performer and a public image have to do with this sexuality, and because of it, I think, judgments about her recorded work sometimes become tangled unwittingly with preconceptions about her person. The first thing that needs to be said on this subject is that whatever one may think of Ronstadt as a sex bomb, it is by no means a false representation of the "real" person—all that public iconography, right down to the airbrushed album covers, is part of the same process whereby she attempts to make herself as alluring as she can.

Now, this flies in the face of many feminists' convictions; for all sorts of good reasons they are deeply suspicious of women who prettify themselves in conventional ways that serve to reinforce male expectations. In my own case, although ideologically and emotionally sympathetic to feminism, I've always enjoyed people of either sex who try to look sexually desirable—*how* they try to do that can vary widely, but the effort itself bespeaks a commitment to style and social generosity that I can respond to. In the case of Linda, what appealed to me about her image back in the late 1960s was the overt blend of good-girl gentility, hippie rebellion, and Los Angeles toughtramp sexuality. I had moved to Los Angeles from Berkeley at the very beginning of 1970. By then I had grown heartily sick of girls in army jackets, and was ready for a little flash.

What makes Ronstadt fascinating in terms of image is not that she is a stubborn holdout for Total Womanhood in an age of guerrilla feminism. It's the tension of the opposites she incorporates. Any fantasy-object (which is what she is for her fans) and any love-object (what she is for her lovers and close friends) have within them the ability to suggest all possibilities: we see our own contradictions mirrored in the other. But Linda embraces more strongly articulated alternatives than most people I know. She is at once sensual and clever, sweet and irrational, vulnerable and strong. Perhaps all of us contain these opposites; it's just that she denies very little of herself, and thus nearly all the facets of her character coexist in a state of high intensity.

It is the strength of these differing aspects of humanity, and their incorporation into one person of uncommon charm, that not only make her unusual as a person but help explain the really quite extraordinary diversity of musical styles that she can successfully encompass. Most interpretive singers (and certainly most singer-songwriters) are identifiable in terms of a specific style or focused concentration of styles. With Ronstadt, the range is far broader. She is often thought of as a country singer, and of course her best work in that idiom (I think of Hank Williams's "I Can't Help It If I'm Still in Love With You" from *Heart Like a Wheel*, with Emmylou Harris's angelic harmony-singing) has made her about the most popular woman country singer of the day—even when she's been downright stingy about including real country songs on her recent albums. She herself regards both the pop songs of her teen years (i.e., the late 1950s and early 1960s, the period of nearly all her oldies covers) and the Mexican *ranchera* style as her principal formative influences. This last, which she learned from records, the radio, and her father, is epitomized by the work of Lola Beltrán, and probably contributes as much to Ronstadt's "belting" style as do opera and the semi-operatic vocalism of 19th-century America. In her own recorded work, the most obvious manifestation of *ranchera* singing is her Spanish-language version of "Blue Bayou," released as a single only under the title "Lago Azul."

Aside from country music, Linda is justly praised for her way with soaring ballads in the folk-rock idiom—"Long, Long Time" from *Silk Purse* and the title track of *Heart Like a Wheel*, to name the two best known, plus all the Souther songs she has sung. This style—and country music, of course—is related to the acoustical folkish material she's recorded, often singing in harmony with Harris or Parton. There was "The Sweetest Gift" from *Prisoner in Disguise*, "I Never Will Marry" and "Old Paint" from *Simple Dreams* and, maybe, "Love Me Tender" from *Living in the U.S.A.* More recently her ballads have evolved into more sophisticated torch songs that suggest the genre of Broadway and cabaret—her own "Try Me Again" and Willie Nelson's "Crazy" from *Hasten Down the Wind*, Kaz's "Sorrow Lives Here" from *Simple Dreams*, and several more. And there are the grander, anthem-like extensions of this style, full of gospel passion, in Tracy Nelson's "Down So Low" and Bonoff's "Someone to Lay Down Beside Me," which end *Hasten Down the Wind* in that order.

If her ballads are most valued by those who collect her albums, it is the covers of early rock and black songs by which listeners to AM radio and purchasers of *Linda Ronstadt's Greatest Hits* know her best. Here her work has been more erratic. "You're No Good" and "When Will I Be Loved" from 1974's *Heart Like a Wheel* may have been brilliant successes. But interpretations of better-known songs like "Tracks of My Tears," "Heat Wave," and "Many Rivers to Cross" (all from *Prisoner in Disguise*) and "That'll Be the Day" (from *Hasten Down the Wind*) were not so good. For me, they still retain an undeniable charm, but her detractors condemn them out of hand. She's been somewhat more consistent recently, suggesting a real growth. To this taste both "Blue Bayou" from *Simple Dreams* and "Back in the U.S.A." from the new album seem only moderately convincing. But "It's So Easy," "Poor, Poor Pitiful Me," and "Tumbling Dice" from *Simple Dreams* are all fine up-tempo covers—with "Pitiful Me" a nice bit of self-parody and "Dice" her best-ever hard rock song—and "Just One Look," "All That You Dream," and "Ooh Baby Baby" uphold that standard on the new album. Except for hard-core disco, it's hard to think of any style she hasn't tried at least once.

Ronstadt has not only become a persuasive interpreter of most every idiom she has assayed, she's also not diffused her image in the process. Singers who try to sing everything generally fragment themselves. With Linda, the end effect is not a grab-bag, but an overarching personal style. Part of her secret is simply an instinctive musicality and a willingness to work hard on phrasing. But in a larger sense it is the very multifaceted cohesiveness of her image that binds the diverse styles together, helping to make them all believable. And at the base of both the music and the image, I think, is the nature of her involvement with people. She may well relate better to individuals than she does to crowds. But audiences clearly can identify with the intensity of her private passions.

Linda has sometimes compared the voice with the kiss; both for her are infallible indices of a personality. In other words, she thinks it's possible to perceive pretty much all you need to know about a person from how his or her voice sounds or how he or she kisses you. I can't speak about her kisses, nor judge her theory about voices in general. But it does seem to me that the key to her own voice's remarkable appeal—quite apart from its sheer strength and quality in the abstract—is the way it mirrors her. People feel they can see into her heart when she sings, and they're right. The range of vocal colors in her singing, from childlike intimacy to punkish yell to commanding assertion to shaky vulnerability, reflects the facets of her private person with infallible candor, and makes her recent public discretion about her private life no real defense at all.

Ronstadt has spoken of herself as a "real seventies person," by which she means that she admits to and identifies with the notion of her music as personal statement rather than political or ideological manifesto. But especially from a musical standpoint, I think she's better thought of as a blend of the sixties and seventies, and perhaps of earlier decades as well. Her singing combines the rhetorical strength of an earlier America, the folkish honesty of the sixties and the frank willingness of this decade to concentrate on personal sentiment. Ultimately what I wish those who are hostile or indifferent to Ronstadt's music would do is try to open their ears—to perceive what she does well without damning it by standards that simply don't apply. Of course, rock can be rebellious and angry, and new wave rock has reaffirmed that part of the music. But it can be softer, too, as can people. At her "shining best," as she once put it, Ronstadt can suggest those extremes better than any singer of our time.

. . .

All of which serves as a prelude to a more detailed discussion of *Living in the U.S.A.* As I indicated early on, it is still too soon after the album's release to say definitively how it ranks in the Ronstadt canon, even if one subscribes wholeheartedly to the notion of hierarchy in such matters in the first place. The actual making of the album was a more difficult process than with some of her records, and she worried in the days after the final mixing and sequencing that the song selection lacked depth. On the other hand, there are no tracks here that seem outright mistakes, which makes it her first disc about which that could be said. And from an interpretive standpoint, this is her finest album yet. On song after song, the singing is both technically commanding and stylistically impassioned.

Living in the U.S.A. is the first-ever Ronstadt record with no string arrangement on any cut. In fact, except for Mike Mainieri on vibraphone on one song and David Sanborn on alto saxophone on two, plus a few background singers, all the music here is made by Ronstadt and her band. This continues the trend begun with *Simple Dreams* of paring down the arrangements from the Gold-Asher days, and reinforces the tendency toward harder rock that Wachtel and Jagger, among others, have encouraged. Conversely, some constants from earlier Ronstadt records are in short supply or absent altogether. Chief among them is the duet-harmony singing with other women, from Parton to Harris to Maria Muldaur to Wendy Waldman. Also missing is any conventional country song. The closest is "Love Me Tender," which will probably be a country hit, given its association with Elvis Presley, but which in musical style is somewhere between a folk song and a nursery rhyme. There are also no extensions here of her earlier explorations of the cabaret-Broadway idiom, or any songs by her.

None of Ronstadt's records has been a "concept album" in the sense of a common theme varied from song to song. Yet so firmly focused is her image and so single-mindedly has she concentrated on love that her records can be used to trace an evolution in her own life from vulnerability and pain to a new-found strength and, even, defiance. *Living in the U.S.A.* doesn't contain a single song that quite fits the old Ronstadt stereotype of the desperately yearning but abused woman who will do anything to get back her man. And, indeed, one suspects that may be what she really means when she worries about the quality of the material on this album—that not only the songs but the new, tough way of singing them have robbed her of a bit of the innocence in herself that she cherishes. *Simple Dreams* had a greater depth of self-revelation, more songs in which the old sorrowing Ronstadt persona retained its vulnerability, even when the expressive terms were more mature both musically and emotionally. On *Living in the U.S.A.* there is one song that continues that development—Souther's exquisite "White Rhythm and Blues." But otherwise that place on the emotional spectrum is taken by two songs that confront the passage of time with a strange, prematurely aged resignation—"When I Grow Too Old to Dream" and "Blowing Away" (or "I'm Blowin' Away," its actual title). Yet both songs are sung with a force that belies the weakness of age. And the other song that confesses to abject depression, "All That You Dream," both ends positively and is couched throughout in an exotic, passionate musical idiom that denies weakness from the outset. Otherwise, the songs here are exultant, intensely personal, overtly erotic or simply tender—which is pretty much the emotional range one has come to expect from a Linda Ronstadt record.

The album's ten songs can be divided evenly between covers of older material and contemporary numbers, and in every case but two direct comparisons can be made either to the original or to the best-known interpretation. The two exceptions are "When I Grow Too Old to Dream," which first appeared in a film of 1935, *The Night Is Young*, and has since come out in innumerable cover versions, and "White Rhythm and Blues," a new, unrecorded Souther song.

"When I Grow Too Old to Dream" has words by Oscar Hammerstein II and music by Sigmund Romberg, and as such is the first song Ronstadt has sung that is a direct representative of the operetta-Broadway tradition I've referred to, even if it did actually originate in Hollywood. Apparently there was a good deal of experimentation in the studio as to just how to sing it and with what arrangement. The solution was an extremely spare combination of Don Grolnick's consoling, patiently plodding piano chords (hardly adjectives that normally characterize the work of one of the finest, most stylistically wide-ranging pianists ever to play in a rock band) and the eerie overlay of Mike Mainieri's vibes. Against this Linda sings the song about as "straight" as she can, "reading right from the lead sheet," as she put it. The result is interesting but not entirely successful. The arrangement serves to defuse the song of its latent sentimentality, and its coldness perhaps underscores the feelings of loss inherent in the lyrics (cf. "I'm Blowin' Away," below). But without the sentimentality the song seems a bit foursquare. And Linda's singing is slightly reminiscent of her version of "Blue Bayou" (another interpretation I didn't much like) in its alternation of low soft singing with high loud singing. Ronstadt went through a period a couple of years ago in concert of overdoing the dramatic effect of shifting suddenly from quiet to loud and back again. Here the bottom part of the voice seems pressed just a bit lower in pitch than is comfortable for her, and the loud singing sounds forced in comparison to what a trained operatic voice could accomplish with this same music. Still, the interpretation is an undeniably interesting one, and the commercial success of "Blue Bayou" proved that a lot of people like just what gives me pause in her singing.

"Love Me Tender" was added to the Ronstadt tour repertory shortly after Elvis Presley's death in August of 1977, and subsequently included in the concert footage in *FM* (although not on that film's soundtrack album). It doesn't appeal to me particularly as a song, but it's sweet enough, and Linda sings it with a nice delicacy (better than Elvis did, with his sagging pitch). Some may find this the most obvious instance on the album of Linda's supposed predilection for sentimentality. For me, the singing is honorable enough in itself, and once again a sparse, telling arrangement avoids all hint of goo. Waddy Wachtel plays guitar and contributes decent harmony singing, and Grolnick's sustained but light-textured organ in the choruses sounds elegiac. Linda cuts Presley's first verse and repeats the chorus at the end, changing words slightly but in no important way from Presley's 1956 original.

Chuck Berry's "Back in the U.S.A." dates from 1959, provides the album's theme and was its first single. Linda's cover falls right about in the middle of her other versions of rock and rhythm-and-blues from this era. The vocal is nicely energetic, and the band matches Berry's arrangement, with Grolnick doing a lovely job of invoking Johnny Johnson's original piano part. Linda's version does without the doo-wop "uh-uh-uh's" and "oh yeah's" that fill up the gaps in the original, which she and her collaborators found dated, and replaces Berry's fadeout with a not-all-that-interesting coda. The singing provides a decent example of Ronstadt's way of coarsening her naturally "clean" vocal production when she feels the need to project a tougher persona—as on the syllables "God," "box" in "jukebox" and the second "I'm" in the phrase "I'm so glad." But this is nothing new for her; the most obvious previous example was the recurrent growl on the word "fall" in "It's So Easy" from *Simple Dreams*.

What's missing in this "Back in the U.S.A." is the easily seductive lilt that Berry and his band attain. In a live performance of the song in May of 1978 at the Oakland Coliseum, just after they'd recorded it, Linda's band launched into the music at breakneck speed and maintained it throughout. Linda apologized later for the tempo, but it lent the proceedings a hectically improvisatory quality that is preferable to the stiffness of the recorded version. The stiffness is suggested by Linda's precise flatting of the tag-syllables on the ends of key lines ("-way" in "runaway," "A." in "U.S.A.," "Lou," etc.). Berry flats the same syllables, but it's done casually, as a sexy accent, rather than deliberately. With Linda it sounds calculated and rote.

The final two oldies covers, "Ooh Baby Baby" and "Just One Look," are far better. No doubt some Smokey Robinson loyalists won't be able to accept her version of the former. As a pure piece of singing, Robinson's version of this song surpasses Linda's. First, there's the whole issue of the erotic symbolism of the male soprano, a symbolism that has operated with infallible effect since the days of the great operatic castrati in the 17th and 18th centuries. The ethereal sexual yearning of Robinson's voice makes an inevitably different and more distinctive impression than a woman in the same register, especially when combined with his odd but endearing prissiness of enunciation. In addition, Robinson's singing is full of little felicities that heighten the sexual ambience—the delicious hesitation on the second "baby" in the first line of the third chorus, for instance, or the wonderful little ornamental quivers on the words "believe" and "here" in the third verse, or the magical phrasing of "mistakes too I'm" in the second verse. It's the performance of a man at the very end of his sexual tether.

But in a smoother, more luxuriant, more sexually *fulfilled* way, Linda's version works too, and it could very well become a wonderful AM radio make-out song. Like Robinson, Linda makes a fine effect with the switching between a breathy, erotic natural voice and falsetto. And what distinguishes her arrangement from Robinson's is the use of David Sanborn's saxophone, especially as it blends with Ronstadt's vocal coloration in words like "pay" in the first verse (an even more telling instance of that blend comes with the final syllable in the song "Alison," in which Sanborn's sax emerges as if from *within* Linda's last falsetto note).

I've already indicated my feelings about Ronstadt vs. Doris Troy on "Just One Look"—I think Linda's version is superior on every count, and not just because she has the better voice. What Troy does offer is a tough, gospelish blackness of enunciation and phrasing, but I for one don't think that's a necessary ingredient of the song; and Linda's white predatory-female protagonist is fully appropriate. Furthermore, her band plays better and is far better recorded, and the arrangement builds subtly with the addition of tambourine and cowbell, both played by Asher. To cite just one further nicety in the coda that Ronstadt et al. append to the song, listen to the way Linda interrupts the repetitions of "Just one look, that's all it took" in the middle of the word "it" to yowl out an orgasmic "whoa baby."

If Ronstadt has somewhat variable results with her oldies covers, her accounts of contemporary songs here are all persuasive. "White Rhythms and Blues" is another of those John David Souther compositions that Linda sings to near perfection. Whether or not Souther can finally achieve a viable performing career, he has certainly found a rare interpreter in Ronstadt. The music of this song boasts a fine melody and a host of exquisitely crafted subsidiary details, and the lyrics, too, seem rich and evocative, especially the full title phrase, "Black roses, white rhythm and blues." Metaphors don't always have to be precise to be evocative. That phrase in Souther's song will strike some as unspecific, as will the title of Warren Zevon's "Mohammed's Radio." For me, despite all the differences in the poetic and musical feeling of the two songs, they both suggest something about a mixture of darker passion and surface charm that is very close to Linda as an artist and a person.

The arrangement is spare yet telling in the best manner of her past two albums, with another of those autumnal, slow-moving organ lines that reinforce the slightly chill, lonely feeling of much of the disc as a whole, and a restrained pedal steel guitar part from Dan Dugmore. Linda's singing, apart from her general sympathy for Souther's music and its idiom, is full of lovely touches. The enunciation on the word "lose," to take one tiny example, is a classic case of the Americanness of her accent. The yearning sound of the voice being let out on words like "stay," "whole," and "your eyes" are typical examples of Ronstadt's command of balladic rhetoric. And her own background singing at the end, merging with Wachtel's electric guitar on the repeated phrase "Black roses," makes a magical effect. The only reservation I have is the falsetto on the line "I don't know what else I can do." Linda argues with some logic that the character in the song is showing her weak side at that point, and hence the falsetto becomes metaphorically appropriate. But it doesn't sound very attractive to me, even though it's handled tidily enough from a technical standpoint.

Her choice of Eric Kaz's "I'm Blowin' Away" offers an especially interesting comparison. The best-known version of this song is Bonnie Raitt's (which Linda says she's never heard, even though the two women are friends), and most rock critics of the sort I've been referring to throughout this essay think of Raitt as a positive corrective to all the faults they perceive in Ronstadt—in fact, the several critics with whom I've spoken about *Living in the U.S.A.* all prefer Raitt's version. Raitt sings in her usual warm, direct, honest manner; for her the song becomes a consoling, rolling anthem. She achieves this by her tendency to elide lines and words, chopping short one note and hurrying on to the next; by the repetition of the chorus at the end; by an arrangement full of sustained strings and French horns and by a production that turns the harmonies of Emmylou Harris, Jackson Browne, and Souther into a small chorus (and blurs their individuality in the process).

Next to this, Linda's account may sound tense and rigid. The arrangement is far sparser, beginning with an eerie pedal steel effect from Dugmore and full of odd, distancing touches, such as the dabs of conga-drum color that Russ Kunkel occasionally applies. Linda's singing fits this mold. It is tight and self-contained, with what sounds like a greater amount of echo (although that may be partly a psychological illusion). The song in this version is no anthem at all, but a series of isolated phrases, cold and distant. Yet in two ways Raitt's version is more austere than Ronstadt's. She sings the recurrent word "shadows" in the chorus on a high C which drops to the F a fifth below. This is an extremely stark effect, hardly softened by the quick G grace-note that she interposes before she actually reaches the F. Ronstadt sings both an A and a G on her way down from C, puts more weight on those notes and holds them longer. The result is altogether softer, and more conventional. The other major difference in the way the two women handle the actual materials of the song (as opposed to their arrangements and singing styles) is that whereas Raitt repeats the chorus at the end, with its refrain of "Shadows keep taking my love/and leaving me," Ronstadt does the final chorus only once, and then appends a final sentence of "You keep taking my love/and leaving me."

Given the traditionally creative role performers play in popular music, neither woman can really be said to be more faithful to what Kaz intended. If the unusualness of the precipitous C-to-F drop in Raitt's version seems preferable, Ronstadt's switch to "you" at the end is more controversial. Ronstadt's detractors may well complain that this is yet another instance of her failure to comprehend an abstract or cosmic metaphor unless it's reduced to the most immediate personal terms. But it seems to me that in switching from "shadows" to "you" as the agent of the protagonist's despair, Linda keeps the more universal implications of "shadows" and achieves a powerful dramatic effect in the sudden personification. The device is precisely the same as Neil Young's abrupt shift to the personal in his "Cortez the Killer." In more general terms, there can be no denying the musicality and beauty of Raitt's account of this song, and, perhaps, its lesser self-consciousness. But for me Ronstadt has by far the more distinctive voice, and the coldness and agony of her version strike closer to the essence of the song. That essence is reinforced by all sorts of details in the phrasing, from the hymnlike inflection of the line, "My life has lost its mystery," to the desperation and passion of the full-voiced attacks on syllables like "wild" and the "sha-" in "shadows." Listen, too, to the way she chops off her voice on such words as "romanced" and "away," twisting the pitch down with a grimness that would do justice to a pioneer woman. Linda Ronstadt is not often thought of as an intellectual singer, and perhaps the process by which this version evolved was intuitive. But as an interpretation it's downright smart.

The performance of Little Feat's "All That You Dream" by both her and the band not only far surpasses the original, but ranks among their finest efforts. Little Feat's recording is only functionally sung and not very interestingly arranged. Ronstadt sings the song with an exact yet unstudied command of pitch (especially important with this song's highly chromatic vocal line) and tough, defiant persona. The toughness is reinforced by several devices—the familiar growls, slurred diction and precise touches of vocal color here and there, as in the switch to falsetto on the word "you" and the tendency to let sustained notes shift through several changes of vowel-sound (most impressively on the final syllable of the word "everyone"). The highlight of the arrangement is Dan Dugmore's pedal steel guitar break, the closest to progressive synthesizer-rock that a Ronstadt song has ever come.

This leaves two more songs, and they may very well be the ones that provoke the most vituperation in reviews by critics who see in Ronstadt the antithesis of all that is strong and rebellious and macho in the best new rock. Those songs are Elvis Costello's "Alison" and Warren Zevon's "Mohammed's Radio." Costello is one of the most respected of the British new-wave rockers, and both in his music and in interviews he has posited himself as a scourge to cleanse the world of 1970s pop pap—he's even specifically identified Ronstadt as a principal purveyor of that pap. And quite apart from their stances within the polemics of late-1970s rock, there is the question of whether this particular song should be sung by a woman.

As far as the first issue is concerned, all I can say is that Linda's version works for me. Costello doesn't actually sing the song very well, although admittedly this ballad's mere existence within the rest of his repertory, which is heavily weighted toward uptempo rockers, makes its own kind of statement. Of course Costello fans could argue that polished singing is beside the point; "Alison" is indeed partly a matter of the projection of an attitude through phrasing and inflection. But it's also a beautifully crafted song, both in lyrics and music—which Costello will surely admit when he calms down. As might be expected, Linda's singing and the arrangement (especially the interaction with Sanborn) are elegantly shaped. What's surprising is the punkish aptness of her phrasing, which manages to echo Costello (she didn't really feel she understood the song until she experienced the full impact of Costello as a performer at a concert at Hollywood High) and add something of her own.

But *what* of her own? In Costello's version the song makes clear if emotionally complex sense, as a song from a man to a woman he has loved, now sees as superficial but deep down loves still. Costello's own guardedness about overt tenderness fits the singer's persona ideally—the song's rich sentiment owes much to its very refusal to be sentimental. But Linda is not only a woman, she has very often pushed the element of sentiment in her music to the point that many of her detractors consider her a hopeless sentimentalist. I have generally found her sentiment to be unsentimental (which no doubt means that I am a sentimentalist myself), so that aspect of her "Alison" doesn't bother me. But it did take me a long time to get used to the idea of a woman singing this song. It can only reach its full emotional depth when the intensity of the protagonist's feelings toward Alison becomes fully manifest. It would seem hard to understand a woman singer's barely contained feeling for Alison unless the woman were herself deeply in love with her. But that seems to imply a bisexual love triangle, which not only needlessly complicates an already complex song, but introduces a disconcerting lesbian element into Linda's public image (the combination of a commanding voice and girlish charm has indeed won her a good many gay women fans).

Here is one case in which knowing a performer can be helpful in purely aesthetic appreciation. After a long and vigorous explanation from Linda as to how she conceived the song and what she thought of intense friendship between women, and even an analysis of the particular woman friend she had in mind as Alison—an aggressive, insecure, selfish, generous, and beautiful young girl who in her own way is very much a punk—it's begun to make sense. There are some who simply don't bother about such questions of persona in the first place. But for those of us who do, "Alison" not only now seems logical in Linda's version, but far more appropriate for her than, say, Lowell George's "Willin'" from *Heart Like a Wheel* or "Carmelita" from *Simple Dreams*.

Which brings us, finally, to Zevon's "Mohammed's Radio." This is both the capstone of the album and an artistic breakthrough for Ronstadt as a singer in the same way that Karla Bonoff's "Someone to Lay Down Beside Me" was on *Hasten Down the Wind* (as an anthem of mature womanhood) and "Tumbling Dice" was on *Simple Dreams* (as a hard-rock war cry of independence). It represents not only an overpowering piece of singing and an inspired arrangement, both far truer to the song than Zevon himself can muster, but also the first time Linda has attempted with sovereign success a song that transcends the humanistic, amorous-psychological basis of her music and moves into the realm of metaphorical abstraction. Yet her detractors think her version of "Mohammed's Radio" is one-dimensional and uncomprehending, with the metaphorical implications of the lyrics reduced to their most obvious and trivial meanings.

It should be inserted here that my feelings about the song are conditioned in part from having heard it several times during her August, 1978, tour. Although Linda says she far prefers working in the studio to singing on stage, it often happens that her live versions of songs just recorded improve during the subsequent tour. That certainly happened with "Tumbling Dice," as documented in the live performance on the *FM* soundtrack, and it makes her and Asher's continued resistance to a live album debatable. The live performances of "Mohammed's Radio" were not only sung and played with even greater passion than on record, but they dispensed with the slightly obvious and clichéd wailing female soul duo on the choruses and included such niceties as the word "alas" pitched higher and hence still more intensely.

Still, the disc version is fine enough, and it's hard once again to avoid the notion that those who can't appreciate it are the victims of their own preconceptions. Linda Ronstadt is known as a singer of boy-girl homilies; therefore it's impossible she could tackle a song like this with any perception. Reinforcing that bias is another problem. All four of the people whom I know to dislike her "Mohammed's Radio" are in some way associated with *Rolling Stone* in New York, and in an interview for that magazine she analyzed the song in words that were more breezy than profound. Her tone may have made her critics even more convinced than before that for her this song is simply a little ditty about listening to rock on the radio. But to me she's talked with some fluency about the song's multiple meanings. And in any case, one has to pull back from preconceptions and behind-the-scenes information and simply listen to what one hears. The devices artists use to make their art are just that—devices. The fact that Maria Callas talked inarticulately about the characters she portrayed hardly detracts from her status as the greatest operatic actress of the century, nor does Beethoven's peculiar brooding about his nephew compromise his music's universality. Even if Linda does use her own psychological tools to get inside a song—even if she approaches the abstract through the personal— that hardly matters if the result is as overwhelming as it is here.

As with "White Rhythm and Blues," the words of "Mohammed's Radio" may not be susceptible to precise analysis—in fact, were such analysis possible, the song might well seem unevocative—and yet may still strike one as emotionally true. This song *is* about the redemptive power of rock and roll. But it's also about rock as escapism, about the place of blacks within a white culture, about mystical religion and the driving force of the irrational beneath society's troubled surface.

Linda's version works so well in part because of the minimal role that ironic inflection plays in this particular song and in part because of the primary function of music in determining the essence of *any* song. In "Mohammed's Radio" the multiple meanings are inherent in the words, and in the relationship between the words and music, rather than a function of the singer's delivery. What makes opera and song such a complex and fertile business is this three-way interchange. Music is both the deepest and most emotionally intense of the arts; independent of words it is rarely successful as a medium for wit and irony. Words lack music's emotional power but can be far more focused; the combination of words and music, then, can function as a dialectically potent artistic marriage. (Richard Wagner, who articulated many of these ideas in his theoretical works and then realized them in his music dramas, liked to link words with the masculine principle and music with the feminine.) A singer can freight the words with still further layers of complexity by way of vocal color and inflection. And thus a woman (already linked archetypally with emotion, if you're a Jungian or Wagnerian) who sings can tap profound depths beneath our everyday existences. If the woman in question is already one whose whole life revolves around emotion, you begin to get some hint of the wellsprings of Linda Ronstadt's appeal.

In the past, however, she has sometimes had trouble with songs in which a composer-interpreter's vocal personality has been an essential ingredient of the song, or if the song has had a heavy component of irony built into both the words and their potential interpretation. For both these reasons perhaps the all-time least successful Ronstadt cover version was her account of Randy Newman's "Sail Away" on her *Don't Cry Now* album of 1973. Some critics find hints of a mordant irony on Zevon's part in "Mohammed's Radio" that make the passionate directness of Ronstadt's performance seem misconceived—above all his very use of the word "alas." For me, though, whatever irony Zevon may possibly have intended seems decidedly secondary, and in any event is in no way denied by Linda's interpretation. Besides, Zevon's voice and singing style, while effective enough for emphatic rockers, are far too limited to suggest much subtlety. The same critics see a real ambivalence on the part of the Zevon protagonist: He recognizes the redemptive power of music but simultaneously distances himself from it, especially in the "village idiot" stanza, in which rock seems to have reduced its devotees to escapist vegetables. This may well be part of the song, but for me it's more of an accent than a central meaning. In any event Linda recognizes this particular ambivalence very clearly, and has even heightened its ambiguity by two minor textual alterations. The second verse in Zevon's original begins, "You know the sheriff's got his problems too/And he will surely take them out on you." Linda broadens the second phrase to make it "me and you." Later on in the same verse the "village idiot" appears; the idiot is masculine for Zevon and feminine for Ronstadt.

The real secret to the song lies in contemplating the words *in conjunction with the music*, and not in the abstract, as I think too many rock critics are prone to do. The music here is not rock and roll in the ordinary sense, even with the refrain of "Don't it make you want to rock and roll/All night long." Instead it's a dirgelike anthem, a rolling, inexorable attestation to the darker, more passionate side of life. It is this passion, power, and even rage Linda and her band capture so perfectly—and without necessarily denying the distancing implications inherent in the "village idiot" passage, since those implications remain inseparable from the words themselves.

As for the band and the arrangement, Zevon's version (on which Wachtel played lead guitar) pales by comparison. His production fails to realize whatever hymnlike potential might have been latent in the use of Lindsey Buckingham and Stevie Nicks for the harmonies on the chorus, and Bobby Keyes's sax solo sounds even more irrelevant than does Linda's soul duo. Ronstadt's musicians attack the music with a real ferocity. The whole hard-edged, weighty, metallic quality the band has taken on since Andrew Gold's departure is completely appropriate here both to the song and the singing.

Ultimately, though, it is Linda who makes this interpretation so special. The vocal range suits her exactly, and here her growing artistry of the past few years reaches a new height, with beauty of voice, strength of persona, and intensity of delivery all at the service of the music. It is a performance in which the vocalism illuminates the material, transforming it in a way that its creator could never himself achieve. As such it reaffirms the place of interpretation in contemporary popular music, and provides an experience of enormous emotional import for any listener able to open up and respond to the glory of great singing.

ONAN'S GREATEST HITS

(WANKER 0000)
1978

DAVE MARSH

The English have the perfect word for it. They call it wanking. The word isn't as descriptive as its counterparts in American slang (we say: jerking off, beating meat, pounding pud) but it's more poetic. Considering how central wanking will be to a desert island existence, the poetry is actually quite functional.

The problem with desert island fantasies is that they're so goddamned impractical. To approach this chapter as an existential decision about what music I'd really prefer to be stranded with, it would be necessary to spend the rest of my life walking around with a cassette of *Who's Next* in my pocket. (It's difficult enough to pack when you've got a month's notice.) And anyway, at such a juncture, even loving rock obsessively, there are other priorities that come well ahead of it: like a fifth (or a case) of Remy Martin and a carton of Pall Malls. I'm not gonna drink fermented coconut juice and smoke palm fronds just because some editor had a notion.

This particular question has a strategic limitation, too. Rock is not like a book, which can be appreciated even without candlelight, if you get up before dark. (One of the advantages of civilization is that you might not.) But you can't exactly sharpen your fingernail and decode the information on a disc, using your sinus cavities as an amplifier. What comes with *this* fantasy (face it) is a cassette deck and a lifetime supply of Duracells. Not quite traveling light, is it?

Anyway, my idea of an island on which to be stranded is Manhattan, or, in a pinch, Great Britain. Something paved, at least. A desert island's only advantage is that it would probably be the one place where you could avoid being kicked around by corporations. So I've declined to choose an album that would be possible to assemble corporately, at least during the current epoch. Call it *Wanker's Delight (Onan's Greatest Hits)*, music devoted to the adolescent's favorite pastime. Divided, naturally, into a soft side and a hard side.

Rock, they say, is about fucking. That's a laugh. Ball to that beat and you'll wind up bruised. And the singers are always bleating about being left lonely, which is less conducive to interpersonal sex than its hairy-palmed alternative. The real truth is that rock was invented by teenagers with pimples, and acned adolescents are mostly getting it on with their fingers. This is the secret reality of rock sexuality—what all rock listeners have in common—which is probably why so many of us have Catholicism and Judaism in our backgrounds. If Portnoy had been ten years younger, he'd have had a ten-transistor radio in there with the liver. And Philip Roth might have written a rock opera rather than a novel—or (I can hear the gallery) rock criticism rather than either. *Mea culpa.*

Not that I feel guilty, exactly. As my colleague Robert Christgau pointed out to me, for the act itself, pornography of a more literary or visual order is desired. Music lacks a kinetic dimension; at least with a book, you have something to do with the other hand. But, as it turns out, a great deal of my favorite rock is about wanking, at least in a general sort of way.

Still, I kept to a fairly strict set of rules in assembling the record that dare not speak its name. First of all, the songs had to fit onto a single LP. The final collection runs a bit on the long side—something more than 45 minutes—but not inconceivably so. Secondly, it had to be music I'd prefer to listen to. The fact is, I'd rather be stranded with these songs than with Linda Ronstadt in the flesh.

I was interested in wanking as a matter of solitude; that ruled out the Supremes' handjob classic, "Buttered Popcorn," and Eddie Cochran's "Sitting in the Balcony." But mostly, I wanted to explore the outer limits of wanking as a theme in rock. So, while I regret the omission of Jimi Hendrix's "Love or Confusion" and Percy Sledge's "Just Out of Reach (Of My Two Empty Arms)," songs like the Atlanta Rhythm Section's "Imaginary Lover" and Jackson Browne's "Rosie," which are fables literally concerning self-abuse, are less sorely missed. Nor did I want to get too obvious or crude—so neither the Miracles' "Come On Do the Jerk" nor the Capitols' "Cool Jerk" (dance records, ha ha) are here. Grin's "Slippery Fingers," Faye Adams's "Shake a Hand" and Sam and Dave's "When Something Is Wrong with My Baby" were left off for similar reasons, while the Band's "The Weight," the Zombies' "She's Not There," and Chuck Berry's "Sweet Little Sixteen" finally seemed just too abstract. But with those titles, you don't even have to have a dirty mind to get the picture, though if you lack a certain kinky turn of thought, why you're interested in rock—or being stranded on a desert island—is beyond me.

But even the most salacious minds can sometimes make a slip. In 1973, I reviewed a Bruce Springsteen concert for *Newsday*, the Long Island family newspaper, and quite unthinkingly quoted the lines from the first verse of his "Blinded by the Light" which conclude with an adolescent pumping into his hat. Nobody cut it out—much to my surprise the next day—and nobody ever made a comment about it, at least not to me. Perhaps they never knew, or were too embarrassed if they did. Though I have always wondered —too embarrassed for me, or for themselves?

I feel about the same this time. Nevertheless, here is *Onan's Greatest Hits*, a record which neither Warner Communications nor CBS is likely to release in our lifetime.

Soft Side

"The Beat"   Elvis Costello
"I Want You"   Bob Dylan
"Pictures of Lily"   The Who

"Only the Lonely"   Roy Orbison
"In My Lonely Room"   Martha and the Vandellas
"Party Lights"   Claudine Clark
"He Ain't Give You None"   Van Morrison

HARD SIDE

"Whole Lotta Shakin'"   Jerry Lee Lewis
"Mona (I Need You Baby)"   Bo Diddley
"Shake"   Otis Redding
"A Hard Day's Night"   The Beatles
"Goin' Home"   The Rolling Stones

It is appropriate that the album opens with Elvis Costello, the youngest artist here, rather than one of his more celebrated colleagues. "The Beat" confirms the continuing presence of masturbation in the rock tradition—it's a 1978 song—and especially the continuing interest in the theme by major artists. One of the interesting things about researching this record was discovering that wanking is a more prominent theme among very famous rock performers than among obscure ones; with the exception of Claudine Clark, there is virtually no singer represented here who is not a household word, at least in the rock community. One wonders, of course, what drives our greatest stars to write such songs—is it merely reminiscence, or is it part of the terrible price they pay for fame and consequent isolation? Either way, they deserve it.

Ostensibly, of course, "The Beat" is addressed to a girl or woman. But this only demonstrates how cautiously even New Wave (or "Punk") artists have had to be when dealing with this taboo topic. It is quite clear, certainly, what Costello is referring to in the chorus when he talks about good boys never playing with their "toys." And the insanely repetitive organ triplet, which stands alone for the first few bars of the bridge, is another kind of clue.

Elvis Costello is best known for his rampant hostility, which borders on sociopathy (the far side of the border, at that), and his version of the wank fantasy is extremely vengeful, though it is expressed personally, rather than with the generalized societal hostility of "A Hard Day's Night." It's also interesting that on Costello's *This Year's Model*, "The Beat" is followed by "Pump It Up," which is not a song about a gas station attendant. (I knew one of the latter, in my high school days, who insisted his name was Jack Mehoff. He used to eat lit cigarettes.)

Costello is a man at war with his psyche. The verses of "The Beat" counsel moderation, and some sort of conciliation with humanity. The chorus mocks this asserted wisdom, which is one of the reasons the misanthrope Costello is so perfect for desert island reverie. Listening to him, you might feel almost cheered by banishment from society.

Bob Dylan's "I Want You" is also desperately psycho-dramatic— the singer again has no self-control, a typical wanker's symptom— but here, he seems to be longing for a loved one. But Dylan's love object is far too perfect to be merely another person. (With that early reference to the Queen of Spades, one hesitates to be too insistent concerning gender.) As in Eastern mysticism, Dylan refers to the Beloved—and as in mysticism, the Beloved is intimately connected to the Self. Lyrically, the references to horns in the first verse are clearly phallic, as is the symbol of the "broken cup" in the second verse. ("Broken cups" indicate spillage—of liquids or, perhaps, seed.) But the musical motif in this song that gives away its true or inner theme is the drumming—particularly the solo beats at the beginning. Masturbation, of course, is intimately connected to drumming, since it is one of man's most primitive forms of percussion. (Compare Kenny Buttrey's rhythm patterns here with the anonymous stutter-step on Claudine Clark's "Party Lights," for instance.)

The Who's imagery is far less obtuse. In fact, it's as brazen as a pimple cream commercial. "Pictures of Lily" may be the only hit record (well, it made number four in England) that is explicitly about wanking. It is also one of the Who's finest songs: Keith Moon's drumming is pure clotted cream, and Pete Townshend's guitar rumbles along like an adolescent id itself. Perhaps the record's most brilliant passage is John Entwistle's climactic trumpet ejaculation in the bridge.

"Pictures of Lily" is a tribute to modern, progressive parenthood.

The singer is having difficulty sleeping so his father pastes pictures of Lily on the wall above the son's bed. The cure works:

Pictures of Lily, made my life so wonderful
Pictures of Lily, helped me sleep at night
Pictures of Lily, solved my childhood problem
Pictures of Lily, helped me feel all right

But pop hasn't reckoned with his son's susceptibility to infatuation. The boy falls in love with Lily, and when he goes to ask dad where he can meet her, he replies: "Son, now don't be silly. She's been dead since 1929." The song ends in mournful confusion, Townshend bashing away at his guitar like a maniac. This is typical of the Who—and I would not want to be anywhere, no matter what the population, without something from this group. It cheers me up—compared to Pete Townshend's psychological fables, I always seem the picture of health.

"Only the Lonely" is not a song about masturbation, but masturbation may be the only solace for an artist whose persona is as desperately paranoiac as Roy Orbison's. All of Orbison's songs are in some way maddened by his fantasies— in "Running Scared," he reaches a peak of terror by imagining that his girl might some-day see a guy she'd like more than him, and cools himself out only by imagining she'd finally come back to him, anyhow. But "Only the Lonely" presents the lover isolated in the most exquisite sense: it is the perfect setting for the utter self-pity that so often accompanies wanking, as Roy mourns pathetically about how only someone so desolate as he could possibly understand his plight. In its way, this record is every bit as bombastic as the Who's, except that rather than Townshend's guitar and Moon's drumming, Orbison copes with strings that pound furiously and vocal choruses that sing "dum-dum-dum-dumdee-doo-wah," which is perhaps a gibberish equivalent of "How goddamn dumb we all are." I have no notion of what Roy Orbison's adolescence might have been like, something for which I am profoundly thankful each time I hear this song.

The only rock song more abject in its self-pity than "Only the

Lonely" is the Beach Boys' "In My Room." It is not included here, not because we don't know what most of us were up to in our teenage sanctums, but because Brian Wilson sounds too completely out of it to find his tool, much less play with it. (Readers who have not heard this record are advised to take a Valium and listen to it now, before I spend all my credibility.) More importantly, I think if I heard "In My Room" on a desert island, there would be no other recourse than suicide.

The logical substitute for "In My Room" is Martha and the Vandellas' much brighter "In My Lonely Room," which has less to do with privacy than with romantic failure. Her guy is fooling around, of course, and right in front of her eyes. She goes home and cries. Well, actually, this song has nothing to do with jerking off. It's just that Martha Reeves was one of the three or four most powerful voices in the history of rock and roll, and anyway, my room was where I used to do it. (The bathroom was cold, and we had a big family who resented long-term occupancy.) Which is why "In My Lonely Room" is here. In loving memory, as the English are wont to say of Buddy Holly. Who would have understood.

The inclusion of "Party Lights" is more purposeful. It makes a simple point: *They drove us to it!* Their nagging, their prohibitions—all of it left us no recourse. And I am reminded of this, over and over again, as Claudine Clark looks out her window and watches the party across the street that her mother will *not* let her attend. I wish I could say that "Party Lights" represents the female perspective on masturbation, but my understanding of women sexually stops far short of that. (If I knew women better, the rest of this chapter would be a lot less well-informed, probably. You count your blessings, I'll count mine.) Also, "Party Lights" is one of rock's great one-shots, which is a nice wanking metaphor, too.

Side one closes with "He Ain't Give You None," in which Van Morrison grapples with the problem of understanding women and comes up short. I haven't understood a Van Morrison lyric since "Gloria," so if you can figure out what it all means, write the publisher. But maybe the way the music builds has something to do with why this song felt like it belonged here. It's real pretty and real demented—by the end of the song, Morrison sounds like he really has grown hair on his palms. And maybe there *is* something to "He Ain't Give You None" in the way of metaphor. What's this business about Old John of Curzon Street who "flogs his daily meat"? Curzon is in Mayfair, London's wealthiest district—surely Van isn't implying the guy's a *pimp*, in those posh precincts? But there is only one other explanation . . .

Side two is much more direct in its emotions. Compared to Jerry Lee Lewis's "Whole Lotta Shakin'," for instance, even Elvis Costello and the Who seem discreet. "Whole Lotta Shakin' " is so defiant, its rhythms so insistent, Jerry Lee so transcendently free of guilt at his emission of pure lust that the song may fairly be construed as this album's anthem. As such, it sets the tone of this side, which eschews the mild diffidence and perplexity of some of side one for sheer ribald revelry. If there is any doubt of these songs' connection to the matter at hand, simply slip into the rhythmic groove each of them offers as its central delight.

"Mona" has been done by a variety of singers, but no one has improved on Bo Diddley's original—except possibly Bruce Springsteen, in his epic on-stage performance, and then he has to incorporate both "Not Fade Away" and "Gloria," plus his own "She's the One," to pull it off. This is Bo's beat at its heaviest, and also a superb pre-coital fantasy. (In my experience, Mona is one of of those names, like Aloysius, that nobody has much anymore and if someone does, you're better off to avoid them, but Bo has no such scruples.)

Sam Cooke's "Shake" was a great dance record, but Otis Redding's interpretation of it—particularly on *Otis Redding Live in Europe*, which is what I have in mind here—is more outright in its carnality. All those "got-ta, got-ta" grunts and shrieks need no explanation, except for the incredibly naive. Whether Redding refers to a consummated passion, or a solitary one, is hardly the issue; in context, this is perfect.

Similarly, "A Hard Day's Night" is probably exactly what it seems to be. But in their appropriation of Little Richard's groove, the Beatles do not neglect the difficulties the working-class male has in finding time for sexual fulfillment. You know, by now, what the only alternative can be. This song seems jolly—and when you think about it, maybe it is—but there's also an untapped reservoir of anger and frustration implicit in the music, which undercuts the cohabitive import of the lyrics.

The climactic item, however, is the Rolling Stones' "Goin' Home," the longest tribute to his own sexual prowess that Mick Jagger has ever written. Wanking is not always a matter of frustration or alienation, of course. For Jagger and the Stones, it is—like everything else—an expression of narcissism. In the trippy days of the sixties, this song may have been taken as a metaphor for fucking—"Goin' home" as the return to the womb, and all that—but this singer is far too confident of success for that. There is an utter absence of humility in "Goin' Home," and the manner in which the harp and drums continuously build while Keith Richard's guitar strokes to a furious conclusion is telling. Fourteen years of observation of the Stones at work have not convinced me, at any rate, that Mike Jagger finds anyone but himself truly exciting, in a sexual sense. Whether this is a result of Jagger's delusion or his honesty is open to question, in certain circles, but there is no question that it's true: Mick Jagger is the world's greatest exponent of self-love.

There are other Jagger songs that tell the same tale with equal effectiveness, and more concisely—for one, "Rocks Off," in which Jagger confesses that he only gets his rocks off when he's dreaming. (Dreaming of who? Well, who is the one person who's always in one's dreams?)

But for all its over-inflated self-importance, "Goin' Home" is the only song in the history of rock and roll that could end this album. Stranded on a desert island, going home is all you have to look forward to, and there's nothing you can do about it but lie back and enjoy yourse f.

DEDICATED TO YOU

THE "5" ROYALES (KING 580)
1958

ED WARD

As I remember Winston-Salem, North Carolina, in the summer of 1962, it was hot, and the air was thick, not only with humidity, but with a smell that I remember pervading the South, and can no longer describe. I was on vacation with my parents and sister, and we'd just come from Kitty Hawk, a place that was completely empty, like I imagined Cape Cod must have been before it was discovered. Winston-Salem, though, was a city I'd never heard of that was as packed and congested as New York at its worst. The heat seemed to be pressing the people down toward the sidewalk, and we were stuck in traffic.

I'm not sure why it surprised me that everybody was black. I was a fervent (verbal) supporter of civil rights and read the *Times* every morning in study hall to see how things were going down South. I knew—certainly I knew this far into the trip—that blacks and whites were kept separate as much as possible. But there was something different about the black faces I saw that set them apart from the faces of the people I worked with at the church-sponsored reading program in Harlem. Maybe it was the heat, maybe not.

Our destination, as we sat in traffic, was just outside of town, the factory that dominates Winston-Salem: R. J. Reynolds, maker of Winston, Salem, Camel, and the rest. Although signs through-out the state advertised CIGARETS 25¢, I noted that none of the black people in the lunchtime throng were smoking. Nor was any-body at the factory, a huge, one-story industrial park-style build-ing. It was air-conditioned inside, with slippery varnished wooden floors. A guide showed us around, and I remember the rolls of filter, the long sheets of cigarette paper, and the packages folded and filled in seconds. I was a real factory-tour buff at the time, and this was one of the best I'd had.

In mid-tour, however, the Cokes I'd been drinking to fend off the heat took hold in the air-conditioning. The guide pointed to his left, and I walked toward the bathrooms. And that's why Winston-Salem has stayed in my memory so long: in 1962, in a building that reeked of the upward mobility of the "New South," I stood in front of two doors marked MEN and $\frac{\text{MEN}}{\text{COLORED}}$, and felt a pain in my stomach. I knew I had a choice to make, and I sus-pected that whichever choice I did make would be the wrong one. If I went into MEN, I would be betraying my principles, but what if I went into $\frac{\text{MEN}}{\text{COLORED}}$ and the guide or some other RJR employee saw me? Or if, through some chance, a black man took offense at my presence on his turf? My parents' oft-repeated adjuration "Don't rock the boat" rang in my bladder, and I clenched my jaw, knowing that some day I'd pay this debt. (In fact, I did sooner than I expected: on my way out, I took a long drink from the colored water-fountain. Nobody noticed, either.)

The tour finished, I refused a free pack of cigarettes in favor of a Winston pen. We got back in the Buick, and we drove away.

That same day, almost a thousand miles away in Memphis, Tennessee, a middle-aged black man was straddling a chair, his arms folded on top of its back, his chin gingerly resting on his arms. He'd drawn the curtains in the motel room he sat in, a habit he'd acquired over a decade ago so he wouldn't have to look at the drabness of the rooms he rented. On the bed, illuminated by a streak of light that escaped between the drawn curtains, sat his cousin, a year or two younger than him, and next to him, a Bible.

It was open, and there was enough light in the room that the man could see the blocks of red print alternating with the black.

No words were passing between them, although the man on the bed looked worried, and there was just the slightest suggestion that he was about to cry. They had been staring at each other like this for fifteen minutes, neither one uttering a sound. The man on the bed lowered his eyes, then looked up again. The man on the chair sat up slowly, unfolded his arms, and placed his hands on his thighs. He sighed. "Okay Clance," he said, "I'll go phone Willie, and when the boys get back, tell 'em to stick around—we got a meetin'." The man on the bed bit his lip and lowered his eyes. All he could do was nod. His cousin stood up and put the chair back under the dressing-table, eyes on his shoes. As he touched the doorknob, he heard the man on the bed speak in a raspy voice. "Pete, I'm sorry. You know I'm sorry, but it's . . ." Pete turned his head. "Yeah man, I know."

God's will, Pete thought, as he stepped out into the summer afternoon, God's will that after fifteen years it ended like this, with him shuffling across the parking lot of a colored motel in Memphis, not too anxious to reach the pay phone located outside the motel office, but this is the way it should have been, and he had to do what had to be done. Funny, that's one thing he and Clarence and the other guys had always had, and it's probably the thing that kept them together as solid as they'd always been. He'd even written a song about it, and he could hear Clarence singing it as he had so many times:

> *I'd rather hear it coming from you, yourself*
> *Than to hear it from someone else*
> *And if there's anything you want to tell me*
> *Why don't you SAY IT!*

His hand clutched a guitar-neck that wasn't there. Boy, he thought to himself, could I rip off a lick on that motherfucker now! I *need* to rip one off. But first I gotta call Willie.

"Home of the Blues," purred the phone. "Uh, Willie Mitchell, please." "Mr. Mitchell's in the studio—may I say who's calling?"

"Pete Pauling." "Oh, hi, Pete—hold on, please," and she put him on hold. Say it, his mind kept singing, even if it hurts me. The fingers on his left hand moved, but no strings resisted. I could sure play that boy now, he thought, I surely could. Well, count your blessings, Pete. You ain't out in the cold, and you ain't gonna be, thanks to your friends. Willie's gonna be sad that it ended, but it won't be like the end of the world for him, either. Those last records didn't hardly make a dent, and maybe Willie was right about the way things been changing. Groups ain't getting it any more, Willie kept telling him, at least not the kinda stripped-down group you got. Oh, sure, now and again a group like the Sensations would get a hit with something like "Let Me In," which, it's true, was just like their old stuff, almost, but the rest of it was all twist shit and those big production numbers. Teenagers didn't care about how good you could sing—hell, they didn't care about nothin', from the sound of it.

"Pete! My man!" He snapped back to awareness. "What's the good word, Pete?" Say it, Pete. "Willie, I, uh, been talkin' to Clance . . ." "Oh, he finally told you, huh? Yeah, man, he called me last night, and I told him that you own the name and all that, and if you wanna dissolve it legally, you gonna have to, uh . . ." "Well, I think we gonna do it." "Pete," Willie said after an awkward pause, "like I keep tellin' you, you're worth just as much, if not more, as a songwriter. You still havin' hits with your songs, and the "5" Royales ain't had a hit in four years! Tell you what, come in tomorrow and we'll talk about it, okay?" "Naw, Willie, not right away. I gotta think about some shit, so I think me and Clance and any of the other boys that wants to gonna drive back to Winston-Salem. I ain't seen mama in a while, and I . . . I dunno. I call you in a couple weeks, okay?" "Sure, Pete," Willie said, worried. "Anything I can do, call me collect." "Yeah. Yeah." Pete hung up the phone. Well, that was that.

He stood outside the phone booth looking off across the road, not really seeing anything, just breathing as if he had to marshal his strength to make that long walk across the parking lot again. He might have stood there forever if he hadn't heard a white disc-jockey's voice quacking out of a car radio. "That's Neil Sedaka with

our number one song, 'Breaking Up Is Hard To Do.' " Pete snapped
his head up and snorted. No shit, he said, chuckling, as he walked
back to his room, no shit.

In 1962, it really had been over fifteen years since Lowman "Pete"
Pauling had begun his varied and successful show-business career.
As it almost always did, it started in church, with three of his
cousins and a friend of theirs forming a gospel quintet. Since the
interior of North Carolina is divided between agricultural space
and textile factories, there must have been hundreds of tiny
churches and tent revivals to which the group could have traveled,
opening for bigger acts or providing the musical interlude for a well-
known evangelist with whom they had connections. The Royal Sons,
they named the group, and their show-stopper, the song that
walked 'em, made folks have church, was an adaptation of an old
hymn by Thomas A. Dorsey that the Norfolk Jubilee Quartet used
to do, all about sitting at the bedside of a neighbor who was about
to cross the swelling tide. Lowman would hold the long bass notes
while he played nervous, angular lines on his guitar, and his cousin
Clarence would ask the neighbor to tell Jesus he was coming over,
too, and the ladies would rocket off the pews, hands in air, eyes
squeezed shut, a sinuous motion snapping their bodies upward from
the base of the spine, shrieking words that were and weren't words
until the ushers or their neighbors laid on the hands, sometimes
catching the spirit themselves. When the song ended, there would
be a dampness in the air, a funky smell sometimes, and the arpeggio
Lowman plucked for the song's end would be answered with a few
"Yas Lawd"'s and the ubiquitous rising inflection of a "Waaal?" The
church would be silent but for some sniffling after that, and it would
be up to the organist or piano player to break the mood so the
preacher could speak.

Lowman learned how he could use pieces of chords played on
his guitar to fill in the tiny holes in the vocal parts, and he listened
closely to the big-time groups they played with, picking up some of
their vocal tricks and taking them back to the Sons' rehearsals.
One night they caught the ear of someone from Apollo Records—
maybe Bess Berman herself—and were told that if they could make

it up to New York, they had a contract. If? Apollo in 1948 was the biggest gospel label in America, riding high on the virtually impossible success of Mahalia Jackson's "Move On Up a Little Higher," a song that had sold well over a million copies and was still selling. If? The Royal Sons would make it to New York if they had to walk until their feet were bloody stumps to cut a record for Apollo. And which song to cut? "Bedside of a Neighbor," with "Journey's End" on the flip.

But the Royal Sons who cut Apollo 253 (that was the record's number) were already changing. Two original members, William Sanders and Anthony Price, had stayed behind in Winston-Salem, and the Tanner Brothers, Eugene and John, replaced them. New York turned their heads right away. They got more worldly, more cynical. Like all the greenhorns before them, they courted respect with a vengeance, and probably worked harder at it because they had touched down in *the* hippest place in the world, Harlem. The women who walked those streets bore no resemblance to the heavy-hipped countrified girls who had sought them out after tent shows down home, and a lot of the men weren't even mildly deferential to white people.

Another thing people didn't do there was buy old-timey gospel records like the Royal Sons made. On gospel shows, they were stuck toward the bottom of the line-up, and any gospel observer will tell you that nobody ever shows up for the early innings of such shows except very old ladies (and, nowadays, white people). Hip young people never went to gospel shows. Hell, half of 'em never went to church.

So the Sons were stuck cutting records that didn't sell, with a contract to fulfill for Apollo. The decision they made was probably not a tortured one. Most likely they really wanted to go where the action was, where the chicks hung out. In the early 1950s, that meant they should cut blues. Not blues in the country sense, not even blues in the Wynonie Harris/Roy Brown/Big Joe Turner sense, but the kind of music that was getting known as "rhythm and blues." The group sound was catching on in New York, with such pioneer vocal groups as the Ravens and the Five Keys scoring hits as early as 1946.

Clarence was probably the last holdout, but he surely saw the advantages for himself. He was the front-man, the one the spotlight focused on, especially during the ballads. He relented, and in mid-1952, the Royal Sons met with Bess Berman and told her that they'd decided to become a blues group called the "5" Royales. Lowman had gone to work writing songs (and rewriting gospel songs) and came up with some pretty wild stuff, including a number about laundromats, those new places people took their clothes and had an attendant do them in a machine, called "Laundromat Blues," where he praised his laundromat baby, who put him in a spin. The first couple of sessions were cut with tenor-man Charlie "Little Jazz" Ferguson, late in 1952. They didn't go exactly as Lowman had hoped. He thought that Jazz spent too much time honking his horn, and he was mad that he was hardly allowed to play any guitar.

When Bess Herman heard "Baby, Don't Do It," she knew she had a hit, and even though it was Thanksgiving week, she released it. Sales went nuts all over the country, and the hit carried through the Christmas season and on into the next year. Lowman never did find out how many copies it sold, but it was over a million. The "5" Royales were always busy doing stage shows including—sweet revenge—the Apollo, where they'd languished at the bottom of so many Sunday afternoon gospel bills. In the spring, they went back into the studio to cut some more with Jazz, and the first release out of this was a plaintive ballad, "Help Me Somebody," with Clarence wailing his heart out so strong that you just had to remember the church.* It was too intense, and they followed it right away with "Crazy, Crazy, Crazy," a song that was silly, silly, silly, but was a lot of fun to do on stage.

That was another thing they were learning. In a gospel show, you had to wait till the audience got the Spirit before you could cut up your own self, but with blues it was different—you *started* by cutting up. And could the "5" Royales cut up! Hank Ballard, whose Midnighters were second to none in lasciviousness, the first vocal group to have their records consistently banned, always freely admitted that his group stole moves wholesale from the Royales

---

* Nine years later, this was the last song they cut with Willie Mitchell.

and still couldn't come close to them at their most outrageous. Attired in powder-blue, pink, or white jackets, white shirts, black bowties and dark pants, they'd go nuts—leaping into each other's arms, humping the mike stands, Lowman playing the guitar with his tongue, Clarence doing somersaults, skinny Johnny Tanner doing splits. But they were always in tune, always right on it on time. Audiences ate it up, and pastors in some of the towns they played denounced them with uncommon fury.

Finally, Apollo awarded them an unusual honor: an album entitled *Rockin' with the "5" Royales*, Apollo's first non-sacred long-player. The artwork was terrible (five rocking chairs), but the music was right there. Unfortunately, not long after its release, Apollo began to run out of steam, something it kept doing for the next ten years. An independent label, it was seldom able to keep up with the rest of the market. Sure, it had Mahalia, but gospel sells slow and steady, and doesn't give the quick, high-volume spurts you need to build the cash-flow. Without the cash-flow, your promotion department begins to fall apart, and without it, you don't get airplay.

Thus, after a show in Cincinnati one night, the Royales were approached by a very slick-talking black man who said he worked for King Records. He'd been watching them for some time, he said, and thought that Mr. Nathan could offer them a better deal than they were getting at Apollo. Lowman muttered that in his opinion that wouldn't be too hard to do. Furthermore, the man said, King had ties with some really superior booking agencies, and could get them on tours that didn't dissolve at midpoint, leaving you stranded in Keokuk with no way to get back home. He knew they'd seen a couple of those (and he suspected that Lowman suspected they were doing another one), and before long Lowman was shaking his hand, agreeing to come in and talk to Nathan Monday morning.

Syd Nathan was certainly one of American pop music's more unlikely heroes. Very nearly blind, with a temper that seemed to have no upper limit, he was an ordinary guy doing one of the few things (dry goods, importing) that Jews were allowed to do in German-and-Wasp-dominated Cincinnati, and doing okay but not great. At the age of fifty, his blood pressure had risen so high that his doctor urged him to retire or get into a business that wouldn't irritate him so much. For reasons known only to himself, he chose to start a record company, and began recording the hillbilly artists who broadcast on WCKY, in Covington, Kentucky, across the river. As the King roster grew, Nathan began signing blues artists like Wynonie "Mr. Blues" Harris, Roy Brown, and the Dominoes, and, since he owned a good chunk of the publishing, he began urging country songs on blues artists and vice versa, resulting in some doomed hybrids (the bluegrass Stanley Brothers' version of Hank Ballard's "Finger Poppin' Time" comes to mind) as well as some brilliant ones (Moon Mullican's Western bop rendition of Bull Moose Jackson's "Cherokee Boogie," and Freddie King's inspired reworking of a steel guitar classic, "Remington Ride"). Racial barriers never meant a whole lot to Syd Nathan, and whites and blacks played on the same sessions, country and rhythm and blues.

Located in a red brick factory building on tree-lined Brewster Avenue, on the fringes of a multi-racial (but heavily black) ghetto, King was just the place for the Royales. It was big enough to have clout, and small enough that the artists all seemed like a family. House songwriters would pitch your songs right along with theirs to people on and off the label, and they seemed to have a real good ear for what an artist could do with a song. The recording studio was state-of-the-art, with big, expensive RCA microphones, a mixing board, and, later, even a four-track recorder. The engineers seemed to know what they were doing, and the recordings came out much clearer than the ones the "5" Royales had made for Apollo.

Of course, there were disadvantages, too. For one thing, with so many artists in a field to promote, sometimes the promotion men didn't do such a good job, losing your record in the pile they were delivering to the stations. Second, Nathan had a terrible habit of type-casting you, and, having decided the Royales were clowns, had them cut a slew of novelty tunes. (They weren't alone, as Lowman found out while waiting to see Nathan one day. He began talking to a hillbilly singer named Jimmy Osborne, who'd had a huge hit with "The Lonesome Death of Little Kathy Fiscus," based on a newspaper story. His A&R man had stuck him with tragedy after tragedy, and Osborne was watching his career shrivel. "Ain't my fault the public gets tired of dead kids," he'd bitched at Lowman, who nodded sagely.) Some of these songs were delightful, like "School Girl," the tale of an insatiable female minor with a nice, explicit chorus:

> (Would she?) You think she wouldn't?
> (Could she?) Aw, you think she couldn't?
> (Will she?) You think she won't?
> (Do she?) You think she don't?
> (Oh!) Oh! (Oh!) Oh, but she did.

(There are people around today who would kill for a film of the routine the Royales performed when they did this tune.) But most of the novelties, like "Monkey Hips and Rice," "Right Around the Corner," and "Mohawk Squaw" were pretty ordinary.

Lowman knew they could do better. He knew the public knew, too, because they hadn't had a hit since "Too Much Lovin'" dented the bottom of the R&B charts in September, 1953, when they were still on Apollo. He knew that the sincerity of "Help Me Somebody" was a strong point they hadn't exploited, and that Clarence could get the girls swooning when he sang something like "When You Walked Through The Door" or "Tears of Joy." Lowman also wrote a different kind of love song, one that dealt with real things men felt that the ooh-baby-be-mine sort of song didn't come close to, like the fact that men could be weak, or that you gotta let your girl get hers, too. This last idea had become a song called "Get Something Out of It," and boy, it was such a weird song that if the guys hadn't sung their asses off on it, Syd'd never have let it out, even as a B-side.

In the four years since their last hit, the group had toured with dozens of package shows, working their way down the bill as time passed. First Johnny Tanner's brother Eugene had quit in disgust, and then Windsor King, who'd been a Royal Son with Lowman and Clarence, split. There wasn't much money to pay them off, and there wasn't much to offer a new guy in the way of fame and fortune. But there were always those to whom the lure of the bright lights was irresistible, and Lowman's spirits raised considerably when he auditioned Obediah Carter, who was as extroverted and ebullient on stage as Johnny Tanner, and handled the tenor parts right up into a show-stopping falsetto, even higher than Windsor had gone. Eugene they replaced with Johnny Moore, a sober, quiet guy who kept tabs on the guys' drinking and served as the group's money-man after Lowman discovered that he had a phenomenal memory for details. From the wildest to the mildest, Lowman would think sometimes, watching them sleep on the converted schoolbus that hauled the colored groups from show to show.

Finally, one hot summer afternoon in the King studio, Lowman decided that the time had come to make the big change. He started them off with a novelty, just so Syd could say that the session hadn't been a total waste, but then he pulled out one of his most soulful ballads yet, "Tears of Joy," which featured an unbelievable, complicated acappella opening and one of Clarence's best vocals ever. Lowman insisted on using his guitar on this session, and he warned the sax player to keep his distance, a warning Obediah underlined by patting his back pocket. Then Lowman started clapping—one, clap, three, clap/one, clap, three, clap—and as soon as they had it, he threw in a chant—Think!, clap, Think!, clap—and then he started snaking around with his guitar. An hour later, it was done. It was easily the best thing they'd ever waxed, and Lowman had been so ecstatic by the second take that he'd woken up the sax player to take eight in the middle. They knocked off one more ballad for good luck, called it a day, and went off to a joint in Kentucky to celebrate.

"Think" was released five years to the day after "Baby, Don't Do It," and it duplicated the earlier record's odd staying power. They even got a very ritzy supper-club New Year's Eve gig out of it, but more important, they were back on top of the bill wherever they played. Lowman, more confident now, was getting further out there with his guitar, because he had accidentally bought a Gibson Les Paul Signature. It was impossible to play pear-shaped Charlie Christian lines on such a wild axe, impossible to play those gospel-style arpeggios, either, unless you were turned way down. Turned up, it screamed, the "too hot" pickups overloaded, and when you played block chords, the effect was positively orchestral. Lowman had bought it for its solid body (important when you threw it around the way he did on stage) and its creamy white color, but the more he fooled with it, the more crazy ideas he got. They tried them out in rehearsal, and one song in particular, "Say It," became a showcase for freakish guitar sounds. Lowman worked up a routine where he'd beg, get down on his knees, with the guitar standing straight up between them as he squeezed out the licks, finishing by turning it all the way up and putting it behind his head so that the strings faced the amplifier and it squealed with feedback. It worked.

There was another song, too, that he wanted to do, but it was important to him, and it was giving him trouble. Lowman had married a fine lady in Winston-Salem a couple of years back, a nurse with a degree from Tuskegee that had gotten her a good job at Winston-Salem's colored hospital. She was incredibly understanding, insisting that the boys eat and sleep when they'd pull in at 4 a.m. after an all-night drive from the last stop on a tour, drunk, babbling, high on tea and bennies, glad to be home. Her very presence would invest civilization even in Obediah, who would slow way down and start calling her ma'am. She was an especially good influence on Lowman, who loved her so much that sometimes he'd imagine she was leaving him and he'd write songs that pleaded, begged, and boasted. Or he'd imagine he'd just met her and write one of his worshipful love ballads.

But what he wanted to do with *this* song was to talk about her as she really was, not as some fantasy figure; how she was so good to him, stuck by him, and put up with his weird life. He had a tune, they had harmonies, but all Clarence did was sing nonsense syllables and the few verses Lowman had come up with. In desperation, he turned to Ralph Bass, a King staff songwriter, and together they commandeered a rehearsal room and sang and played the song over and over until the song fell together and all the words fit. The lyrics still weren't the best Lowman or Bass had ever written, but Lowman was proud of the entire first verse, and the melody, coupled with a guitar line that didn't quite fit, made you want to hear the song again and again.

On the day of the session, Lowman showed up with another

guitar player, and the Royales were certain he'd lost his mind until the other guitarist took his instrument out of its case. Johnny Tanner took one look at it, did a comic double-take, and said "Whaaaat is that?" "That," said Lowman, "is a Fender Precision electric bass guitar." "Oh, no, Pete," said Clarence, "you ain't gonna fuck up a session that's this important with some damn fool idea of yours." But they struck up the new tune at Lowman's insistence, and the new guy played quietly and subtly, except in one or two places where his support buoyed the song up unexpectedly and, they all had to admit, made it sound better.

"You clowns are ready, we can cut some phonograph records," the recording engineer said through the intercom. The group was eager to do the new song the new way, so after the usual mike balancing to make sure the instruments didn't overwhelm the vocals, Clarence stepped up to his microphone and half-sung, half-spoke the words that would make him immortal:

> *This is dedicated*
> *To the one I-I*
> *Love.*

Lowman burned on the guitar, the bass man did his part, and Clarence and the Royales sang with all the churchy fervor they could come up with. They did three takes, but that was just for safety's sake. Even the engineer caught the spirit, and remarked "Gittin' hot, gittin' *hot!*" after they listened to the playback. Next, they decided to do a gospel tune Lowman had rewritten as "Don't Be Ashamed to Call My Name," which had some pretty haphazard lyrics (the second verse is a nursery rhyme, for instance), but which allowed Lowman and the bass player to get a real nice chunga-chunga-chunga bop-BOP! riff going in between the lines. Lowman's guitar playing on this number got pretty extreme, so that when he announced "Say It" as the next tune, Johnny Moore looked at Johnny Tanner and rolled his eyes heavenward, but they shrugged and went into it. About half-way into the first take, the engineer interrupted to tell Lowman that his guitar was distorting, so he should turn it down. "I want it that way," he snapped, but the guy was insistent, so Lowman made a show of turning the amp down, turning the guitar up with his pinkie so the engineer couldn't see, and of course this made it distort just as much as before. After four aborted takes, Lowman and the engineer, a skinny white kid just out of the Signal Corps, were almost at blows, so Johnny Moore went into the control room and talked to him. "Do it any damn way you please," the intercom finally barked, "just do it. Take five."

Take five went without a hitch, and Lowman miraculously kept his final solo under enough control so that while the guitar roared, it didn't go into the squealing or buzzing it sometimes did, although the amp made a frying noise that showed up on the tape. Lowman listened to the playback with his eyes closed, and when it was over, the engineer asked him if he wanted to do another take. Lowman toyed with him for a minute just to worry him, and then he declined in favor of going back in and knocking off a novelty.

He did, however, insist that "Say It" be released as a single before "Dedicated to the One I Love." He thought it was a bigger hit (he was also the sole writer), and was the direction he wanted the Royales to go in, but the public disagreed. Some radio stations wouldn't play it because it sounded too much like a blues tune, although not enough like one to put it on the late-night blues hour, and others rejected it just because it was too weird. The folks at King didn't sweat promoting it, because they knew there was a stone hit in the can, and in April, 1958, they released it.

Over the years, Lowman Pauling probably made more money off of his half of "Dedicated to the One I Love" than he made off of all his other songs combined. The "5" Royales took it to the top in 1958, the Shirelles did likewise—but on the pop charts, too!—in 1961, and the Mamas and Papas did it yet again in 1967. Somewhere along the way, a third name appeared on the credits and quickly vanished, because Ralph Bass was nobody to steal a song from—he knew that game backwards.

Right after the "Dedicated" session, the "5" Royales posed for a group photo in color, because King had decided to release an album. In the picture, the Royales, dressed in pink tuxedo jackets, white shirts, and baggy blue trousers, stand by the acoustic tile of the studio wall. Lowman is in the center, his Les Paul tucked into his right armpit, and he is hunched down slightly, smiling into the camera. To his right stand Obediah Carter and Johnny Tanner, leaning way back with their arms spread out, and on his left Clarence and Johnny Moore mirror them, although they aren't leaning back quite as much, and they're very slightly out of focus, Clarence staring a bit above the camera. They all look pleased.

They should—an album, even that late in the game, was a very special tribute for a group that didn't "cross over" to the white charts, the way Frankie Lymon and the Teenagers or the Del-Vikings did. King only released albums on their biggest-selling acts, like Little Willie John, Hank Ballard and the Midnighters, Earl Bostic, and Bill Doggett. Of course, albums didn't make up much of the record market in 1958, with the focus being on singles and EPs, but *Dedicated to You* sold pretty well, probably because it had two "million-sellers" on it.*

The "5" Royales were now stars at King; 24" x 36" posters of them were sent to sepia record stores, and they were accorded respect by deejays, record executives and, aspiring stars alike. One youngster who seemed to worship them was a small, wiry kid from Georgia, an ex-boxer whose group, the Famous Flames, was patterned after the "5" Royales in many ways. Their guitarist, Cleveland Lowe, played in a style similar to Lowman's but without his inventiveness, and when the vocalists, John Terry, Sylvester Keels, and Bobby Byrd harmonized, the sound was very much like the Royales. The kid's name was James Brown, and Lowman had never seen such a little bundle of confidence, just as he'd never had anyone follow him around the way this kid did. Lowman didn't always care for the kid's music—"Please Please Please" was plenty emotional, for instance, but where was the story, where was something for the listener to identify with?—yet he had a sense that he might be on to something. "I'm gonna record some of your stuff someday, Pete," James often said, and Lowman would say, "Just don't scream the words, boy," and they'd crack up.

"Cross country tours are nothing new to the "5" Royales, and

---

* There was no regulatory body to verify claims of million-sellerdom in those days, but in this case it seems entirely likely that it is true.

with each stop they set records for attendance," said the liner notes on *Dedicated to You*, and for once a set of King notes told the truth. One memorable tour combined them with James Brown, Hank Ballard and the Midnighters, Little Willie John, Otis Williams and the Charms, and Bill Doggett, whose band provided support for the vocalists. It was a King All-Stars tour, and the Royales alternated top billing with James Brown, depending on which act was bigger in the town they were playing. Meanwhile, King, impressed with the sales of *Dedicated*, and eager to cash in on the success the group was having on the road, threw together another album, *The "5" Royales Sing For You*, an indifferent mixture of old and new stuff that infuriated Lowman, because he knew there was much better stuff they could have released. It didn't even have a hit on it, so it sold less than 10,000 copies, and is nearly impossible to find nowadays. Also, the hysteria surrounding a package tour like they were on made it impractical to sell albums from the stage or in the lobby like you could do at a gospel show, so they couldn't even get rid of them that way.

When the tour deposited them back in Cincinnati in July, 1959, the group cut a couple more sessions, and Lowman felt sure he had a hit in one or two of the songs. Either the heart-stopping ballad "Miracle of Love," with Clarence singing stronger than ever before, or "My Sugar Sugar," which really rocked, would take off. He also spoke to Syd Nathan about the album fiasco, and together with the head of the rhythm-and-blues artists-and-repertoire department he programmed King 678, *The "5" Royales*, so that it featured some of their very best songs ("School Girl," "When You Walked Through the Door," "Get Something Out of It," "Wonder Where Love Has Gone"), as well as the ones they had just cut. King put it out as soon as "Miracle of Love" began to take off, and the Royales went back on the road.

What they didn't know was that "Miracle" took off, but it didn't stay launched very long. King scrambled among the tapes and released "Tell Me You Care," a pretty indifferent ballad with the Royales singing out of tune, backed with "Wonder Where Love Has Gone," a better song, on the B-side. When it flopped—which was quickly—they put out "My Sugar, Sugar," and things began looking better right away. It wasn't a hit, exactly, but it wasn't really a dud, either. And in those days, it took a bit longer to find these things out, since the rhythm and blues record business hardly made enough money to warrant demographic or market research. Even so, a pattern was emerging.

One night, as they were leaving the backstage of a show, a teenager had called Obediah "an old Caldoniafied nigger," and the rest of the guys had to hold him back to keep him from outright throttling the kid. Back on the bus, they shunned the usual card game and huddled together to talk. "Kid's got a point, you know," said Johnny Moore. "We ain't gettin' any younger, and we ain't even havin' that many hits these days. They don't put the right records out, and they don't promote 'em right, and sometimes they do okay, you know, but lately they ain't even been doin' that well. Pete, you told me you couldn't even get Nathan on the phone that time you needed dough to get Obediah out of jail in Lake Charles. I betcha they drop us real soon. We better be lookin' out for somethin' else to do." "Go back to the church," mumbled Clarence. Lowman looked at him hard, and then grinned. "Sheeeit, walkin' old ladies, is that your style, homeboy? Cuz if it is, you can go, but me, I can just think back to a couple hours ago, and I can see those people yellin' and screamin' just like they always have. So what if some young punk don't like us? There's always somebody don't like you. They don't like you because you ain't the Dixie Hummingbirds or they don't like you because you ain't the symphony orchestra or they don't like you because you ain't Nat King Cole. But I know, even if y'all don't, that we ain't seen this thing to the end yet, that we got some more years yet before we can call it a day, and if you don't want to do it no more, go on ahead and go, and I'll hire me some niggers that do want to do it." There was a silence in the bus after this outburst, and even the card game lowered its collective voice. Nobody knew what to say. After all, Lowman was right, the crowd did dig it, but about the rest of it . . .

In June, 1960, they found out. Their contract came up for renewal, and King passed on its option. Their last two singles, "I'm With You" and "Why," had been dead on arrival. Syd Nathan apologized, and kept repeating that he was a businessman, and if it were a purely personal decision they'd be welcome to stay forever, but he didn't look Lowman in the face when he shook his hand and wished him well. And then—irony supreme—the "5" Royales were without a record label in the same month that the very label that had dropped them released one of Lowman's songs done by that skinny kid who'd kept saying he'd do it, and they sat by and watched James Brown rocket to the top of the charts with his eccentric version of "Think." James had become quite a star since '56, and yet he always remembered the people who'd helped him out. He had been irate when he'd learned about the Royales being dropped, but he didn't feel he was secure enough in his position at King yet to make waves. He did his best to see that the group kept working the road, and he assured Lowman that he'd do something for them as soon as he could. Lowman thanked him, but wondered just how much James could do, now or ever.

Even without a label, things weren't too bad for the "5" Royales. Unlike the rock and roll audience, the rhythm and blues audience is very devoted. Once you've shown your stuff, you can be assured of people coming to see you for quite a while. They'll keep you going through dry periods of up to ten years, so long as you'll sing your hits, do your act, and try not to act too bored when you do. They'll fill a club over and over, and there will be enough of them so you'll get asked back next time you're in the vicinity, just so long as that isn't too soon. The Dells have been living this way since 1955, the O'Jays and the Manhattans almost as long. If by 1960 the sort of music the "5" Royales did best was on its way out, at least among youngsters, there was still a market for their talents as live performers on the much-maligned chitlin' circuit.

It was after one of these gigs that they met young Willie Mitchell, who led the house band and did some producing at Home of the Blues, a small Memphis label with leasing deals at several larger labels. He'd become a "5" Royales fan after he'd bought a copy of their last album in a drugstore, and, with the Shirelles heating up the charts with their version of "Dedicated," he felt the Royales deserved another chance. (Syd Nathan, never one to pass up a buck, re-released the Royales' version). They cut several songs

for Mitchell, and he put them out. They sounded tired, even though
Clarence's vocal on the new version of "Help Me Somebody"
completely eclipses the one they hit with on Apollo. But Mitchell
had an idea, one he was sure would give the "5" Royales a new
start. He called Lowman in Winston-Salem, and three days later,
they were checked in to the Blue Bird Motel, Memphis's finest
colored motel. It was summer, and it was hot.

As Lowman crossed the parking lot, the sounds of traffic receded,
and the clanking of the motel's air conditioner got louder. He saw
that the station-wagon was back, which meant that Johnny,
Obediah, and Johnny were back. Was this gonna be hard? He
realized that he didn't know, himself. Maybe the right question
was how hard is this gonna be? He didn't want to go in the door.
He didn't want to have to look into their faces, didn't want to have
to answer their questions, didn't want to have to pay them off and
then turn his back and walk away on all of it.

And it was just then that a feeling, both warm and cool, swept
over him. It seemed to start simultaneously at the bottom of his
belly and in his heart, reaching out arms and turning once like the
hands of a clock. As if from a distance, he felt himself exhale, and
the feeling redoubled, hugging him from within. He witnessed the
sound of the blood in his temples without really feeling that he was
in them, and then he exhaled again, and a drop of sweat fell cold
from his hair onto his neck, and he inhaled, and he exhaled, and he
knew he was home again.

Eight eyes looked up when he walked into the room, but nobody
spoke for a long while, and, of course, it was Johnny Moore who
broke the silence merely by saying "Hey, Pete." Lowman suppressed
a strange chuckle and sat down on the dressing table. "Well, y'all,
I guess you know why we're here." "It's cool, man," Obediah said.
"We been seein' it comin', but we knew you had to see it on your
own time, Pete. But it's cool." Well, no shit, he thought, and then
he said it: "Well, no shit," flat like that. They were all smiling by
now, even Clarence, who'd winced at the profanity, and he spoke
next. "Pete, git your axe and let's sing a song, brother." Lowman

grabbed his cousin's glance with his own, and narrowed his eyes to see if there were double-dealing in it, but there wasn't. And he knew which song it would be, a song about parting, of course, but a song of hope, and he unpacked the Les Paul while the tiny Fender Princeton amp warmed up, and suddenly he realized where the feeling he'd had had come from.

He gripped the neck and played the G arpeggio as he'd done so many times, and they started to sing, but much slower than they usually did:

> *I was sitting by the bedside of a neighbor*
> *Who was just about to cross the swelling tide*
> *And I asked him if he would do me a favor*
> *Kindly take a message to the other side.*

Somehow it didn't jump like it used to, but somehow that didn't matter any more because the jump had been replaced by some other quality that meant just as much. The guys were taking chances with the harmony that Lowman had only dreamed about, and yet it stayed in there, and he was playing a guitar obbligato against the verses that seemed to go everywhere at once, but clung to the sound nevertheless. He had never heard Clarence sing like this, and he wasn't sure but what he might not want to hear him sing like this again. They were all singing like, well, not like their *lives* depended on it, somehow, but like something else of equal importance did. And, as Lowman steered the chords around that final plagal cadence, that instrumental a-men, he caught sight of what it was, and something inside of him rejoiced, because he knew that now, even this far down the road, it would never, never leave him, and it never did, never again.

I made all of that up. Not all of it, actually, but most of it. The part about me at R. J. Reynolds is true, but the rest of it only touches down here and there. I didn't really do any research before I wrote it, partially out of laziness, partially because I didn't quite know where to go for some of the information. I did call Winston-

Salem information to see if Lowman Pauling was listed, and found out that there were quite a few Paulings, but no Lowman. The next day, quite by accident, a friend told me that he'd seen his obituary in the January, 1974, issue of *Jet*, and that it hadn't said much. He also told me that James Brown had produced some sessions with a group called the "5" Royales (Bootsy Collins, who played bass with Brown, remembers playing these sessions, and told me that "those songs was some *bad* boys, too"), but King hadn't released anything, and that there exists a record by "Lowman Pauling and the Royalton" on Federal. But I never called Winston-Salem back once I'd ascertained the approximate names of the guys in the group (approximate because my only sources are a maddeningly incomplete reissue record with terrible liner notes and a book on "oldies" that's riddled with inaccuracies), even to see if Clarence's last name was Paul or Pauling. I never called the performing-rights societies (ASCAP or BMI) to see who gets Lowman's royalties, failed to follow up a lead that Ralph Bass is working for TK Productions in Chicago, and didn't seek out James Brown or Hank Ballard for recollections.

I don't feel particularly terrible about this crime against scholarship, especially because the body of songs that Lowman Pauling left behind on his records has already given me more to think about and enjoy than I could ever top, except with a time-machine and a ticket to one of their shows. I enjoy looking at them on the cover of *Dedicated to You*, an album I bought because the guy in the record store told me it was "rare," and wondering who they were, how they felt, what sustained them, and what happened to them. I'd like to read a "real" article about them, with interviews and information about the sessions, and maybe some greying out-of-focus photos from some fan's Brownie camera as illustration, but I'm not the guy who's going to write it.

There's another reason I don't feel bad about the lengthy counterfeit above, and it's a bit more difficult to explain, although it's a corollary to the first reason: I think that the mystery has been completely taken away from rock and roll, that it has been over-explained, over-analyzed, and, in the process, it has become effectively neutered, incapable of shock and joy. I think that for many "rock" artists, the impulse toward fun has been smothered by an increasingly rigidified sense of what is and what isn't acceptable, destroyed by a flock of vultures who won't be sated until the corpse is picked clean, the roll removed from the rock, and every secret, no matter how trivial or irrelevant to the creative act, is laid bare. And when the self-censoring impulse provides the shadow between the impulse and the act, you're dead, Jim, but you just don't know it.

Unfortunately, the audience for current rock and roll has bought right into this process. People expect exegesis as a preamble to pleasure, and accept obfuscation and pretension as necessary components of both art and entertainment. Programmed by an insidious process that started before Woodstock, they have become passive consumers, confusing novelty with innovation, an attitude fostered by "rock critics" who unreasonably demand that an artist never fail, constantly better his work, and provide complete access to his thoughts and actions at all times. Of course, the androids who produce "alternative" FM radio are as much to blame for this as the critics, since they, too, would rather present mediocre new product by an artist than play the old stuff, even if it's less self-conscious, and less "important" than the new. The music that is the end-product of this process is undanceable, for the most part,* has lyrics that are often about nothing at all and show no inspiration from real-world experience, and clearly shows that it was constructed bit by bit in the sterile atmosphere of a very complex recording studio. The roll, the fun, the noise, the craziness, is gone. Yet people still buy it, identify with it, and go see it performed. It's amazing to me that so many people fell for this so quickly, and with so much seeming pleasure, and that it's generated the amazingly lucrative industry that it has. The book you hold in your hands is testament to this, as, I suspect, is the fact of your holding it.

I'm not innocent in this affair, either—far from it. I began writing about rock and roll a dozen years ago because at the time it was the only way a young writer without newspaper experience

---

* The portion of it which aspires to being art music, as opposed to dance music, is (with exceptions) lamentably out-of-touch with the goings-on in real contemporary art music, yet it gets ten times the press.

could break into print. Right along with my peers, I declared "rock" to be the "art of our times," and wrote more than my share of fatuity and fustian. At the time, I guess none of us realized that we were digging our own graves, that the "rock press" would soon become a ghetto from which most of us could not escape. We were told by editors and writers that there are certain things "rock critics" shouldn't even attempt (like serious analysis, or reporting or criticizing anything at all outside the music biz), and we were held in contempt by a journalistic establishment that perceives the rock press as the most ass-licking, weak-spined, corrupt sector of the Fourth Estate, an impression the rock press itself has done almost nothing to rectify or change. It has narrowed its focus so much that it has spawned an entire generation of readers oblivious of its own accomplishments in fiction, art, drama, politics, "serious" music, movies, comics, science, and sports—not to mention the lives and works of past artists, thinkers, and performers whose ideas inspire the present. Talk about a desert island! I cannot bring myself to believe that rational, thinking human beings have voluntarily brought this to pass, but the voices of protest are so muted, and there is so little being done about it that it's an almost inescapable conclusion.

The more time I spend with "rock" (a term I hate as much—or had you guessed?—as I hate being called a "rock critic"), the less it means to me in many ways. There's too much missing from it. I know because I remember the sense of joy I experienced when certain events of my life coalesced around a rock and roll song, or the sense of adventure I felt as an eight-year-old, tuning in Alan Freed or Harlem's WLIB to hear real "teenage" music. It never occurred to me—then or later—that I was part of a community, because I wasn't. I never believed that the words to a rock and roll song could give me any insight into how to live or love, because they couldn't do anything but suggest, no matter what the rock critics say.

Hey, the poets of our time are poets, not rock lyricists; the musicians who will leave a mark are musicians, not rock musicians; the story-tellers of our time are writing fiction and journalism, not rock criticism; the important artists of our time are artists, not rock artists. If their lives or works of art touch rock and roll, well and good, and damn near unavoidable, but please don't confuse cause and effect, form and content, or structure and meaning. There's a big wide world out there—don't you want to know about it? There are people who are a lot more exciting than anyone you've seen on television—don't you want to know what they're doing?

Maybe I'm an idiot, but I am, despite everything, cautiously optimistic about the future of this country's cultural life. I'm just enough of a believer in the human animal to feel that, just as America's eaters have begun rejecting Wonder Bread for the real stuff, there is bound to be a reaction to the insipidity of America's cultural diet. Entertainment is as essential as vitamin C, but it won't work in the absence of serious artistic endeavor and intellectual activity, and I'd like to believe that people are becoming dimly aware of that fact. Of course, I've got a vested interest there, too. I would like to make enough dough writing so that I could stop regarding such things as clothing and medical care as luxuries. At the moment, the things I want to do, the values I hold dear, the goals I want to reach in my life are out of fashion. If—and this is a hard one—I can keep the bitterness that sweeps over me when I see what my peers have made out of this culture from overwhelming me and poisoning my attitudes, if I can stay alive and healthy, mentally and physically, until the pendulum swings back and what I do—hell, what I *am*—becomes socially acceptable again, there is literally no telling what I, and all the other people like me who are wasting their talents on trash and ephemera or hiding out and waiting, might be able to accomplish.

> *Life can never be*
> *Exactly like we want it to be*

Lowman Pauling and Ralph Bass wrote that one afternoon in Cincinnati. I'll buy that, but I'll never give up believing that it can be more like I want it to be than it currently is, and that, with help, I can make it that way for myself and help others do it for themselves. The freedom to let my imagination roam that the very best music—including the very best rock and roll—gives me has become an important element of the help that I need to do it right. That's all I need to know about it, and all you need, too.

TREASURE ISLAND

GREIL MARCUS

My colleagues whose essays you have read were placed in a privileged position: they were obliged to confront destiny only with an eye to their own pleasure, sustenance, or, as the case may be, enlightenment. But someone must put selfishness aside—someone must take responsibility for *the tradition*. The desert island question, after all, has always had its corollary: the Martian question. That is, Were a Martian to land on Earth and ask you the meaning of rock and roll—a likely prospect, given the Chuck Berry record NASA shot into space a while back—what would you play to explain? And this question, forcing the respondent into a position where he or she must represent the human spirit to an alien, has never been nearly so manageable as the desert island conundrum.

You start, perhaps, with "She Loves You." "That," you say with pride, "is rock and roll!" But what if the Martian doesn't catch on? What if he/she/it is a musicologist, and wants to know where "She Loves You" came from, or where it went? Or what if, after spinning "She Loves You," you think of "There Goes My Baby," and find yourself saying, as you inevitably will, "Hey, wait a minute, you gotta listen to this . . ." You and the Martian will be there for a long time.

For these reasons, and because recent research has shown without a doubt that Martians *love* to land on godforsaken places (where do you think all those big heads on Easter Island came from?), my choice of an artifact that could represent all of rock and roll is all of rock and roll. Or my version of it, anyway.

For the long list that follows, I tried to rethink the story of rock and roll, in terms of spirit, not sales (though luckily the two come together more often than one has any right to expect). I tried to think of all the singles and albums that would leave essential gaps in that story were they passed over, and didn't worry about a few historical gaps (such as, What about Hank Ballard or the Mamas and the Papas? Well, what about them? They just don't live up to that spirit, despite what you—or I—might have thought at the time).

When a performer's contribution to the story (not his or her career) could be fairly summed up by a single record, I looked for that record. A lot of artists, particularly rock's founders, arrived with a style and never really changed it; I generally left out the two or ten first-rate LPs a performer made if there was one that genuinely spoke for all of them, going farther only when a definite shift in style or themes demanded it.

The length of annotation from artist to artist, or the number of entries an artist receives, is meaningless as to the performer's "importance." It took me more space to fix the Clovers' place in the story than the Coasters' because the Clovers are more obscure, not because they are more interesting (and in fact my criterion was the record, not the artist; a lot of people have been enormously influential, at least for a time, without ever making a record that deserves inclusion—one need only think of Iron Butterfly, or Bill Haley). Most singles aren't annotated because space prohibited it and because singles stand on their own, so many of them glorious one-shots from performers with only one thing to say, or worth hearing.

Though I relied on a lot of greatest hits packages, I included only a few anthologies by various artists, and then only when they collected music unreleased in any other form, or when, as anthologies, they made a statement as coherent as a good one-shot single. Most of the records cited are original releases, and many (and many of the reissues, too) are out of print. Almost all of the singles were hits, and are easily available on oldies collections, and many of the albums have been reissued in one form or another. I've omitted information on such collections and reissues simply because they generally remain in print for less time than it takes a book to go through the press. It's a seeker's game, anyway.

On notation: entries are alphabetical by artist; when the artist's name appears in an album title, there is generally no separate noting of the artist's name (i.e., *The Best of the Animals*). Non-U.S. releases have been included only when a record wasn't issued in the U.S., or when it came out in a form inferior to the version I've chosen (the case with many early Beatles and Rolling Stones LPs, which were often jumbled by American labels); when not the U.S., country of origin is indicated after the label is noted (i.e., CBS/UK). When two labels are listed for a single (i.e., Downey/ Dot), the first is the label on which the record was originally released, the second the label that, usually about a month later, picked it up and made it a hit. When there is more than one date after an album entry (i.e., 1950/1960, or 1950–1955/1960), the first date(s) indicates the years the music was originally released, the date following the slash the year the album in question was released. And, when there are two dates, but no third date following a slash (i.e., 1950–1955), it means I wasn't able to determine when the album in question was released, but only when the music on it, usually various singles, first appeared.

The rest of this book, then, is my idea of the best of rock and roll, slightly more than thirty years of it. If this seems like a lot to squirrel away on some lonely island, a treasure held against someone to play it for—just think of how much stuff Robinson Crusoe hauled off that shipwreck of his.

JOHNNY ACE, *Again . . . Johnny Sings* (Duke). The first rock and roll
ghost, this deep-voiced ruler of the blues ballad died in a game of
Russian roulette, and sang as if he saw it all coming. 1952–1955.

FAY ADAMS, "Shake a Hand" (Herald). 1953.

Crossing the Red Sea with the Adverts (Bright/UK). Head-down, into-
the-wind punk from a band with the humor and determination to
make you think their album title wasn't altogether a joke. 1978.

ALLMAN BROTHERS BAND, *Eat a Peach* (Capricorn). The endless
boogie didn't wear out, but it was stopped in its tracks. Following the
violent deaths that broke the band, one noticed the reveries, guitarists' bids for peace of mind: the after-the-rain celebrations of "Blue
Sky," and the ageless, seamless face of "Little Martha," front-porch
music stolen from the utopia of shared southern memory. 1972.

ANGELS, "My Boyfriend's Back" (Smash). 1963.

The Best of the Animals (MGM). When I first heard this group announced on the radio, I laughed out loud at their name—and then,
as "House of the Rising Sun" crawled out of the radio, shut up. This
was trash R&B from Newcastle, England, and especially when the
focus shifted from American blues to savage pleas for release from
working-class slums, more powerful than it had any right to be. 1964–
1965/1966.

ASHTON, GARDNER & DYKE, "Resurrection Shuffle" (Capitol). 1971.

THE BAND, *Music from Big Pink* (Capitol). Frontier sounds from bar-band vets who brought rock back to roots much older than "Slippin' and Slidin' "—though sometimes that too was thrown in. The album was an American mystery (crafted by Canadians, nailed in place by an Arkansas drummer); the clue might have been found off the record, in something like "The Coo Coo," an ancient hillbilly ballad about an omen as predatory as it was beautiful. 1968.

——*The Band* (Capitol). A heartland adventure, with mysteries re-placed by road maps, good booze, and dirty stories. "Up on Cripple Creek" was its center—and in American folklore, Cripple Creek is like the Big Rock Candy Mountain, a place where all fears vanish beyond memory. This record took you there; it also showed you why you had to make the trip. 1969.

——*Rock of Ages* (Capitol). On stage, with Allen Toussaint's horn charts and Marvin Gaye's "Don't Do It"—the sound of a storm warn-ing. With their own "Get Up Jake," the tale of a man who would have slept through it. 1972.

BEACH BOYS, *Best of the Beach Boys, Vol. 2* (Capitol). A concept album about middle-class teenage boys in pursuit of California girls—but only to validate their own honor. 1962–1965/1967.

——"Be True to Your School"/"In My Room" (Capitol). Brian Wilson didn't so much create a California myth as get the details of its pop life right. Irony must have been in there somewhere, but at the time, you could have fooled me. 1963.

——"Fun, Fun, Fun" (Capitol). 1964.

——*Beach Boys' Party* (Capitol). Trash heaven, summed up by "Bar-bara Ann" (lead vocal by Dean of Jan &), a shaggy dog story about doo-wop that after more than ten years feels better than anything on *Pet Sounds*—or *Sgt. Pepper*. 1965.

——"Wouldn't It Be Nice" (Capitol). 1966.

——*Wild Honey* (Capitol). Shaken by Brian's collapse after his at-tempt to top the Beatles, the group, heading into many years in the wilderness, gathered for one last gesture. Deceptively modest, it was no less utopian than "Surfin' U.S.A." Just listen to "Country Air." 1967.

BEATLES, *Live! at the Star-Club in Hamburg, Germany* (Bellaphon/ W. Germany). With years in Liverpool clubs hanging over them, they stood on the edge of world conquest. But they didn't know that, and so, with the arrogant wit that would carry them through the decade, they played only for the next drink. It was the crassest, most brutal rockabilly, straight legacy of Presley, Perkins, Richard, and Vincent, manhandled into a sound that was authentically new—and more than a little scary. Recorded 1962/released 1977.

——*Please Please Me* (Parlophone/UK). With a shout of "One, two, three, *faah*!," Paul McCartney kicked off the first cut of their first album, and for millions, it was the cry of the music coming home. Lennon-McCartney originals ("I Saw Her Standing There," the slashing title song, the incandescent "There's a Place") sealed the triumph, and with an urgency the audience had—and has—all but forgotten. Number one in the UK for thirty consecutive weeks. 1963.

——*With the Beatles* (Parlophone/UK). After this, it was all over. With its doomy, take-it-or-leave-it sleeve, the album was an act of force, leaping out of silence with "It Won't Be Long" and battering to a close with John Lennon's titanic version of "Money," perhaps the toughest piece of rock of all. Threatening, absurd, determined, innocent and bitter, it broke the history of the music in half. Number one in the UK for the next twenty-two consecutive weeks. 1963.

——"I Want to Hold Your Hand" (Capitol). 1964.

——"She Loves You" (Capitol). 1964.

——*A Hard Day's Night* (Parlophone/UK). Side one, the soundtrack music, was hot stuff; side two was unnerving. "Things We Said Today" and "I'll Be Back" were mature, careful, deadly—the first hints of Art, and proof the Mop Tops were . . . smart! 1964.

——*Beatles for Sale* (Parlophone/UK). By now the toast of about eight continents, their rebellion dimmed by the Rolling Stones, they sang with great confidence, with an easy joy. But "What You're Doing" pressed on toward the still-unimaginable *Rubber Soul*, and "Eight Days a Week" remains the most beatific record ever made. 1964.

——"Help!"/"I'm Down" (Capitol). 1965.

——"Yesterday" (Capitol). 1965.

——"Day Tripper" (Capitol). 1965.

——*Rubber Soul* (Capitol). Exchanging assault for seduction, they delivered the most serious love songs, exploring contingency, ambiguity, pleasure, and guilt. Where before they had taken pop music by storm, here they remade it from the inside out. Their best album. 1965.

——*Revolver* (Capitol). Classy, arty, but gleaming with intelligence: saved from its pretensions (as the next album would not be) by the golden rain of "And Your Bird Can Sing" and the embrace of "Here, There and Everywhere." 1966.

——"Strawberry Fields Forever"/"Penny Lane" (Capitol). A curse on childhood, lifted on the flipside. The first concept 45? 1967.

——"I Am the Walrus" (Capitol). *Sgt. Pepper* strangled on its own conceits; after those conceits were vindicated by world-wide acclaim, John, Paul, George & Ringo made this single, radical where The Greatest Album of All Time was contrived, passionate where it was brilliant. It stands as a signpost to a future never quite reached; *Sgt. Pepper* was a Day-Glo tombstone for its time. 1967.

——*The Beatles* (Apple). The "white album," cut following manager Brian Epstein's death and their infatuation with and (save George) rejection of the dread Maharishi: a tour de force, masterpieces scattered like crumbs, and a preview of the breakup to come. It contained their hardest rock in years, both musically, with "Yer Blues" and "Helter Skelter," and emotionally, with John's "I'm So Tired." As one who began playing rock and roll before he heard Elvis, he meant it. 1968.

——"Don't Let Me Down" (Apple). Overlooked on release, this was to be their last shining moment. John was not exactly singing to his audience—this was Yoko's song—but he might have been, and after ten years, one can hardly hear the tune as anything but an honest and worthy farewell. 1969.

BEE GEES, "Holiday" (Atco). 1967.

BELMONTS, "Tell Me Why" (Sabrina). 1961.

——*Cigars, Acapella, Candy* (Buddah). Dion's old back-up singers return with the ultimate rock and roll lullaby. The music was unaccompanied by instruments, and strictly from the fifties—the sound of men who were forced to grow up. 1972.

JESSIE BELVIN, "Goodnight My Love" (Modern). 1956.

More Chuck Berry (Chess). From the Originator, the Brown-Eyed Handsome Man, the St. Louis Flash—fourteen performances, *all* your favorites, that will forever define the spirit and the form of rock and roll. Also issued as—*Chuck Berry Twist!* 1955–1960.

Richard Berry and the Dreamers (United Superior). First-rank anarchy from a forgotten pioneer of the crazed style that was Los Angeles black rock. He carried the cool-as-a-corpse lead on the Robins' (later Coasters) historic "Riot in Cell Block #9," followed it under his own name with "The Big Break," threw himself on the mercy of the courts in "Next Time," profoundly affected everyone within earshot (Ritchie Valens, the Beach Boys, Frank Zappa, Captain Beefheart), and still sounds strange. 1953–1956.

BIG BOPPER, "Chantilly Lace" (D/Mercury). 1958.

BIG BROTHER AND THE HOLDING COMPANY, "Coo Coo" (Mainstream). 1968.

BIG YOUTH, *Screaming Target* (Trojan/UK). Addled Jamaican stays up all night raving about Clint Eastwood in *Dirty Harry*. 1973.

BOBBY "BLUE" BLAND, "It's My Life" (Duke). 1955.

——*Two Steps from the Blues* (Duke). "You know how it feels—you understand/What it is to be a stranger, in this unfriendly land." Thus Johnny Ace's inheritor of the blues ballad caught the fate of a whole people, as he does on every cut of this record, from "I Pity the Fool" to the horrifying "St. James Infirmary." 1961.

Blondie (Private Stock). Little Egypt lives. 1977.

BLUE RIDGE RANGERS, "Back in the Hills" (Fantasy). 1973.

BLUE SWEDE, "Hooked on a Feeling" (EMI). 1973.

BOB AND EARL, "Harlem Shuffle" (Marc). 1963.

BOB B. SOXX & THE BLUE JEANS, "Why Do Lovers Break Each Other's Heart" (Philles). 1963.

GARY "U.S." BONDS, *Greatest Hits* (Legrand). Along with coolly enshrining Daddy G and the Church Street 5 in the annals of American culture, Bonds supposedly used the sound of jets taking off to give his clattering singles more density. He gave *us* "Seven Day Weekend," "School Is Out" (the follow-up, "School Is In," flopped —not even Bonds could triumph over *that* concept) and "Dear Lady Twist," but there is no more exciting passage in rock than the slow build of pressure that finally erupts into the celebrations of "Quarter to Three." 1960–1962.

BOSTON, "More than a Feeling" (Epic). 1976.

——*Don't Look Back* (Epic). The premise was Jimi Hendrix, but the result was as white as the Beach Boys; the band's triumph was the emotion they were able to get into the soaring guitar lines, the cathedral-like organ, the endless overlays of vocal sound and texture. There was no personality: just an undeniable insistence on the grandeur of the pain and longing of even the most ordinary young men. 1978.

DAVID BOWIE, *Hunky Dory* (RCA). A seductive study of the displacement of pop life, and a fair bid for an English *Blonde on Blonde*. "Life on Mars?" remains the decadent aesthete's first and last question—his whole world is proof there's none here. 1971.

——*Pin Ups* (RCA). Despite noble experiments in the late seventies with *Low* and "*Heroes,*" this flashy tribute to the English scene, circa 1966, remains his quirky triumph—not that he'd ever come up with any other kind of triumph. I mean, who else could sing "Here Comes the Night" like a raving queen and make it sound *right?* 1973.

JAN BRADLEY, "Mama Didn't Lie" (Formal/Chess). 1963.

DONNIE BROOKS, "Mission Bell" (Era). 1960.

BUSTER BROWN, "Is You Is or Is You Ain't My Baby" (Fire). 1960.

JAMES BROWN, "Try Me" (Federal). 1958.

——"Night Train" (King). 1962.

——*Live at the Apollo, Vols. 1 & 2* (King). The Prisoner of Love comes to Harlem and lives up to his name. These albums, the apotheosis of Soul Brother #1, make up a passion play in cold sweat: every moment rehearsed and every moment real. 1962 & 1968.

ROY BROWN, *Good Rocking Tonight* (Route 66/UK). Barely older than Chuck Berry, he remains an almost unknown founding father. He gave the high wail of freedom to Elvis, Jackie Wilson, Smokey Robinson, and countless others, and lived to see them do more with it than he did. 1947–1954/ 1978.

JACKSON BROWNE, "Running on Empty" (Asylum). 1978.

BROWNS, "The Three Bells" (RCA). 1959.

BUCHANAN & GOODMAN, "The Flying Saucer" (Luniverse). 1956.

Buffalo Springfield (Atco). A retrospective drawn from the three albums cut by this sharp, combative, and moody bunch of L.A. rockers, one of whom (Stephen Stills, composer of the definitive "Rock 'n' Roll Woman") almost quit the business when he failed his audition to become a Monkee. (For Neil Young's contribution, cf. Kit Rachlis's chapter.) 1966–1969/1973.

ERIC BURDON & THE ANIMALS, "Sky Pilot" (MGM). 1968.

SOLOMON BURKE, "Cry to Me" (Atlantic). 1962.

JOHNNY BURNETTE & THE ROCK 'N' ROLL TRIO, "Train Kept A-Rollin' " (Coral). 1956.

BURNING SPEAR, *Garvey's Ghost* (Mango). A dub (instrumental) version of the reggae band's *Marcus Garvey*, this is Jamaican surf music —which is to say that slave ships are visible on the horizon. Produced by Jack Ruby, who in an earlier incarnation had his own Caribbean connections. 1976.

BUZZCOCKS, "Spiral Scratch" (New Hormones/UK). 1977.

BYRDS, *Mr. Tambourine Man* (Columbia). The Beach Boys sing Dylan —until "The Bells of Rhymey," when the Sirens sing Pete Seeger. The sound was gloriously lyrical, and called "folk rock," for some reason. 1965.

————*Turn! Turn! Turn!* (Columbia). Protest songs that sound like love songs, love songs crying with loss and memory, all riding on waves of electric guitars. Phil Spector might have liked it; certainly the Byrds liked Phil Spector. 1965.

————"Eight Miles High" (Columbia). 1966.

————*The Notorious Byrd Brothers* (Columbia). Gentle, and just about all melody, this album caught the secret remorse of late sixties rebellion like nothing else. 1968.

JERRY BYRNE, "Lights Out" (Specialty). 1958.

CADETS, "Stranded in the Jungle" (Modern). 1956.

CADILLACS, "Speedoo" (Josie). 1955.

J. J. CALE, "Going Down" (Shelter). 1973.

JOHN CALE, *Vintage Violence* (Columbia). Cale came from the Velvet Underground, but he was also Welsh. Here he began with present-day urban fantasies of isolation and revenge, then drove them back a thousand years until they merged with imprisoned maidens and starving crusaders. It was as if Cale had said, Yes, fear eats the soul, but not if the soul eats it first. 1970.

FREDDIE CANNON, "Palisades Park" (Swan). 1962.

CAPRIS, "There's a Moon Out Tonight" (Planet/Old Town). 1960.

CAPTAIN BEEFHEART AND HIS MAGIC BAND, *Mirror Man* (Buddah). One night's pursuit of the avant-garde, summed up in 19 minutes of "Tarotplane" (the reference is to Robert Johnson's "Terraplane"), a growling, impossibly sustained leap back to the country blues of the thirties—music that was almost as far ahead of its time as it was behind it. Recorded 1965/ released 1973.

————"Diddy Wah Diddy" (A&M). 1966.

————*Trout Mask Replica* (Straight). As unique and true a vision of America as rock and roll has produced, but I know one person who blames a kidney stone attack on it. (Cf. Langdon Winner's chapter.) 1969.

CLARENCE CARTER, "Patches" (Atlantic). 1970.

CELLOS, "Rang Tang Ding Dong (I Am the Japanese Sandman)" (Apollo). 1957.

GENE CHANDLER, "Duke of Earl" (Vee-Jay). 1962.

CHANTAYS, "Pipeline" (Downey/Dot). 1963.

The Chantels (End). The first and most impassioned of the girl groups— Arlene Smith's 15-year-old voice was as great as any in rock, and producer George Goldner's studio would later turn up in Phil Spector's head. "Maybe" and "I Love You So" are still overwhelming, but it's the enormous sound of "If You Try" that cracks open the history of the music to make room for five black girls that most have forgotten, or never heard at all. 1959.

The Ray Charles Story, Vol. One (Atlantic). A towering, inescapable figure, Charles scandalized many black performers when he brought gospel piano and vocals into a secular, even salacious blues context. You can hear his musical personality take shape on these delightful early recordings; the indelible authority that marked his later career is present only in snatches. 1952–1956/1962.

——*Modern Sounds in Country & Western Music* (ABC-Paramount). The preeminent black singer in America, he'd always loved Hank Williams, but here he went beyond him. Williams sang about a home in the sky; Charles sang as one who'd been there, and now suffered exile. 1962.

——*Ingredients in a Recipe for Soul* (ABC-Paramount). Supposedly a compromise to "reach a broader audience" (reaching the broadest possible audience is what Charles's career has been all about), this was mainstream material ("You'll Never Walk Alone," etc.) made over into the deepest expression of longing and anguish. "That Lucky Old Sun" remains a lost masterpiece. 1963.

——"I Don't Need No Doctor" (ABC). "They gave me a medicated lotion/But it didn't SOOTHE my emotion!" 1966.

——*A 25th Anniversary in Show Business Salute to Ray Charles* (ABC). Thirty-six hits: "What'd I Say," the ultimate rhythmic statement; "Georgia on My Mind," the ultimate ballad; "Drown in My Own Tears," the ultimate defeat. Listening, one realizes that it wasn't simply Charles's mastery that allowed him to define soul music before it was named—it was also his warmth. 1953–1971/1971.

CHIFFONS, "One Fine Day" (Laurie). 1963.

CHI-LITES, *Greatest Hits* (Brunswick). Sixteen rich, graceful versions of a crucial seventies black persona: anti-macho, thoughtful, accepting, honest. A leap over the Wilson Pickett swagger of the mid-sixties right back to the shattered heart of Bobby Bland—sexual politics in profound harmony. 1969–1972/1972.

CLAUDINE CLARK, "Party Lights" (Chancellor). 1962.

DAVE CLARK FIVE, "Catch Us If You Can" (Epic). 1965.

DEE CLARK, "Raindrops" (Vee-Jay). Featuring the supreme rock couplet: "There must be a cloud in my head/Tears keep falling from my eye-eye." 1961.

The Clash (CBS/UK). Unsettling English punk: rock and roll busted up with echoes of *Trout Mask Replica*, and reassembled according to sprung reggae rhythms, all tumbling down in the caterwauling vocals and guitar rave-ups of "Police and Thieves." The momentum was purely political: this record meant to organize a youthful community that had appeared out of nowhere. 1977.

——"Complete Control" (CBS/UK). Produced by Lee Perry of Jamaica, and one of the most powerful hard rock records of all time. 1977.

CLEFTONES, "Heart and Soul" (Gee). 1961.

JIMMY CLIFF, "Vietnam" (A&M). 1970.

——*The Harder They Come* (Mango). Soundtrack to a reggae film that as a rock and roll movie outran *Jailhouse Rock*, the set collected the best of Jamaica's rhythm masters and cut through the miasma of the early seventies with the freshness and vitality—not the bravado —that Berry, Richard, and Fats brought to the mid-fifties. Child of New Orleans rock (itself formed partly by Caribbean sounds), the music was mournful (the Melodians' "Rivers of Babylon," Cliff's "Many Rivers to Cross"), defiant (Cliff's "You Can Get It If You Really Want"), desperate (the Maytals' ferocious "Pressure Drop"). The Rolling Stones would have killed to make this record. 1972.

CLOVERS, *Their Greatest Recordings—The Early Years* (Atco). Combining vocal anonymity and catchy material, the Clovers now sound like essential doo-wop product; "Love Potion Number Nine," a late Coasters-style hit, sparks this LP as an anomaly, as does the paralyzing blues guitar on "Down in the Alley." The deep appeal of the group is in the way it disappears into and thus perfectly represents one of rock's founding genres—that, and the fact that the Clovers had the most lugubrious bassman in history. 1951–1959/1971.

COASTERS, *Their Greatest Recordings—The Early Years* (Atco). Stepin Fetchit as advance man for black revolt, with script by two Jews, Jerry Leiber and Mike Stoller. Out of scores still remembered, their best lines: "It's gonna take an ocean/Of calamine lotion." From "Riot in Cell Block #9" to "Little Egypt," *this* was rock 'n' roll. 1955–1961/1971.

——"What About Us"/"Run, Red, Run" (Atco). Stepin Fetchit drops his mask, and pulls a gun. 1959.

EDDIE COCHRAN, "Summertime Blues" (Liberty). 1958.

COMMODORES, "Machine Gun" (Motown). 1974.

CONTOURS, "Do You Love Me" (Gordy). 1962.

——"First I Look at the Purse" (Gordy). 1965.

The Best of Sam Cooke (RCA). Along with a few others, he invented soul music, but only Cooke could have made "Chain Gang" sound both slick and true. Interestingly, the number that has grown most over the years is "Wonderful World," which could have been written by Buddy Holly. (Cf. Joe McEwen's chapter.) 1957–1962/1962.

——"Another Saturday Night" (RCA). 1963.

——"A Change Is Gonna Come" (RCA). The greatest soul record ever made—released just after Cooke was shot to death—and a tender, terrifying prophecy of what the racial changes already at work in the land would cost; a prophecy, finally, of what they would be worth. (Cf. Tom Smucker's chapter.) 1965.

ALICE COOPER, "Eighteen" (Warner Bros.). 1971.

ELVIS COSTELLO, *My Aim Is True* (Columbia). Bad news boy, Buddy Holly after shock treatment, he emerged out of England simultaneously with the disappearance of his namesake. Just twenty-two, master of every rock and roll move, he sang of neurotic retreat, sexual disorientation, social pathology, the death of God, and denied everything. 1977.

——& THE ATTRACTIONS, *This Year's Model* (Columbia). With his new little band heading straight into the wilderness of punk, his pop sensibility heated up and produced music that recalled the wit of Randy Newman and the raging momentum of Bob Dylan in his glory years. This was an urban horror story, thuggish fury hiding an edge of compassion, and it all came to a head in "Radio, Radio," wherein the misanthrope joined his audience—if only to tell its members they had nothing to lose but their chains. 1978.

COUNTRY JOE AND THE FISH, "Bass Strings"/"Section 43" (Rag Baby). 1966.

COUNTS, "Darling Dear" (Dot). 1954.

Fresh Cream (Reaction/UK). This was the roar of the country blues, juiced with Eric Clapton's English electricity, an awesome sound. 1966.

CREDENCE CLEARWATER REVIVAL, "Proud Mary" (Fantasy). 1969.

——*Green River* (Fantasy). Stuck in the suburbs of San Francisco and dreaming of the Mississippi, John Fogerty crafted a timeless vision of America: a white boy (Fogerty) and a black man (Fogerty's heroes: Howlin' Wolf, Little Richard) sharing a raft, drifting south, finding friendship, defeat, fear, and salvation. In other words, Elvis's Sun singles, without their innocence. 1969.

——*Willie and the Poorboys* (Fantasy). The rural echoes were still there, but the action shifted to the city, and all the warnings in *Green River*'s "Bad Moon Rising" came true. 1969.

——"Up Around the Bend" (Fantasy). 1970.

CRESTS, "Step by Step" (Coed). 1960.

CROSBY, STILLS, NASH AND YOUNG, "Ohio" (Atlantic). 1970.

The Crystals Sing Their Greatest Hits! (Phil Spector International/ UK). Unlike the Ronettes, this perfect girl group, led often by Darlene Love, had no image, just passion—and, despite the S&M leanings of a couple of cuts here, an unconquerable warmth. Their soul went into their hits, and "Da Doo Ron Ron" (Spector called it "a little symphony for the kids"; he could have called it a little A-bomb), "He's Sure the Boy I Love," and "Then He Kissed Me" are in the souls of all who've heard them. 1961–1963/1975.

CUFF LINKS, "Guided Missle" (Dootone). 1957.

JOHNNY CYMBAL, "Mr. Bass Man" (Kapp). 1963.

DANLEERS, "One Summer Night" (Mercury). 1958.

SPENCER DAVIS GROUP, "Gimme Some Lovin'" (UA). 1966.

DESMOND DEKKER & THE ACES, "Israelites" (Uni). 1969.

DELLS, "There Is" (Cadet). 1968.

DELL-VIKINGS, "Whispering Bells" (Dot). 1957.

DEREK & THE DOMINOS, *Layla* (Atco). The two great guitarists of the era, Eric Clapton and Duane Allman, raising an epic tapestry of romantic blues—an anguished and somehow heroic statement, just before the fall. 1970.

JACKIE DESHANNON, "What the World Needs Now Is Love" (Liberty). 1965.

DIAMONDS, "Little Darlin'" (Mercury). 1957.

BO DIDDLEY, *Got My Own Bag of Tricks* (Chess). The King of Raunch (true godfather to the early Rolling Stones?) can pack almost as many classics into a greatest hits set as Chuck Berry: their charm is grimier, for Bo's greatness is in his shamelessness. Sly growls like "Cops and Robbers" or even "Who Do You Love" pale next to "Say Man," which is right up there with the most ridiculous records ever to crack the Top 40. 1955–1963/1972.

DION, "Abraham, Martin and John"/"Daddy Rollin' (In Your Arms)" (Laurie). 1968.

——*Everything You Always Wanted to Hear by Dion and the Belmonts —But Couldn't Get!* (Laurie). Sizzling Italian doo-wop from the Bronx—the dynamics of "I Wonder Why" were faster than sound— that turned into rough, wailing post-Presley hard rock when Dion went solo. Priceless stuff. 1958–1963/1975.

FATS DOMINO, *Legendary Masters* (UA). Not a legend, like the rest of rock's founders, but a song and dance man, the shape of his whole career can be heard in the piano intro to "The Fat Man," his first hit. 1950–1961/1971.

DOMINOES, "Sixty Minute Man" (Federal). 1951.

——*The Dominoes Featuring Clyde McPhatter* (King). No hits but heavenly music from the group that virtually fathered doo-wop. In emotion if not style, McPhatter's clear teenage tenor went back to the shaken gospel of Blind Willie Johnson, forward to the eroticism of Elvis; no rock singer's touch has been more delicate, or more doomstruck. 1950–1953/1977.

RAL DONNER, "Girl of My Best Friend" (Gone). 1961.

DONOVAN, *Sunshine Superman* (Epic). An original, he summed up the mindlessness of the hippie, but also the expansive delight of the hippie's playful idealism. His precise evocations of Arthurian England, bad trips, and haute demimonde scene-making would have been nothing without the evocativeness of the settings provided by producer Mickie Most, who made each song the signpost of a different world. Those worlds were mostly benign—but not in the still-scary "Season of the Witch," where Donovan stretched out his syllables until they hung over you like a curse. This was as sure a warning as the horrors breeding within the idealism as the Stones' "Gimme Shelter," and a lot more prescient. 1966.

The Doors (Elektra). If the music hasn't worn well—Jim Morrison now sounds inordinately full of himself—at the time it hit with almost the impact of Clyde McPhatter in the early fifties, and trashed the more casual pretensions of the San Francisco psychedelic bands. Including "Light My Fire," "The End," and the lovely "Crystal Ship," this debut album was called "only a map of our music" by the Doors, but it was as far as they got. 1967.

DOVELLS, "Bristol Stomp" (Parkway). 1961.

DR. HOOK AND THE MEDICINE SHOW, "Carry Me, Carrie" (Columbia). 1972.

DRIFTERS, *Their Greatest Recordings—The Early Years* (Atco). Founding black rock: hard stuff with the hilarious "Money Honey," sexy ways with "Adorable" and the almost pornographic "Honey Love," rebellion with the scabrous (and beautiful!) "White Christmas," all shaped by astonishingly intricate vocal backings for the transcendent lead of Clyde McPhatter, whose influence on Elvis was as true as the legacy he left Jackie Wilson, Smokey Robinson, and Al Green. 1953–1959/1971.

——*Golden Hits* (Atlantic). A wholly different group—led by Ben E.

King, Rudy Lewis, and Johnny Moore—that dominated the charts with sophisticated yet tough string arrangements of romantic yet brittle Brill Building songs ("There Goes My Baby," one of about a dozen "greatest records ever made," "Up on the Roof," "On Broadway," "I Count the Tears"), and in the process came up with as apt an orchestration of teenage life as the Beach Boys. 1959–1964/1968.

Dubs, "Could This Be Magic" (Gone). 1957.

Bob Dylan, *Bringing It All Back Home* (Columbia). His high school rocker's past well buried, the king of folk music heard the Beatles, hired a band, and replied with an edgy, madly funny set of songs about the failure of rational humanism in these United States. He also made the charts, and bought some new clothes. 1965.

——"If You Gotta Go, Go Now" (CBS/Netherlands). Recorded 1965/ released 1967.

——*Highway 61 Revisited* (Columbia). Like a rolling stone, if a Minnesota Isaiah calling down the spirits of Hank Williams and Robert Johnson could be a Rolling Stone. This was an explosion of vision and humor that forever changed rock, and a piece of music that stands as its signal accomplishment. It was also a journey through America (with a stop at a Mexican border town and a destination beyond the law), a map of its traps and glories. 1965.

——*Blonde on Blonde* (Columbia). The journey completed—if not over—the new king of rock stepped back and offered dandy's blues, vivid, highly charged, insular, destructive, tempting: the sound of a man trying to stand up in a drunken boat, and, for the moment, succeeding. His tone was sardonic, scared, threatening, as if he'd awakened after paying all his debts to find that nothing was settled. 1966.

——*The Royal Albert Hall Concert.* The sound the dandy made onstage with the Hawks, when together they performed as the greatest rock and roll band in the world—and, for their time, as the loudest. Recorded 1966/ bootlegged 1971.

——*The Basement Tapes* (Columbia). Having pushed to all known limits, he went into retreat, settled in with the Hawks (now calling themselves the Band), and rewrote American music as a pilgrimage to the confessional, broken up by stops at the bawdy house. It was intimate and echoed, probing the farthest Appalachian hollows, bursting with rock and roll drama, insisting on mysteries their author would eventually flee along with the rest of us. Recorded 1967/ released 1975.

——*John Wesley Harding* (Columbia). As Paul Williams wrote, it was as if he came out of the oblivion of pop retirement, went south to where it all began, and reinvented rock and roll as it might have sounded just days before Elvis made his first record. 1968.

——"Lay Lady Lay" (Columbia). 1969.

——"Knockin' on Heaven's Door" (Columbia). 1973.

——"Most Likely You'll Go Your Way and I'll Go Mine" (Asylum). 1974.

——*Blood on the Tracks* (Columbia). After years of desultory albums and haphazard inspiration, he roared back, and what returned was the intensity of his performance, the impossibility of getting out of his way. As he always had in his best moments—ever since he discovered that more linked Carl Perkins, Dock Boggs, Blind Lemon Jefferson, and Little Richard than separated them—he sang in a voice that brought home menace and acceptance, age and rebirth, terror and peace, dust to dust. 1975.

EAGLES, "Hotel California" (Asylum). (Cf. Grace Lichtenstein's chapter.) 1977.

EASYBEATS, "Friday on My Mind" (UA). 1967.

EDSELS, "Rama Lama Ding Dong" (Twin). 1961.

TOMMY EDWARDS, "It's All in the Game" (MGM). 1958.

ELASTIC OZ BAND, "Do the Oz" (Apple). 1971.

ELDORADOS, "At My Front Door" (Vee-Jay). 1955.

ELEGANTS, "Little Star" (Apt). 1958.

SHIRLEY ELLIS, "The Name Game" (Congress). 1964.

LORRAINE ELLISON, "Stay With Me" (Warner Bros.). 1966.

EQUALS, "Baby, Come Back" (RCA). 1968.

EVERLY BROTHERS, *Original Greatest Hits* (Barnaby). Perfect songs from Boudleaux and Felice Bryant let two mother's-son Kentucky punks—stuck between Elvis and Frankie Avalon—dramatize a generation's worth of high school anguish, longing, and glee. 1957–1961/ 1970.

FAIRPORT CONVENTION, *Fairport Chronicles* (A&M). Folk-rock out of *Bleak House, Morte d'Arthur,* and the Basement Tapes: guitarist Richard Thompson wrote straight from the plague years, and the incandescent Sandy Denny spoke for Emily Brontë's ghost—though now one hears her own. Starting at Stonehenge (pictured on the cover of this superbly compiled retrospective), they told the emotional history of Albion, pausing here and there for a romp through "Million Dollar Bash," a bow to Dion, a nod to Buddy Holly. 1968–1972/1972.

MARIANNE FAITHFUL, "As Tears Go By" (London). 1964.

——"Sister Morphine" (London). 1969.

FALCONS, "You're So Fine" (Unart). A good record, but included for the rolling piano notes that open it—salvation in ten seconds flat. 1959.

CHARLIE FEATHERS, "One Hand Loose" (King). 1956.

BRYAN FERRY, "*These Foolish Things*" (Atlantic). An outrageous set of oldies covers, where Dylan's "A Hard Rain's A-Gonna Fall" sounds trashier than Lesley Gore's "It's My Party." Thanks to Ferry's Dracula-has-risen-from-the-grave voice, one of the decade's funniest productions, but since all that melodrama only glamorizes the pathos that ultimately rises to the surface, also one of its most bizarrely moving. 1974.

——*The Bride Stripped Bare* (Atlantic). Or, The Revenge of Lust, a tale that leaves all parties free to live out their cruelest, most self-pitying fantasies, and then to pay for them. An extraordinary dramatic achievement, with a sound so rich and full of presence it's a wonder almost no one listened. 1978.

SONNY FISHER AND THE ROCKING BOYS, *Texas Rockabilly* (Ace/UK). Bitter, world-weary white R&B out of Houston, music of sexual boasting and social defeat. The pace was slow, compared to the stuff Sam Phillips was turning out at Sun, but more sinuous; the bite came from Fisher's unfriendly drawl and Joey Long's guitar, which suggested nothing so much as a very poisonous snake. 1955–1956/1979.

FIVE DU-TONES, "Divorce Court"/"Shake a Tailfeather" (One-derful!). 1963.

FIVE KEYS, "The Glory of Love" (Apollo). 1951.

——*The Five Keys* (King). On the downslide of their career, this elegant black quintet caught the end of one era and the beginnings of the next, moving with great passion from the doo-wop that had brought them fame to (with "Dream On," the best Jerry Butler record Jerry Butler never made) the man-alone tragedy that was the essence of early soul. 1959–early sixties/ 1978.

"5" ROYALES, *Dedicated to You* (King). A black vocal group, with a guitar player. Once upon a time, Eric Clapton would have paid to hold his coat. (Cf. Ed Ward's chapter.) 1958.

FIVE SATINS, "In the Still of the Nite" (Standard/Ember). 1956.

FLAIRS, "Foot-Stomping Part I" (Felsted). 1961.

FLEETWOOD MAC, *Greatest Hits* (CBS/UK). Despite memorable forays into hard pop ("Oh Well") and early soul ("Need Your Love So Bad"), this troubled British band took the white blues cult farther than anyone else; there isn't a guitarist in the world who wouldn't claim the terrible, shattered peace of Peter Green's "Love that Burns" for his own. 1968–1971/1971.

——*Fleetwood Mac* (Reprise). Carried up the charts by "Over My Head," a seventies "Tonight's the Night," this was a showcase for the broken romanticism of Christine McVie, the premier white female singer of the decade. 1975.

——*Rumours* (Reprise). By now an unlikely team of English veterans and young Californians who ruled the Top 40, they paid for their success with the collapse of two marriages, and held on to it with a set of love songs so blasted and unflinching (especially "Gold Dust Woman" and "Go Your Own Way," which stand as the best rock ever to come out of Menlo-Atherton High School) they made a fair match for those of *Blood on the Tracks*. 1977.

THE FLEETWOODS, *Greatest Hits* (Dolton). Close harmony from two girls and a boy, and the flipside of teen rebellion: the sound of awful yearnings, quiet defeats, of a love always just out of reach. 1959–1961/1962.

Let's Take a Sea Cruise with Frankie Ford (Ace). They dumped a white pretty boy on Huey Smith's crack New Orleans band, and then discovered the pretty boy could sing out of the top of his head and make lines like "I pawned my pistol, I pawned my watch and chain/ I would pawn Roberta but Roberta can't sign her name" seem realistic. With the strange "What's Going On," in which Frankie shows up at his girl's house to find it surrounded by cops, is forced to run for his life, and never does find out what happened. (Cf. Jay Cocks's chapter.) 1960.

FOUR DEUCES, "W–P–L–J." (Music City). 1955.

FOUR SEASONS, "Walk Like a Man" (Vee-Jay). 1963.

FOUR TOPS, *Greatest Hits* (Motown). Once past the optimistic romance of "Baby I Need Your Loving" and "Without the One You Love," they became Motown's gloom-masters, hell-bound and brave. Their greatest hit was "Reach Out I'll Be There," which Levi Stubbs sang as if he were calling to a buddy in a firefight. 1964–1967/1967.

ARETHA FRANKLIN, *I Never Loved a Man the Way I Love You* (Atlantic). This album shocked the music world. The down-to-the-ground guitar, the wake-the-dead horns, the surging attack—she made it all seem secondary, and she also made the Rolling Stones sound like little kids. More directly than Ray Charles or anyone else, she brought the apocalypse of gospel into pop, reaching for love with the desperation, urgency, and grace with which she once reached only for salvation, and thus made love and salvation seem like the same thing. 1967.

——*Aretha's Gold* (Atlantic). Containing four cuts from *I Never Loved a Man*, and included here for "(You Make Me Feel Like) A Natural Woman," "I Say a Little Prayer," and most of all for the long fall of "Ain't No Way," now heard as a premature epitaph for a career that was already cracking when this record was released. 1969.

STAN FREBERG, "The Old Payola Roll Blues" (Capitol). 1960.

FREE, "Wishing Well" (Island). 1973.

ALAN FREED, *Rock 'n Roll Dance Party* (Coral). An answer record to Stan Freberg's "Payola Roll Blues," even though it was released first. 1957.

BOBBY FREEMAN, "Do You Wanna Dance" (Josie). 1958.

DON GARDNER AND DEE DEE FORD, "I Need Your Loving" (Fire). 1962.

MARVIN GAYE, *Super Hits* (Tamla). Motown's Mr. Suave cut his groove with a string of rough-edged pop R&B classics, from the churchy "Can I Get a Witness" to the immortal "Hitch Hike." Perhaps the most charming of Berry Gordy's stable of singers, he seemed too endearing to carry real force—until "I Heard It Through the Grapevine," which crept out of the radio like pop voodoo. After that (see singles below), whether he was singing about politics or sex, his commitment seemed limitless. 1962–1969/1970.

——"Inner City Blues" (Tamla). 1971.

——"Let's Get It On" (Tamla). 1973.

——AND TAMMI TERRELL, *Greatest Hits* (Tamla). Gaye made records with a number of women; the best were cut with the late Tammi Terrell, whose death has been the subject of almost as much speculation as that of Marilyn Monroe. The team is best remembered for "Ain't No Mountain High Enough"—a masterpiece of affection, and, oddly, not much of a hit—but their story wouldn't be complete without their aching revival of "For Your Precious Love," not to mention "You're All I Need to Get By." 1967–1969/1970.

LESLEY GORE, "You Don't Own Me" (Mercury). 1963.

GRAND FUNK RAILROAD, "We're an American Band" (Capitol). 1973.

GRASS ROOTS, "Where Were You When I Needed You" (Dunhill). 1966.

Grateful Dead Live at the Pyramids (Arista). Who knows what it'll sound like: the concept is staggering. Recorded 1978/release pending.

DOBIE GRAY, "Drift Away" (MCA). 1973.

GREAT SOCIETY WITH GRACE SLICK, *Conspicuous Only in Its Absence* (Columbia). You want the fabled San Francisco Sound? The Jefferson Airplane never got it down on record, but on the live side of this album, featuring a cataclysmic version of "Somebody to Love," the Great Society did. Recorded 1966/released 1968.

AL GREEN, *Greatest Hits* (Hi). In the Memphis tradition of spare, direct, unadorned rock—a tradition born at Sun in the fifties and nurtured at Stax in the sixties—Green emerged as the true heir of Otis Redding. Yet he was a better songwriter, a cooler presence; he had none of Redding's bravado and none of his bathos. Green sang about limits: he came to make his plea and then give thanks. This odd combination took him to the top of the charts again and again, most memorably with "Look What You Done for Me," a song that might have been about impotence but is surely the only rock and roll record that can be called vulnerably virile. 1971–1974/1975.

——*Call Me* (Hi). Like all great pop singers, Green trashed barriers. This LP, surely his best, combined Hank Williams, self-penned gospel, and soul that was mainstream only because there was no one else left to sing it. "Funny How Time Slips Away" seemed to draw from every era of black music without imitating any; Green took the whole history of rhythm & blues on his shoulders with this tune, and carried it like a coat he'd had made especially for him. 1973.

——*The Belle Album* (Hi). The soul man as supplicant as exile. Coming off a violent incident that left a woman dead and his career up in the air, Green turned to Jesus, but unlike almost every other singer, white or black, who'd done the same thing, he didn't proselytize. Instead, wandering through country bars and down southern back roads, he let you share a sense of peace; he even made you feel you'd helped earn it. 1977.

GUESS WHO, "Share the Land" (RCA). 1970.

GUITAR SLIM, "The Things That I Used to Do" (Specialty). 1953.

HACKAMORE BRICK, *One Kiss Leads to Another* (Kama Sutra). Long before the Ramones, this New York band, with more wit and a better sense of rhythm, had all they reached for well in hand. My favorite moment comes when the singer's girl falls out of the window during a drag race; he doesn't notice because he's humming along with the radio, which is playing their song. Like that girl, these modern Coasters-cum-Velvet Underground vanished without a trace. 1970.

HARPTONES, "A Sunday Kind of Love" (Bruce). 1953.

JOYCE HARRIS, "No Way Out" (Infinity). c. 1960.

WILBERT HARRISON, *Let's Work Together* (Sue). The Kansas City Man after ten years in oblivion, weary-voiced and open-hearted. Performing as a ragged, barely amplified one-man-band, he sang from the netherlands of R&B, where defeat reaches its limit and turns back for the last good kiss. This was the sort of music folklorists record on street corners, but somehow, Harrison got a hit out of it. 1969.

DALE HAWKINS, "Susie-Q" (Checker). 1957.

RONNIE HAWKINS, "Who Do You Love" (Roulette). 1963.

SCREAMIN' JAY HAWKINS, "I Put a Spell on You" (Okeh). 1956.

HEART, "Crazy on You" (Mushroom). 1976.

HEARTBEATS, "A Thousand Miles Away" (Rama). 1956.

JIMI HENDRIX EXPERIENCE, *Are You Experienced?* (Reprise). This record didn't simply change the way the guitar was played, or merely explode the ambitions of the music. Its best songs—"Purple Haze," "I Don't Live Today," "The Wind Cries Mary"—represent a titanic struggle to reconcile tradition and innovation, black rock and white. Brave, reckless stuff. 1967.*

——*Live at Monterey* (Reprise). While on the first side Otis Redding plays it safe for the elite white audience at the Monterey Pop Festival, on the flip Hendrix claims his music, turning "Wild Thing" and "Like a Rolling Stone" into fair equivalents of what your parents were afraid would happen if you hung out with blacks. Recorded 1967/ released 1970.*

——*Electric Ladyland* (Reprise). A sprawling, mighty mess, with the spirit of "Voodoo Chile" entering into "All Along the Watchtower," in which Jimi eats Dylan alive and, like the whale vomiting up Jonah, spits him out better for the experience. 1968.

CLARENCE "FROGMAN" HENRY, "I Don't Know Why, But I Do" (Argo). 1961.

HERMAN'S HERMITS, "A Must to Avoid" (MGM). Not only a good record, but a classic of rock phrasemaking. 1967.

JESSIE HILL, "Ooh Poo Pah Doo" (Minit). 1960.

JUSTIN HINES AND THE DOMINOES, *Jezebel* (Island). Buddy Holly's shade surfaced after his death in many forms. This still-waters-run-deep reggae group was one of the more unlikely. 1976.

HOLLIES, "Bus Stop" (Imperial). 1966.

*This entry by Dave Marsh

BUDDY HOLLY, *The "Chirping" Crickets* (Coral). His debut album, released under the name of his group: a fifties *Rubber Soul*. 1958.

——*The Complete Buddy Holly* (MCA Coral/UK). A cheat, given the Draconian selectivity of this section, but included because you can actually sit down and listen to all six LPs, from imitation-Elvis Texas demos to posthumous New York overdubs. And how could I leave out "Well . . . All Right" or "Crying, Waiting, Hoping"? 1954–1959/1973.

JOHN LEE HOOKER, *Detroit Special* (Atlantic). Hooker has put out scores of albums in his thirty-year career; all I've heard are good, because all feature his crawling kingsnake guitar, his pounding foot, his stoic, doomy rage. As a bluesman he has never catered to rock— except to sit in with Van Morrison, who has always catered to Hooker. 1951 & 1963/1972.

HOTLEGS, "Neanderthal Man" (Capitol). 1970.

HOWLIN' WOLF, "How Many More Years" (Chess). The Sun sound— before Elvis. 1951.

——*Howlin' Wolf* (Chess). Mississippi terror, Chicago Back Door Man, the late Chester Burnett rode the blues like a man breaking a mustang; the blues never gave an inch, but the Wolf was never thrown. The purest rock in blues dress ("Going Down Slow," "Down in the Bottom," "Wang Dang Doodle," "You'll Be Mine"), this album, with the famous rocking chair on the cover, inspired a generation. The first LPs by the Rolling Stones were honest attempts not to catch up with it, but simply to come close enough to holler and be heard. 1959–1962.

IMPRESSIONS, *The Vintage Years* (Sire). Jerry Butler and the Impressions (led by singer, writer, and guitarist Curtis Mayfield) started out together; pursuing separate careers, they defined the failing heart, the pleading desire, that was Chicago soul. This set collects their music from "For Your Precious Love" and "Gypsy Woman" in the fifties to "Only the Strong Survive" and "Freddie's Dead" more than ten years later—yet their supreme moment came almost at the beginning, with Butler's delicate and hopeless "He Will Break Your Heart," led every step of the way by Mayfield's guitar. 1958–1972/1976.

ISLEY BROTHERS, "Shout" (RCA). 1959.

——"This Old Heart of Mine (Is Weak for You)" (Tamla). 1966.

JACKSON 5, "I Want You Back" (Motown). 1969.

——"The Love You Save" (Motown). 1970.

MICK JAGGER, "Cocksucker Blues" (Ruthless Rhymes Ltd./W. Germany). Recorded 1970/ bootlegged 1976.

The Best of Elmore James (Sue/UK). Compatriot of Robert Johnson, from whom he took his style (though he took only a small part of Johnson's), he found fame in Chicago, when he was ready to rock. This set collects his best sides, made for the Fire label. Not a deep singer, he had humor, a fine sense of blues classicism, and most of all the careening drive of his electric guitar. When he died in 1963, only forty-five, disciples like the Rolling Stones and the Yardbirds were already wired to his amp. 1956–1962.

The Best of Tommy James and the Shondells (Roulette). The Elton John of his time, he began imitating "Be-Bop-a-Lula" and ended psychedelicizing his sound with "Crimson and Clover," which was at once a statement of utter abstraction and a natural number one: exactly what Brian Wilson has been aiming for, lo these many years. 1966–1969/1969.

JAMIES, "Summertime, Summertime" (Epic). 1958.

JAN & DEAN, *Legendary Masters* (UA). Comedians, until in less than a year (summer '63 through spring '64) they knocked off "Surf City," "Drag City" ("Fuck City" remains unreleased), and the monumental "Dead Man's Curve," and became Southern California mythmakers in spite of themselves. After which they went back to being comedians, until in less than two years Jan rammed a truck and knocked off the top of his head. 1958–1968/1971.

JARMELS, "A Little Bit of Soap" (Laurie). 1961.

JAY AND THE AMERICANS, "Cara Mia" (UA). 1965.

JEFFERSON AIRPLANE, "Runnin' Round This World" (RCA). 1966.

JEWELS, "Hearts of Stone" (Imperial). 1954.

ELTON JOHN, "Tiny Dancer" (Uni). 1972.

——*Goodbye Yellow Brick Road* (MCA). The great sweep of pop romanticism from a great pop fan who dominated the pop charts of his time. Conceived in hype, he lived up to all of it, proving, as he does here with "Love Lies Bleeding," that he too was born to rock. 1973.

——"Philadelphia Freedom" (MCA). Supposedly written as a tribute to Billie Jean King's tennis team, and a work of genius. 1975.

JOHNNIE AND JOE, "Over the Mountain, Across the Sea" (J&S/Chess). Oddly ignored today, but an unquestionable match for "In the Still of the Nite" and "Earth Angel." 1957.

JANIS JOPLIN, "Kozmic Blues" (Columbia). A number of recordings were made that captured her power, including "Ball and Chain" from the Monterey Pop Festival in 1967—but none have ever been released. This, along with "Coo Coo," listed under Big Brother, came closest. 1969.

KALEIDOSCOPE, *Side Trips* and *Beacon from Mars* (Epic). L.A. eccentrics, kin to the Band, they didn't so much combine country blues, hillbilly murder ballads, loud music and cajun stomps as place them side by side—still proving those disparate rural forms were similarly effective as sources of passion and regeneration in an urban world. A very old kind of fatalism hangs over the sound: the fatalism of Appalachian snake-handlers. 1967.

KALIN TWINS, "When" (Decca). 1958.

PAUL KELLY, "Stealing in the Name of the Lord" (Happy Tiger). 1970.

CHRIS KENNER, *Land of a Thousand Dances* (Atlantic). Trance-like black Indian singing countered by producer Allen Toussaint's elegant horn and piano arrangements, falling together in unstoppable syncopation and creating hits: the emblematic title tune, "I Like It Like That" and the amazing "That's My Girl." In other words, the rock utopia turns out to be the Crescent City. 1961–1966/1966.

ERNIE K-DOE, *Mother in Law* (Minit). The all-time novelty hit, plus a definitive summation of early sixties New Orleans R&B, courtesy of producer Allen Toussaint, as usual. 1961.

B. B. KING, "The Thrill Is Gone" (Bluesway). 1969.

BEN E. KING, "Stand by Me" (Atco). 1961.

CAROLE KING, *Tapestry* (Ode). A rough, intimate, broken-voiced testament to endurance and desire, and after all the years King spent as the anonymous melodist behind so many unforgettable songs ("One Fine Day," "When My Little Girl Is Smiling," "Some Kind of Wonderful"), a shock. 1971.

KINGSMEN, "Louie, Louie" (Jerden/Wand). 1963.

The Kinks' Greatest Hits! (Reprise). The hardest rock of the British invasion, and probably the meanest. 1964–1966/1966.

——"Sunny Afternoon"/"I'm Not Like Everybody Else" (Reprise). 1966.

——*Something Else by the Kinks* (Reprise). Commercial failure turned head Kink Ray Davies back on himself. What he found were the futile aspirations to gentility harbored by the English working class: the pain of living within limits one could not afford to damn, because that would mean admitting they existed. To end this sad tale, he offered "Waterloo Sunset," one of the most beautiful songs in all of rock, the brief life of a man whose only pleasure comes from the lovers he watches from his window. It was a finale of a piece with the rest of the story, and also its transcendence. (Cf. Janet Maslin's chapter.) 1968.

——"Lola" (Reprise). 1970.

——"The Way Love Used to Be" (Reprise). 1971.

——"20th Century Man" (RCA). 1971.

KNICKERBOCKERS, "Lies" (Challenge). 1965.

GLADYS KNIGHT AND THE PIPS, "Midnight Train to Georgia" (Buddah). 1973.

SONNY KNIGHT, "If You Want This Love" (Aura). 1964.

LED ZEPPELIN, Zo-So (known as "Led Zeppelin IV") (Atlantic). Deservedly the most popular hard rock record ever made, inspired by Robert Johnson and the Druids, with a bow to "Book of Love," this music meant to storm Heaven, and it came close. 1971.

CURTIS LEE, "Pretty Little Angel Eyes" (Dunes). 1964.

LEFT BANKE, "Pretty Ballerina" (Smash). 1967.

JOHN LENNON, "God" (Apple). 1970.

JERRY LEE LEWIS, Ole Tyme Country Music (Sun). A cruel misnomer: taken from his auditions for Sam Phillips, this is one long Louisiana roadhouse stomp. Recorded 1956/released 1970.

——Rockin' Up a Storm (Sun/UK). Twenty-eight of the biggest from the Great Sinner and His Pumping Piano. "Whole Lotta Shakin'" remains the ultimate statement, but when "Lovin' Up a Storm" was first played on the radio the National Weather Service picked it up and named a hurricane after it. 1957–1962/1974.

SMILEY LEWIS, "One Night of Sin" (Imperial). 1955.

GORDON LIGHTFOOT, "If You Could Read My Mind" (Reprise). 1970.

LITTLE ANTHONY AND THE IMPERIALS, "Hurt So Bad" (DCP). 1965.

LITTLE EVA, "The Loco-Motion" (Dimension). 1962.

LITTLE PEGGY MARCH, "I Will Follow Him" (RCA). 1963.

Little Richard's Grooviest 17 Original Hits! (Specialty). Anarchy in the U.S.A., about the time the Sex Pistols were born. This was some kind of unhinged New Orleans R&B, at first anyway, but even Fats Domino must have wondered what the hell was going on. (Cf. Jay Cocks's chapter.) 1955–1958/1969.

——"I Don't Know What You've Got But It's Got Me" (Vee-Jay). 1965.

LITTLE WILLIE JOHN, "Need Your Love So Bad" (King). (Cf. Joe McEwen's chapter.) 1956.

LOVE, "Alone Again Or" (Elektra). 1968.

DARLENE LOVE, "A Fine, Fine Boy" (Philles). 1963.

LOVIN' SPOONFUL, *Do You Believe in Magic* (Kama Sutra). The tune that asked the question also defined its terms, and the old blues and jokey new folk songs that filled out the album did well enough. That John Sebastian never learned to frown rather compromised his contemplation of the abyss, but in the glory days following the Beatles' arrival, who needed the abyss? 1965.

———"Summer in the City" (Kama Sutra). 1966.

NICK LOWE, *Pure Pop for Now People* (Columbia). Or Chuck Berry for Perverts. 1978.

ROBIN LUKE, "Susie Darlin'" (International/Dot). 1958.

BARBARA LYNN, *You'll Lose a Good Thing* (Jamie). A young woman's Louisiana blues, shaped by the pop premises of New Orleans: the sound of going down slow, but not all the way. 1963.

LYNYRD SKYNYRD, *Street Survivors* (MCA). Leaving brutal mortality-play hits like "Saturday Night Special" in their wake, this Florida guitar band barnstormed America throughout the seventies until they were destroyed in a plane crash. This was their last and best LP: aching, emotionally mature, the guitars striking fire and drawing blood. 1977.

LONNIE MACK, *The Wham of That Memphis Man!* (Fraternity). The first to see the limitless rhythmic possibilities of Chuck Berry's then-obscure "Memphis," he was an early guitar hero, and guitar heroics are mostly what this set is about. But it ends with an open wound: "Why," a soul ballad so torturous, so classically structured, that it can uncover wounds of your own. Mack's scream at the end has never been matched; God help us if anyone ever tops it. 1964.

MAGAZINE, "Shot by Both Sides" (Virgin/UK). 1978.

MAGIC SAM, "21 Days in Jail" (Cobra). 1958.

MAJORS, "A Wonderful Dream" (Imperial). 1962.

Manfred Mann's Earth Band (Polydor). Highlighted by a synthesized version of Randy Newman's "Living Without You" and the sad story of a man looking for a job after an atomic war, this was the decade's most successful attempt at "progressive" music—probably because the musicians never lost their sense of humor. 1972.

MARCELS, "Blue Moon" (Colpix). 1961.

BOBBY MARCHAN, "There Is Something on Your Mind" (Fire). 1960.

MAR-KEYS, "Last Night" (Satellite). 1961.

MARSHALL TUCKER BAND, "Can't You See" (Capricorn). 1973.

MARTHA AND THE VANDELLAS, *Greatest Hits* (Gordy). "Dancing in the Street" will be sung (and rewritten—see the Stones' "Street Fighting Man" and Springsteen's "Racing in the Street" for the story so far) as long as rock lasts, and it wasn't even their best. "Love (Makes Me Do Foolish Things)" is as quiet a testament to vulnerability as the music has produced, but you can hear a smile in it; "Heatwave" may be Motown's masterpiece. The furious call-and-response between the Vandellas and Martha ("Go *ahead*, girl!"), the devastatingly complex yet uncompromised syncopation, the absolute confusion and affirmation of Martha herself—rock has never been any stronger, and all who've covered this tune have made fools of themselves. 1963–1965/1966.

MARVELETTES, *Greatest Hits* (Tamla). Motown's only true girl group: sassy, sexy—thanks to a bit of U.S. Bonds in the sound, very tough, thanks to sneaky catch-phrase lyrics, very smart. But no producer or lyricist could have guaranteed the high swoop at the end of "Playboy," the unexpected delight of "Danger Heartbreak Dead Ahead," or the happy longing of "Beechwood 4-5789," a tune Brian Wilson was likely answering when he wrote "I Get Around." 1961–1966/1966.

DAVE MASON, *Alone Together* (Blue Thumb). Just out of Traffic, he joined with Eric Clapton to pursue the legacy of Cream, and caught it. 1970.

John Mayall's Bluesbreakers with Eric Clapton (London). Almost fifteen years ago, the words "Clapton Is God" began to appear on London walls. This is why. 1965 (UK)/1967 (US).

MAYTALS, *Monkey Man* (Trojan/UK). Rough roots reggae from a three-man vocal group who offered heart-of-darkness visions cut with wild good humor, all carried by a beat Huey "Piano" Smith would have appreciated. Sure-fire smash: "African Doctor." 1971.

——*Funky Kingston* (Island). A landmark in the history of rhythm & blues, because of the 478th valid version of "Louie, Louie," an impossibly soulful cover of John Denver's "Country Roads," but most of all because of the title song. It began with ragged, seemingly African chants, then conquered the territory that once belonged to "Hold On, I'm Comin'," and finally slammed home; the cryptic, scattered story-line—driven by music so infectious and a vocal so alarming you couldn't bear not to understand—had something to do with why reggae was born in Jamaica and why it could never really thrive anywhere else. Thus, like all great pop, the tune drew a line, and allowed every willing soul to cross it. 1975.

PAUL McCARTNEY & WINGS, *Band on the Run* (Capitol). Pure pop for all people, bursting with hooks—and underneath the shiny surface, pretty hard stuff. With "Jet," the most exciting single of its year, though all who heard it will die without knowing what it was about. 1974.

MC5, *Back in the U.S.A.* (Atlantic). The vinyl equivalent of a Silvertone stereo, with politics to match. 1970.*

GEORGE McCRAE, "Rock Your Baby" (TK). 1974.

BARRY McGUIRE, "Eve of Destruction" (Dunhill). 1965.

WAYNE McGINNIS, "Rock, Roll & Rhythm"/"Lonesome Rhythm Blues" (Meteor). 1956.

DON McLEAN, "American Pie" (UA). 1971.

CLYDE McPHATTER, "A Lover's Question" (Atlantic). 1958.

MEADOW-LARKS, "Heaven and Paradise" (Dootone). 1955.

MEDALLIONS, "The Letter" (Dootone). "Let me whisper, sweet words of dismortality, and discuss the pompitus of love. Put it together, and what do you have? Matrimony!" Weird. 1955.

MELLOWKINGS, "Tonite-Tonite" (Herald). 1957.

HAROLD MELVIN AND THE BLUENOTES, "If You Don't Know Me by Now" (Philadelphia International). 1972.

MFSB, "TSOP" (Philadelphia International). 1974.

MICKEY AND SYLVIA, "Love Is Strange" (Groove). 1956.

STEVE MILLER BAND, *Children of the Future* (Capitol). On side one, a gorgeous (if, as history proved, cynical) celebration of innocence; on side two, a freewheeling (if, as history proved, cynical) celebration of experience, as captured in Chicago blues. 1968.

GARNET MIMMS AND THE ENCHANTERS, "Cry Baby" (UA). 1963.

MINK DEVILLE, "Cadillac Walk" (Capitol). 1977.

The Miracles' Greatest Hits from the Beginning (Tamla). Motown's Renaissance man, Smokey Robinson took less than four years to move from a neat answer to the Silhouettes' "Get a Job" to the soaring "What's So Good About Goodbye," which established him as the finest craftsman (and punner) in rock. He claimed Frankie Lymon as his inspiration, but Lymon only dreamed of sounds like these. 1958–1964/1965.

——*Greatest Hits, Vol. 2* (Tamla). No one broke hearts with Smokey's elegance, or put them back together with his grace. On this most

* This entry by Dave Marsh

perfect of albums, each tune was more beautiful than the last—until "The Love I Saw in You Was Just a Mirage," a song so brilliantly conceived, so carefully written, so indelibly arranged and sung, it made most everything that surrounded it on the radio seem faintly obscene. 1964–1967/1968.

Moby Grape (Columbia). Hard country rock from a golden age San Francisco band—but almost as a clue to their quick disintegration, this flawless debut LP turned a strange corner near the end ("I'll just lay here, and decay here," moaned a voice), and, as it closed, with the crazed, receding visions of "Indifference," dropped straight into an exalting and dangerous psychic anarchy. As such, it caught the true spirit of the Haight at just that point where it turned back on itself. 1967.

Moldy Goldies: Colonel Jubilation B. Johnston and His Mystic Knights Band and Street Singers Attack the Hits (Columbia). "Secret Agent Man" is croaked to the half-time beat of "Rainy Day Women" and mixed with "Columbia, Gem of the Ocean"; a demented hillbilly utters "The Name Game" as if he's sure it holds the secrets of the universe. Cut right after the sessions for *Blonde on Blonde*, when producer Bob Johnston and his pals were still glued to the ceiling. 1966.

MONOTONES, "Book of Love" (Argo). Ultimate one-shot, single of singles. 1958.

MOODY BLUES, "Go Now" (London). 1965.

JOHNNY MOORE'S THREE BLAZERS, "Merry Christmas, Baby" (Exclusive). 1949.

VAN MORRISON, "Brown Eyed Girl" (Bang). 1967.

——*Astral Weeks* (Warner Bros.–Seven Arts). Belfast: childhood, initiation, sex and death—and Richard Davis's bass. (Cf. Lester Bangs's and M. Mark's chapters.) 1968.

——*Moondance* (Warner Bros.). "Ray Charles was shot down, but he got up"—or, into the mystic, with one foot digging into the American earth. (Cf. M. Mark's chapter.) 1970.

——*Van the Man* (Amazing Kornyphone). Blazing live performances ("Friday's Child"!) on one side, and a riveting, unspeakably gentle instrumental ("Caledonia Soul Music") on the other. Recorded 1970–1971/bootlegged 1974.

——*Tupelo Honey* (Warner Bros.). The brooding black Irishman celebrates true love, and walks down Broadway in his hot pants. But were they pink? 1971.

——*Saint Dominic's Preview* (Warner Bros.). The brooding black Irishman strips off his hot pants and dives into the sea. Visions clash: the selfishness and fraud of Aemrican life, the helpless fury of Belfast, the distant call of an even older homeland—and, ending it all, the absurd but irresistible promise of "Almost Independence Day." (Cf. M. Mark's chapter.) 1972.

——*"It's Too Late to Stop Now"* (Warner Bros.). (Cf. M. Mark's chapter.) 1974.

——*Veedon Fleece* (Warner Bros.). Drifting ballads, Blakean journeys. If the piano on "Linden Arlen Stole the Highlights" was a prayer, "You Don't Pull No Punches But You Don't Push the River" defined a quest that will always be out of Morrison's reach—for he can never stop pushing. 1975.

——*Into the Music* (Warner Bros.). Which means, perhaps, that Morrison must wait for the river to come to him. He pushed hard in the last years of the decade—junking some LPs, releasing others—and finally, after missing badly, stepped forth as if he had been overwhelmed: by the clarity of faith, the endless renewal of sex, the ordinary mysteries of romance. Summoning the cadences of "Madame George," he grabbed hold of it all in the eight minutes of "When the Healing Has Begun," and rode it home. 1979.

MOTHER EARTH, *Living with the Animals* & *Make a Joyful Noise* (Mercury). A wry hippie R&B band that nevertheless reached for the country side of the dial, they were led by Tracy Nelson, whose "Down So Low" came from places Janis Joplin never got to. 1968 & 1969.

MOTHERS OF INVENTION, *Absolutely Free* (Verve). Is there any facet of American popular culture Frank Zappa hasn't pissed on? If so, write and tell him what it is, and he'll get a beer out of the refrigerator and unzip. From "Concentration Camp Moon," a prescient satire of hippies, to the anti-disco culture "Dancin' Fool," he's been there. On this early effort, though, the wit was liberating, the noise of the band not merely Absurdist but actually absurd—and, all questions of smugness aside, who could resist a high school anthem called "(I've Got My) Status Back, Baby"? 1967.

The Motown Story (Motown). The history of James Jamerson's bass playing, on fifty-eight hits. 1958–1970/1970.

MOTT THE HOOPLE, "All the Young Dudes" (Columbia). 1972.

——*Mott* (Columbia). With pointed, dramatic rock and Ian Hunter's sardonic songs and vocals—virtually every moment rooted somewhere on *Highway 61 Revisited* or *Blonde on Blonde*—this hard-luck

British band caught the noble weariness of those who kept the faith in a time when it had to seem only they believed. Hunter must have smiled when he saw the punks of the late seventies reach the audience he was sure had to be out there somewhere—smiled, and wondered if anyone remembered "I Wish I Was Your Mother," a shatteringly beautiful horror story that no punk has touched on record, though Sid Vicious may well have lived most of it out. 1973.

MOVE, "Do Ya" (UA). 1972.

MUSIC MACHINE, "Talk Talk" (Original Sound). 1966.

MYSTICS, "Hushabye" (Laurie). 1959.

JOHNNY NASH, "Some of Your Loving" (ABC-Paramount). 1960.

——"I Can See Clearly Now" (Epic). 1972.

NATIONAL LAMPOON, *Radio Dinner* (Banana-Blue Thumb). The Persecution and Assassination of Bob Dylan, John Lennon, and Joan Baez, held together by two preppies earnestly explaining how George Harrison's 1971 Concert for Bangladesh showed them exactly where the seventies are *at*, man. 1972.

RICKY NELSON, *Legendary Masters* (UA). The best rockabilly a Hollywood kid could buy, and I'd take it over Eddie Cochran's or Johnny Burnette's. Pick to click: "Be Bop Baby." 1957–1963/1971.

——"Garden Party" (Decca). 1972.

NERVOUS NORVUS, "Transfusion" (Dot). 1956.

AARON NEVILLE, "Over You" (Minit). 1960.

——*Tell It Like It Is* (Par-Lo). Pop blues from New Orleans: light on the surface, deadly at the bottom. Neville's high tenor conveyed an acceptance of life's worst in the sardonic "Jailhouse"; in the incomprehensible "Space Man," he countered with a Mardi-grassed refusal to believe in anything but life's best. 1967.

New York Dolls in Too Much Too Soon (Mercury). Marvelous rock archaeology, combined with churning affirmation in the face of a void they couldn't have done without. With "Human Being" as a last word, they made history if not the charts. (Cf. Robert Christgau's chapter.) 1974.

RANDY NEWMAN, *Sail Away* (Reprise). "The ship? Great God, where is the ship?" 1972.

THUNDERCLAP NEWMAN, "Something in the Air" (Track). 1969.

NUTMEGS, "Story Untold" (Herald). 1955.

O'JAYS, "Love Train" (Philadelphia International). 1973.

OLYMPICS, "Dance by the Light of the Moon" (Arvee). 1960.

ROY ORBISON, "Ooby Dooby"/"Go, Go, Go" (Sun). 1956.

——*All-Time Greatest Hits* (Monument). "I knew his voice was pure gold," Sam Phillips of Sun Records said of the Texas rockabilly. "I also knew if anyone got a look at him he'd be dead inside of a week." Thus, Roy kept his shades on, and four years later began a string of gorgeously over-orchestrated hits that defined pop romanticism in the early sixties. There were a few winner's songs—"Mean Woman Blues" is the classic—but most offered tragedy so sweet that today, when Bruce Springsteen strains for notes he can't hit, you know it's not just angst he's in love with, but Roy, too. 1960–1964/ 1972.

ORIOLES, "It's Too Soon to Know" (Natural). 1948.

ORLONS, "Don't Hang Up" (Cameo). 1962.

PACIFIC GAS & ELECTRIC, "Are You Ready" (Columbia). 1970.

GRAHAM PARKER AND THE RUMOUR, *Howlin Wind & Heat Treatment* (Mercury). Harbinger of the English New Wave, with roots in the hardest soul music and ska of the sixties, Parker burned with anger and romance, class resentment and a sense of fate, all powered by a questing spirit that blew away the fog of the mid-seventies. As for the Rumour, they came up with the drama that made Parker's every gesture seem like a last stand. 1976.

——"Discovering Japan" (Vertigo/UK). 1979.

Junior Parker (Charly/UK). Though he went on to a long, rich career at Duke, his early Sun sides (cut under the name of Little Junior's Blue Flames) were most vivid and prophetic. The sizzling "Feelin' Good" sums up the erotic rhythms that, of all elements of R&B, whites have been least able to catch; after a quarter-century, "Mystery Train" still sounds as if its tracks end only at the Styx. 1953/1977.

BILL PARSONS, "The All American Boy" (Fraternity). 1958.

PASSIONS, "Just to Be with You" (Audicon). 1959.

PAUL AND PAULA (originally Jill & Ray), "Hey Paula" (LeCam/ Phillips). 1962.

PENGUINS, "Earth Angel" (Dootone). 1954.

CARL PERKINS, *Original Golden Hits* (Sun). As much as anyone, he defined rockabilly: the snapping guitar, the hillbilly's bid for freedom and excitement, the unexpected bursts of feeling (his cover of the Platters' "Only You") and humor (the Memphis razor follies of "Dixie Fried") that he pushed too far ever to live out. Today he is undiminished as a performer, spared Elvis's fate because it was never he who became famous, but his songs: "Matchbox," "Honey Don't," "Boppin' the Blues," and the tune that begins, "Well, it's one for the money . . ." 1956–1957/1969.

PERSUASIONS, *Chirpin'* (Elektra). A veteran black acappella group, the Persuasions are singers to make you cry, and here they do—with an altogether savage account of the implacable divisions of race in "Willie and Laura Mae Jones," with a heartbreaking celebration of doo-wop in "Looking for an Echo," and with a ghostly, desperate, single-voiced tribute to the fallen Jackie Wilson, "To Be Loved." The story of black rock is in this record. 1977.

PETER AND GORDON, "I Go to Pieces" (Capitol). 1965.

TOM PETTY AND THE HEARTBREAKERS, "American Girl" (Shelter). 1977.

PHIL PHILLIPS, "Sea of Love" (Khoury's/Mercury). 1959.

The Best of Wilson Pickett (Atlantic). Stag-o-lee in a mohair suit, he promoted a sly carnal urgency, but it was "In the Midnight Hour," more plea than brag, that made him immortal. Pickett climbed mountains, crossed rivers, braved storms, all within his room, until the door opened and love came tumbling down. As Jon Landau said, this was not a classic, it was an epic. 1959–1967/1967.

GENE PITNEY, "Every Breath I Take" (Musicor). 1961.

——"Mecca" (Musicor). 1963.

PLASTIC ONO BAND, "Cold Turkey" (Apple). 1969.

PLATTERS, "My Prayer" (Mercury). 1956.

POLICE, "So Lonely" (A&M/UK). 1978.

POPPY FAMILY, "That's Where I Went Wrong" (London). 1970.

ELVIS PRESLEY, *The Sun Sessions* (RCA). They ranged far back into the hills, kept the radio tuned to the latest Memphis blues, and thus, on five singles, Elvis, guitarist Scotty Moore, bassist Bill Black, and producer Sam Phillips performed "the giant wedding ceremony," marrying white culture to black, and invented rock and roll. It was as if all the contradictions of American music had been resolved in a dream; as Nik Cohn has written, it was also the sexiest thing anyone had ever heard. 1954–1955/1976.

——*Good Rocking Tonight* (Bopcat/Netherlands). Revelatory early takes from the Sun sessions, with unbelievable studio dialogue from the founders. Plus various rockabilly classics and a deadly serious argument between Jerry Lee Lewis and Sam Phillips over the inherent blasphemy of "Great Balls of Fire." 1954–1958/1972.

——*Elvis' Golden Records* (RCA). If the Sun singles created rock, these put it across. 1956–1957/1958.

——*Jailhouse Rock* (RCA). An EP, with "Young and Beautiful" and the wonderful "(You're So Square) Baby, I Don't Care." 1957.

——*Elvis is Back!* (RCA). From the Army, and ready for the blues. 1960.

——"Crying in the Chapel" (RCA). Recorded 1960/released 1965.

——*Elvis' Golden Records, Vol. 3* (RCA). The best of his overblown, irresistible ballads, plus some real rhythm & blues. 1960–1962/1963.

——*Elvis-TV Special* (RCA). The great comeback, ten years after the Army cut his hair, with the live, small-combo, Samson-in-the-Temple version of "One Night," the finest music of his life. 1968.

——*From Elvis in Memphis* (RCA). Mature, soulful, desperate. 1969.

——"Suspicious Minds" (RCA). 1969.

——"Burning Love" (RCA). 1972.

——*A Legendary Performer, Vol. 1* (RCA). *Summa*: from Sun folkways to number-one hits to "Peace in the Valley" to three more staggering shots from the TV special, all ending with "Can't Help Falling in Love." Peace in the valley? R.I.P. (Cf. Tom Smucker's chapter.) 1954–1968/1973.

LLOYD PRICE, "Lawdy Miss Clawdy" (Specialty). 1952.

——"Stagger Lee" (ABC-Paramount). 1958.

P. J. PROBY, "Mission Bell" (Liberty). 1965.

PROCOL HARUM, "A Whiter Shade of Pale" (Dream). 1967.

PROFESSOR LONGHAIR, "Bald Head" (Mercury). 1950.

Put Your Cat Clothes On (Sun/UK). Rare Memphis rockabilly, and startling: "Rockin' Chair Daddy" from Harmonica Frank Floyd, an early avatar; Roy Orbison's "Domino," a prophecy of surf music; Ray Harris's searing "Come on Little Mama"; Jack Earl's "Slow Down," which doesn't; Carl Perkins's title tune (the first rock and roll attempt at a theme that would finally blow its cover with Lou Reed's "I Wanna Be Black")—and more! 1951–1958/1973.

QUIN-TONES, "Down the Aisle of Love" (Hunt). 1958.

RAYS, "Silhouettes" (Cameo). 1957.

REBELS, "Wild Weekend" (Swan). 1962.

MAC REBENNACK, "Storm Warning" (Rex). c. 1960.

OTIS REDDING, *Pain in My Heart* (Atco). His crucial influences were Little Richard and Sam Cooke, but this Memphis R&B is a version of the Sun sound (Elvis was also an influence): clean, uncompromised, and intense, with every emotion from hilarity to devastation fully realized. 1964.

——*Otis Blue* (Volt). He was committed to his calling like few of his contemporaries; that allowed him to make "I've Been Loving You Too Long" more than a love song, allowed him to make it something like a statement of ethics. But it also led him to worry some of his lines to death, and when that happened, you simply heard the band: Al Jackson's remarkably personal drum beats, Duck Dunn's isolated bass, Booker T's rolling piano, and Steve Cropper's guitar accents—or, as on "Rock Me Baby," his rare, X-ray solos. 1965.

——*Dictionary of Soul* (Volt). Meant to sum up the genre, and it did. 1966.

——*Live in Europe* (Volt). The last LP before his death late in the year, with the audience on the verge of a religious experience. The roll-call of hits ends with "Try a Little Tenderness"; you can hear a woman in the crowd cry out to Otis for salvation, and you can hear her get it. 1967.

——*Dock of the Bay* (Volt). Can one call Otis Redding the black Van Morrison when Van Morrison would like nothing better than to be called the white Otis Redding? 1968.

Lou Reed, *Street Hassle* (Arista). The mechanics of compassion, or, as Reed might have it, a recognition of just how bad bad luck can be. (Cf. Ellen Willis's chapter.) 1978.

Revels, "Church Key" (Impact). 1961.

Paul Revere and the Raiders, "Just Like Me" (Columbia). 1965.

Jody Reynolds, "Endless Sleep" (Demon). 1958.

The Many New Sides of Charlie Rich (Smash). A Sun veteran, Bobby Bland's white soul brother found his style on another label, with the sardonic "Mohair Sam" and the despairing "Down and Out." Rich didn't belong with the rockabillies; he sang as if he'd never been young. 1965.

——*The Best of Charlie Rich* (Epic). Later, he fulfilled the promise of Elvis's early ballads, trivializing the country version of heartbreak and making a lot of soul music sound histrionic, offering the bitter acceptance of "Life's Little Ups and Downs," the damage of "Sittin' and Thinkin'," the compassion and lyricism of "Set Me Free." 1968–1971/1972.

Jonathan Richman, "Roadrunner" (Beserkley). 1975.

——and the Modern Lovers, *Rock 'n' Roll with the Modern Lovers* (Beserkley). All-acoustic rockabilly, begging for the strait-jacket (just listen to the incredible "Dodge Veg-O-Matic," and the way Jonathan says "I like to watch it rot"): the closest anyone has come to "Flying Saucers Rock 'n' Roll" since Sputnik. 1977.

Righteous Brothers, "You've Lost that Lovin' Feeling" (Philles). 1964.

Billy Lee Riley and His Little Green Men, "Flying Saucers Rock 'n' Roll" (Sun). 1957.

JOHNNY RIVERS, "Secret Agent Man" (Imperial). 1966.

RIVINGTONS, "Papa-Oom-Mow-Mow" (Liberty). 1962.

MARTY ROBINS, "El Paso" (Columbia). 1960.

VICKI SUE ROBINSON, "Turn the Beat Around" (RCA). 1976.

RODS, "Do Anything You Wanna Do" (Island). 1977.

The Rolling Stones (London). With the best name and the most ominous album cover in the history of rock, they were undeniable before you got their first LP out of its jacket. The music was cool and ruthless: classic R&B stripped of all doubt, the demand for pure aggression and excitement sweeping everything from its path. 1964.

——*12 × 5* (London). English robber barons laying tracks across the U.S.A., they seized huge chunks of right-of-way, foreclosing on modern soul with "Time Is on My Side," careening to apocalyptic heights with "It's All Over Now," and terrifying all opposition as the guitar that opened "Empty Heart" reached out and grabbed your very soul. 1964.

——*The Rolling Stones, Now!* (London). A sexual tour of the Deep South. 1964.

——"Play with Fire" (London). A sexual tour of the English class system. 1965.

——"Satisfaction" (London). A sexual tour of mass culture. (Cf. Simon Frith's chapter.) 1965.

——*December's Children* (London). With "The Singer Not the Song," their first nod at lyricism (at, dare it be said, humility), yet framed by "She Said Yeah," the fastest song they ever cut. 1965.

——"19th Nervous Breakdown" (London). A sexual tour of parental neglect. 1966.

——*Aftermath* (Decca/UK). Like everyone else, they were stunned by *Rubber Soul*; this set, more than fifty minutes long in its UK version, was their answer. For the first time, Mick Jagger and Keith Richard wrote every song, and the "way of life" then-manager Andrew Loog Oldham had promised the Stones would carry forth fell into place. Bohemians roamed London, flashing contempt for all things bourgeois while toying with their ruling-class equivalents. They posited a duel between the sexes, choosing weapons of scorn and humor. Sensitive to the disasters of the world they passed through, they refused its claims anyway. They skirted decadence by the pace they kept, and avoided it because they were driven not by idle curiosity, or even narcissism, but by the most delicate and brutal shadings of lust, given absolute and final form in eleven-and-a-half minutes of "Goin' Home," which they never really did. 1966.

——*Between the Buttons* (London). Like everyone else, they were stunned by *Blonde on Blonde* . . . 1967.

——"Jumpin' Jack Flash" (London). A sexual tour of child abuse. 1968.

——*Beggars Banquet* (London). Worthy of Parnell, but catered by Fortnum & Mason. (Cf. Simon Frith's chapter.) 1968.

——"Honky Tonk Women" (London). A sexual tour of hard rock. 1969.

——*Let It Bleed* (London). Like everyone else, they were stunned—well, impressed—by the fact that the open possibilities of the sixties were on the verge of implosion; this set, beginning with a heroic call to dig in for the long haul ("Gimmie Shelter," which as the greatest rock and roll recording ever made both denied shelter and delivered it), moved through hilarious celebrations of sex, stardom, and tomfoolery, and ended with "You Can't Always Get What You Want," sure watchwords for the seventies: a stirring documentary about the collapse of Swinging London that somehow made the future the Stones were dreading along with their audience seem more than possible—made it seem like honest work. Their best album. 1969.

——*LIVE r Than You'll Ever Be* (Lurch). A searing concert bootleg from Oakland, California, with the definitive versions of "Love in Vain" and "Midnight Rambler." 1969.

——"Brown Sugar" (Rolling Stones). A sexual tour of racist irony. 1971.

——*Exile on Main Street* (Rolling Stones). "Self-conscious public creators careering down the corridors of destiny, burying Mick's voice under layers of cynicism, angst, and ennui" (Robert Christgau), they met the seventies and beat them, two falls out of three. Fave rave, symbolically and in every other way: Robert Johnson's "Stop Breaking Down." 1972.

——*Some Girls* (Rolling Stones). With the awful, suspended longing of "Just My Imagination," the comic rush of "When the Whip Comes Down," and the sleazy, sweaty embrace of the title tune, a sexual tour of everything under the sun. 1978.

Presenting the Fabulous Ronettes Featuring Veronica (Philles). Rock for the gods and the girls' bathroom. (Cf. Jim Miller's chapter.) 1964.

LINDA RONSTADT, "You're No Good" (Capitol). 1975.

Rosie and the Originals, "Angel Baby" (Highland). 1960.

Diana Ross and the Supremes, *Greatest Hits* (Motown). Ten number-one singles: lush, aching, worldly, unstoppable. In 1966 I was appalled when a writer claimed "You Keep Me Hangin' On" was a better record than "Like a Rolling Stone," but it might be true. 1963–1967/1967.

The Roxy London WC2 (Jan.–Apr. '77) (EMI/UK). The birth of punk: rough, unfocused, screeching, and impossibly alive. 1977.

Roxy Music, *Stranded* (Atco). Emerging in the wake of David Bowie, but outclassing him in imagination and humor, Bryan Ferry and his band orchestrated the adventures of a pan-European Don Juan, dropping only the slyest hints that the persona was the disguise of a very scared hustler. Thus the tension was all implicit, but when it broke—as in "Amazona," with the astonishing instrumental stutter that finally cracks into Phil Manzanera's guitar solo—the relief was devastating. 1973.

——"All I Want Is You" (Island/UK). 1974.

——*Siren* (Atco). Don Juan Faces Life. With the band hitting the limits of the music that grew from *Rubber Soul*, Ferry dismantled his lounge lizard act bit by bit, until all that was left was what his entire career had meant to hide: "an average man," but one with enough emotion in him to record for Motown. 1975.

Merrilee Rush and the Turnabouts, "Angel of the Morning" (SpearSound/Bell). 1968.

Safaris, "Image of a Girl" (Eldo). 1960.

Santo and Johnny, "Sleep Walk" (Canadian American). 1959.

Savage Rose, *Your Daily Gift* (Gregar). This odd, intelligent Danish group made a series of striking LPs in the early seventies. Here they anticipated the art rock of David Bowie and Talking Heads, merging the high, bizarrely twisted vocals of Anisette with the threatening, doomy sounds of the band, until all you wanted was peace, and with the title tune gently closing out the album, got it. 1971.

Boz Scaggs (Atlantic). Duane Allman's playing on "Loan Me a Dime" grows from country blues to city blues to the most intense rock; he traces a history of the music, and nothing is dropped along the way. With Peter Green's work on Fleetwood Mac's "Love that Burns," it's the farthest any white guitarist has ever traveled. 1969.

Jack Scott (Ponie). First-rank rockabilly from a Canadian: a lasting marriage of the Sun band sound and the vocal style Elvis used on "I Was the One." Chartbound: "Goodbye Baby (Baby Goodbye)." 1956–1960/1974.

LINDA SCOTT, "Don't Bet Money Honey" (Canadian American). 1961.

SEARCHERS, "Needles and Pins"/"Ain't That Just Like Me" (Kapp). 1964.

NEIL SEDAKA, "Calendar Girl" (RCA). 1960.

BOB SEGER & THE SILVER BULLET BAND, "Night Moves" (Capitol). The mystic chords of memory. 1976.

RONNIE SELF, "Pretty Bad Blues" (CBS). 1957.

SENSATIONS, "Let Me In" (Argo). 1962.

Never Mind the Bollocks Here's the Sex Pistols (Warner Bros.). The return of the repressed: a snarling, nihilistic, altogether heroic act of pop rebellion in the grand tradition of "Hound Dog," *Down and Out in Paris and London,* and *Un Chien Andalou.* Fun, too. 1977.

SHANGRI-LAS, "Leader of the Pack" (Red Bird). 1964.

——"I Can Never Go Home Anymore" (Red Bird). 1965.

The Best of Del Shannon (Dot). There were two versions of early sixties teen life: the Bobby Vee version, where everything works out, and the Shannon version, where *nothing* works out and the kids run scared—from each other, from their parents, from the detectives hired to find them, from *life itself.* Boy, did it sound good. 1961–1965.

SHEP AND THE LIMELIGHTS, "Daddy's Home" (Hull). 1961.

SHIELDS, "You Cheated" (Tender/Dot). 1958.

SHIRELLES, *Greatest Hits* (Scepter). The class of the girl groups, thanks to Shirley Alston's restraint, spare Drifters-style arrangements, and superb songs. "Baby It's You" and "Will You Love Me Tomorrow" enriched countless teenage romances, but "Tonight's the Night" is still the sexiest record I've ever heard. 1959–1962/1963.

SHIRLEY AND LEE, "Let the Good Times Roll" (Alladin). 1956.

SHIRLEY (AND COMPANY), "Shame, Shame, Shame" (Vibration). 1975.

SHOCKING BLUE, "Never Marry a Railroad Man" (Colossus). 1970.

TROY SHONDELL, "This Time" (Goldcrest/Liberty). 1961.

SHOWMEN, "It Will Stand"/"Country Fool" (Minit). 1961.

SILHOUETTES, "Get a Job" (Ember). 1958.

CARLY SIMON, "You're So Vain" (Elektra). 1972.

SKYLINERS, "Since I Don't Have You" (Calico). 1959.

The Best of Percy Sledge (Atlantic). Beginning with "When a Man Loves a Woman"—Sledge never matched it, no one could have—this was soul so deep it seemed to rise slowly from the bottom of the sea, and, as each song ended, to return from whence it came. 1966–1969/1969.

SLY AND THE FAMILY STONE, *Greatest Hits* (Epic). The Lost City of Sixties Rock: a joyful, edgy celebration of a community rooted in black power and white counter-culture, powered by "Everyday People" and blessed by "Everybody Is a Star." 1967–1970/1970.

——*There's a Riot Goin' On* (Epic). The sixties turn into the seventies, and the Lost City burns to the ground. This was Muzak with its finger on the trigger, and it wore a death's head mask. As a statement of pessimism, "Thank you for talkin to me Africa," the album's last word, ranks with "Bartleby"; as music, with Robert Johnson's "Come on in My Kitchen." 1971.

SMALL FACES, "Here Comes the Nice" (Immediate/UK). 1967.

Huey "Piano" Smith's Rock 'n' Roll Revival! (Ace). Forget the stupid title: this is bedrock fury, stone age confusion. (Cf. Jay Cocks's chapter.) 1956–1958/1972.

Warren Smith (Charly/UK). A quirky Sun singer, his heart was in the lonesome wail and ancient modal figures of the Elizabethan ballads Appalachian mountain boys were raised on—and so, while submitting to rockabilly classics like the racist "Ubangi Stomp," he slipped in the fantastic "Red Cadillac and a Black Mustache," and subverted country rock with spooked echoes of "House Carpenter", which was one true source of the music he was paid to make. 1956–1959/1977.

SONNY AND CHER, "But You're Mine" (Atco). 1965.

JIMMY SOUL, "If You Wanna Be Happy" (S.P.Q.R.). 1963.

JOE SOUTH, "Games People Play" (Capitol). 1969.

PHIL SPECTOR, *A Christmas Gift for You* (Philles). The producer as artist, and millionaire, he put $50,000, a shocking sum for the time, into this project, and didn't get it back: still recovering from November 22, America was not in the mood for the loudest—and sexiest—Christmas music in the history of Christendom. With Darlene Love leading the way with "Christmas (Baby Please Come Home)," and the Ronettes, the Crystals, and Bob B. Soxx & the Blue Jeans chasing after her with souped-up standards, America has been listening ever since. 1963.

SPIKEDRIVERS, "Strange Mysterious Sounds" (Reprise). 1967.

Best of the Spinners (Atlantic). With Thom Bell producing, this could almost be Clyde McPhatter's Drifters: the sound and themes are dapper and modern, but the aesthetic is completely intact. 1972–1976/1978.

SPIRIT, "I Got a Line on You" (Ode). 1965.

DUSTY SPRINGFIELD, "Wishin' and Hopin' " (Phillips). 1964.

——*Dusty in Memphis* (Atlantic). Guided by Jerry Wexler, Aretha Franklin's producer, a white English pop singer matches the Queen of Soul in style and Diana Ross in eroticism. 1969.

BRUCE SPRINGSTEEN, *Darkness on the Edge of Town* (Columbia). The great romantic of the seventies makes an album about working-class defeat—and, leaving most of his innocence hanging in the air, comes away ready for a long, uncertain fight against cynicism. 1978.

EDWIN STARR, "War" (Gordy). 1970.

RINGO STARR, "It Don't Come Easy" (Apple). 1971.

STAX/VOLT REVUE, *Live in London* (Stax). The Memphis soul kings and a queen (the MG's, the Mar-Keys, Eddie Floyd, Otis Redding, Carla Thomas) driven past themselves by a near-hysterical audience; a show that ended in glory when the band locked into the horn riff of Sam and Dave's "Hold On, I'm Comin' " and brought down the walls of Jericho. 1967.

STEELY DAN, *Countdown to Ecstasy* (ABC). They burrowed through the decade, scoring scabrous, deeply controlled hits about people for whom control was just a memory. Here, busting up the joint with a ditty about Eastern cults, terrifying the unwary with the inexplicably apocalyptic "Bring Back the Boston Rag," and savaging the rich and the poor in "Show Biz Kids," they turned the Band's second album upside down. If that record showed Americans they couldn't and shouldn't escape their country or their history, this one showed why it likely wasn't possible to fully join either one—and made the prospect sound groovy. 1973.

——*Pretzel Logic* (ABC). This album (named, said *auteurs* Donald Fagen and Walter Becker, for the swastika, because the title song was about Hitler, though not even he would have been able to figure out just how) led a crowd of fans through a land where nothing worked. The only nods to pleasure were tributes to jazz, to the past. The songs were uniformly inspired—colloquial, enigmatic, piercing—and the music, mainstream rock, was untouchable. 1974.

——*Katy Lied* (ABC). Again, the breakdown, but this time it went all the way. The LP began with a (the?) stock market crash, caught a Vietnam vet mulling over a vision that took in a spoonful of junk, Nixon's Cuban connection, and his own ghost, and almost jumped off the planet with the blasted truths of "Any World (That I'm Welcome To)," a song about disenchantment so strong not even suicide could satisfy it. Hidden in all this despair were two of the finest lines rock and roll has produced about itself: "All night long, we sang that stupid song/And every word we sang I knew was true." 1975.

BILLY STEWART, "Summertime" (Chess). 1962.

ROD STEWART, *Every Picture Tells a Story* (Mercury). With his band of eccentric British rockers (Ronnies Lane and Wood, Mickey Waller,

Martin Quittenton), he went after the sound Bob Dylan got on *Blonde on Blonde*; he missed, and the result was the most satisfying album of the seventies: bone-hard rock cut with compassion, humor and friendliness, ballads driven by blues feeling, an explosion of lyricism. 1971.

——"Tonight's the Night" (Warner Bros.). As defined by the Shirelles, but sung from the other side of the fence. 1976.

The Stooges (Elektra). The sound of Chuck Berry's Airmobile—after thieves stripped it for parts. 1969.

Stories, "Brother Louie" (Kama Sutra). 1973.

Barret Strong, "Money" (Anna). 1960.

Surfaris, "Wipe Out" (DFS/Dot). 1963.

Donna Summer, "Hot Stuff" (Casablanca). 1979.

Swamp Dogg, *Total Destruction to Your Mind* (Canyon). A lost masterpiece of late soul: a delicate, crying voice, shining horn charts, and the sensibility of a very addled protest singer—and cuckold. 1970.

Swingin' Medallions, "Double Shot (Of My Baby's Love)" (4 Sale/Smash). 1966.

Koko Taylor (Chess). Blues from the belly—and, with the horrifying "Insane Asylum" (a recasting of "St. James Infirmary" that makes a corpse on a slab seem like a comfort), four and a half minutes of electroshock. 1970.

The Teenagers Featuring Frankie Lymon (Gee). They were big, really big, taken off New York streets to turn front-porch acappella and 13-year-old Frankie's ghetto reveries into bigger money, as the pint-sized prodigy cried "I'm not a juvenile delinquent!" and played god-father to the Jackson 5, who he wouldn't live to see. Why *do* fools fall in love? 1957.

Temptations, *Anthology* (Motown). From the glorious "My Girl" to the exquisite "I Wish It Would Rain," from the "Heroin"-like "Cloud Nine" to the withering drama of "Papa Was a Rolling Stone," the Tempts preserved the tradition of the black vocal group even as they made it their own. Comparable to the Rolling Stones in their absorption of trends and politics while keeping track of the essential business of sex and romance, they were unsurpassed over the long haul. 1964–1972/1973.

Joe Tex, "Hold On to What You've Got" (Dial). 1964.

Them, *Here Comes the Night* (Parrot). Riveting, humorless, no-hope R&B out of Ireland—and, with "Mystic Eyes" and "Gloria," the first signs of Van Morrison's visionary obsessions. 1965.

——*Them Again* (Parrot). Without compromising his pessimism, Morrison turned lyrical, with "Call My Name," "Could You Would You," and "It's All Over Now, Baby Blue," where he outdistanced Dylan's original. It would be some time before he caught up with himself. 1966.

B. J. Thomas, "Rock and Roll Lullaby" (Scepter). 1972.

Carla Thomas, "Gee Whiz (Look at His Eyes)" (Satellite/Atlantic). 1964.

Irma Thomas, "Wish Someone Would Care" (Imperial). From happy-go-lucky New Orleans, and the saddest record in all of rock. 1964.

Junior Thompson, "Raw Deal"/"Mama's Little Baby" (Meteor). 1956.

Peter Townshend, *Who Came First* (Decca). As with the Who's *Who's Next*, which came first, the focus was on enlightenment and politics ("Let's See Action" seemed to be about a revolutionary on a secret mission, but the alternate title is "Nothing Is Everything"). But what Townshend must have really been after, as he overdubbed himself into a complete rock and roll band, was a certain joyousness and a certain toughness: on "Pure and Easy" he found both, and outclassed every record the Who made in the seventies. 1972.

Traffic (UA). Loose, funny, sexy, and dark: a British version of *Music from Big Pink*. It was Dave Mason's record, not Stevie Winwood's —except on "No Time to Live," his highest moment. 1968.

John Travolta and Olivia Newton-John, "You're the One that I Want" (RSO). 1978.

Trashmen, "Surfin' Bird" (Garret). 1963.

Troggs, "Wild Thing" (Fontana). 1966.

Doris Troy, "Just One Look" (Atlantic). 1963.

Tubes, "White Punks on Dope" (A&M). 1975.

Tommy Tucker, "Hi-Heel Sneakers" (Checker). 1964.

Turbans, "When You Dance" (Herald). 1955.

Joe Turner, "Shake, Rattle and Roll" (Atlantic). 1954.

Ike Turner's Kings of Rhythm, *I'm Tore Up* (Red Lightnin/UK). A&R man and bandleader for the Sun label in its pre-Presley blues days, Turner's own music of the time can best be described by the name of the label that reissued it. 1954–1958/1976.

Ike and Tina Turner, "River Deep—Mountain High" (Philles). "That record," said producer Phil Spector, "sounds like God hit the world and the world hit back." 1966.

Conway Twitty, "It's Only Make Believe" (MGM). 1960.

Ritchie Valens, "La Bamba" (Del-Fi). 1959.

BOBBY VEE AND THE SHADOWS, "Suzie Baby" (Soma/Liberty). 1959.

Velvet Underground (MGM). (Cf. Ellen Willis's chapter.) 1967–1969/1970.

——*Loaded* (Cotillion). A last stab: the sound softened, the tone turned pleasing on the surface and mythical beneath it, and Lou Reed produced the songs that would carry him through a good part of the seventies—"Rock & Roll," "Sweet Jane," "Head Held High," and the strange "New Age." Reed's negations had a unique aspect: they were suffused with affection. 1970.

VENTURES, "Walk–Don't Run" (Blue Horizon/Dolton). 1960.

VIBRATIONS, "My Girl Sloopy" (Atlantic). 1964.

GENE VINCENT, *Greatest* (Capitol/UK). The most tortured of the early rockers and the dirtiest, almost forgotten in the U.S.A. at the time of his death in 1971, he seemed totally committed to the beat, to hit and run love, to the most sensual and destructive rockabilly noise. 1956–1959/1978.

VOLUMES, "I Love You" (Chex). 1962.

WAILERS, *Catch a Fire* (Island). Leaders of the abortive reggae invasion, they were Jamaican heroes, a true group with years behind them. Chroniclers of exile, they took homelessness, a secret theme of the blues, as a first principle. Their politics—as a group and as spokesmen—made the incredible "Concrete Jungle" comparable to both "Gimmie Shelter" and "In the Still of the Nite." 1972.

——*Burnin'* (Island). After negation, revolt—not as salvation but as justification. "Get Up, Stand Up" (the real "Street Fighting Man") led the charge; the fast draw of "I Shot the Sheriff," undercut by profound fatalism, hinted at why it might not matter if the charge went in circles. 1973.

——*Bob Marley and the Wailers—Live!* (Island). Often called their island's Rolling Stones because of dark tones and snaking rhythms, the group scattered, and Marley emerged as a performer who recalled no one so much as Bob Dylan in the mid-sixties. Here, he made his way through a racial drama of revenge and compassion with true pop glamour. 1975.

JERRY JEFF WALKER, "Mr. Bojangles" (Atco). 1968.

——"L.A. Freeway" (MCA). 1973.

JUNIOR WALKER, "Shotgun" (Soul). 1965.

JOE WALSH, "Life's Been Good" (Asylum). The Coasters in whiteface —with lotsa money. 1978.

WAR, "Slipping into Darkness" (UA). 1972.

DIONNE WARWICK, "Don't Make Me Over" (Scepter). 1962.

GINO WASHINGTON, "Gino Is a Coward" (Ric Tic/Son Bert). 1964.

MUDDY WATERS, *Sail On* (Chess). This Delta-to-Chicago bluesman chilled the earth with the stark, spidery lines of his masterpiece, "Rollin' Stone," after which he set up for a fifteen-year battle of the bands with Howlin' Wolf. If the fear of God lurks in the rock and roll heart, he helped put it there. 1950–1954/1969.

JOHNNY "GUITAR" WATSON, "Cuttin' In" (King). 1962.

WE FIVE, "You Were on My Mind" (A&M). 1965.

LENNY WELCH, "Since I Fell for You" (Cadence). 1963.

TONY JOE WHITE, "Roosevelt and Ira Lee" (Monument). 1969.

WHO, "I Can't Explain" (Decca). 1965.

——*The Who Sing My Generation* (Decca). They sang it and claimed it. This was British rock so hard-nosed (and, thanks to the feedback chords of Pete Townshend and the hell-bound drumming of Keith Moon, so surprising) it threw off fans as fast as it attracted them, and neither the band nor their audience ever caught up with it. 1965.

——"I'm a Boy" (Decca). 1966.

——*Happy Jack* (Decca). The Who meet the Beach Boys, with unnervingly funny results, especially on "A Quick One While He's Away," their first—and best—"rock opera." 1966.

——*The Who Sell Out* (Decca). Townshend's ability to at once celebrate and expose the most obvious and obscure aspects of pop life threatened the group with artiness, so he put off the day of reckoning with music alternately ethereal ("Rael," "Tattoo") and crushing ("I Can See for Miles"), all couched in a loving parody of British pirate radio. The Who wrote and performed their own commercials; if they could have found a way to slip themselves payola, they probably would have done that too. 1967.

MAURICE WILLIAMS AND THE ZODIACS, "Stay" (Herald). 1960.

CHUCK WILLIS, "It's Too Late" (Okeh). 1956.

——*I Remember Chuck Willis* (Atlantic). When the saddest-voiced R&B singer of the fifties asked, "What am I living for," he made you wonder; when he sang "C.C. Rider" you knew he was never coming back. Dead one year to the day after the latter song made the charts, he didn't. 1956–1958/1963.

WILLOWS, "Church Bells May Ring" (Melba). 1962.

JACKIE WILSON, "Reet Petite" (Brunswick). 1957.

——*Greatest Hits* (Brunswick). Clyde McPhatter's replacement in the Dominoes, then Mr. Excitement, he was master of the lightning knee-drop and its vocal equivalents. Remembered for the spotlight drama of "To Be Loved," the joy of "That's Why," he lives out what time is left to him in a coma, the result of a heart attack suffered on stage as he sang the key lines of "Lonely Teardrops": "My heart is crying, crying—" 1956–1968.

Jesse Winchester (Ampex). Lean and hungry rockabilly from a Tennessean hiding out in Canada: mature, bitter, looking hard for Saturday night, but not exactly trusting it. 1970.

Johnny Winter, *Second Winter* (Columbia). Leaving behind one of the great forgotten albums of the sixties, the albino Texas guitar flash shattered all categories, somehow merging a dozen sorts of blues, classic rock, Dylan's "Highway 61 Revisited," and (in Lester Bangs's words) "Bill Haley preaching Armageddon" into a thrilling personal statement matched only by Eric Clapton's *Layla*. Then, like Clapton, he turned to heroin. 1969.

Wire, *Chairs Missing* (Harvest/UK). The English punk assault broke down so many doors that in Britain anything became possible, and surfacing along with a lot of angry young men and women was a whole new strain of minimalist, highly ironic, wittily existential rock and roll. This band, which hid melodies in almost impenetrable lyrics about dislocation, pleasure, and doom, probably owed more to Jean-Luc Godard's New Wave than to that of anyone else. 1978.

Bill Withers, "Lean on Me" (Sussex). 1972.

Stevie Wonder, *Greatest Hits* (Tamla). Motown put him onstage as the 12-year-old successor to Ray Charles, but he was his own mannish boy, beginning with the ridiculous "Fingertips, Part 2," hurtling across the hilarious "Contract on Love," and arriving with the irresistible "I Was Made to Love Her." Still, no one took him seriously, and so, listening hard to the Beatles and Bob Dylan, he got serious, and people took him less seriously. 1963–1967/1968.

——"Superstition" (Tamla). Number one, and hard rock the Rolling Stones would have envied. 1972.

——*Innervisions* (Tamla). Finally, Wonder's seriousness paid off: he staked his claim to the paradoxes of black culture and the bland certainties of enlightenment, and people took him too seriously. Winner of so many Grammy awards he began handing them out to other artists, he became the most over-rated performer of the decade. This album, containing the extraordinarily bleak "Living for the City" and the searing "Higher Ground," was his best. 1973.

Link Wray and His Ray Men, "Rumble" (Cadence). 1958.

X-RAY SPEX, *Germfree Adolescents* (EMI/UK). A seminal punk band led by one Poly Styrene, who wore braces and screeched like some bizarre New Wave version of Annette, they offered an unfettered attack on teenage self-pity, pop narcissism and grown-up priggishness. With "Let's Submerge," at once a tale of sex and riding on the Underground, they also proved themselves fearless in the face of simple good times—or, for that matter, complex good times. 1978.

YARDBIRDS, *Shapes of Things* (Charly/UK). British R&B without ancestor worship, and you could cut your hands on it. With Eric Clapton or Jeff Beck on guitar, their attack ranged from Elmore James' "Ain't Done Wrong" to "You're a Better Man Than I," a heart-stopping protest song cut in—of all places—the Sun studios in Memphis. 1964–1968/1978.

YOUNG RASCALS, "Good Lovin' " (Atlantic). 1966.

KATHY YOUNG AND THE INNOCENTS, "A Thousand Stars" (Indigo). 1960.

NEIL YOUNG, *Decade* (Reprise). Some music that ranks with the most commercial of the seventies, and a lot that ranks with the most uncompromised. (Cf. Kit Rachlis' chapter.) 1966–1976/1977.

——*Tonight's the Night* (Reprise). Dopers on the run in the 1970s: clattering sounds of teeth in a skull as the connection is made and the connection is broken. 1975.

——AND CRAZY HORSE, *Rust Never Sleeps* (Reprise). Of all bankable stars, Young was most affected by the English punk explosion, perhaps because his own best music had been just as rough. This album— half acoustic meditations on decay and illusion, half hot-metal electricity driving straight through both, was his tribute to the flameout of Johnny Rotten and the death of Elvis Presley, and, almost incidentally, final proof of Young's status as the truest rocker of the seventies. 1979.

The Youngbloods (RCA). Named for a Coasters song, they played quick and tight New York folk-rock. The pastoralism that would later smother the band was present here, but on "Four in the Morning," a lost-love urban horror story, they stomped it like a cockroach. 1967.

TIMI YURO, "What's a Matter Baby" (Liberty). 1962.

Warren Zevon (Asylum). With a cold eye, a boozer's humor and a reprobate's sense of fate, this California rounder put L.A. back on the rock and roll map, and nearly blew the Malibu singer-songwriter crowd right off it. 1976.

ZURVANS, "Close the Book" (End). Release date unknown.

CONTRIBUTORS

LESTER BANGS was born in Escondido, California. Beginning at *Rolling Stone* in 1969, he has written some of the most revelatory and scabrous rock criticism in the short history of the form. An editor of *Creem* for five years, he has also written for the *Village Voice, Ms.*, and other publications, and now lives in New York. His first record, "Let it Blurt," was released in 1979 on the Spy label.

TOM CARSON, born in Germany, is a frequent contributor to the *Village Voice* and *Rolling Stone*. He lives in New York.

ROBERT CHRISTGAU, a New Yorker, is the music editor of the *Village Voice* and author of *Any Old Way You Choose It* (Penguin). Former rock critic for *Esquire* and *Newsday*, his work has also appeared in *The New York Times*, the Washington *Post, Creem, Cheetah*, and other publications.

JAY COCKS writes about rock and roll for *Time*, where he was formerly a film critic. His writing has also appeared in *Take One*, and he is the author of a number of screenplays. He was born in New York and lives there now.

SIMON FRITH, this book's token Englishman, received his Ph.D. from the University of California at Berkeley and now teaches sociology at the University of Warwicke in Coventry. A former columnist for *Creem* and currently a contributor to *Melody Maker*, he is the author of *The Sociology of Rock*, which will be published in the United States by Pantheon, and *Elementary Education Before the Education Act*, which will be published in England by Croom Helm in 1980.

GRACE LICHTENSTEIN is a staff writer for the *Village Voice* and is currently at work on a book about women and adventure. She chronicled her work as Rocky Mountain bureau chief for *The New York Times* in *Desperado* (Morrow), and has written for *Ms.*, the San Francisco *Chronicle*, and many other publications.

M. MARK is Arts editor of the *Village Voice*, where her writing on music and books appears regularly. Born in Waterloo, Iowa, she arrived at the site of Buddy Holly's plane crash, just outside Clear Lake, only hours after the fact.

DAVE MARSH, who describes himself as an aging idealist, was born in Pontiac, Michigan, and edited *Creem* from 1969 through 1973. Since then he has been music editor of Boston's *Real Paper*, record editor of *Rolling Stone*, where his column American Grandstand appears regularly, and has contributed to the *Village Voice* and the Boston *Phoenix*. His book on Bruce Springsteen, *Born to Run*, was published by Doubleday in 1979.

JANET MASLIN is a film critic for *The New York Times*. Her work has appeared in *Rolling Stone*, the Boston *Phoenix*, *New Times*, *Film Comment*, and other publications. She is a member of the National Society of Film Critics.

JOE McEWEN, best known to Boston radio listeners as Mr. C, has written about black music for *Rolling Stone*, the Boston *Phoenix*, and *Black Music*, and is the author of *Sam Cooke* (Sire-Chappell). He is currently working in A&R for Epic Records, and lives in New Jersey.

JIM MILLER, born in Chicago, received his Ph.D. from Brandeis University. Along the way, he contributed often to *Rolling Stone*, the *Real*

Paper and other publications. He is the editor of *The Rolling Stone Illustrated History of Rock & Roll* (Random House), on the one hand, and the author of *History and Human Existence* (University of California), on the other. He is currently rock critic for the *New Republic* and teaches political philosophy at the University of Texas at Austin.

PAUL NELSON was born in Warren, Minnesota, and co-founded the *Little Sandy Review* in 1961. He was an early champion of Bob Dylan's electric music in the pages of *Sing Out*, worked as a member of the A&R staff for Mercury Records, and has contributed to *Circus, Creem,* the *Real Paper,* the *Village Voice,* and *The New York Times.* He is presently record editor of *Rolling Stone.*

KIT RACHLIS grew up in New York and is the music editor of the Boston *Phoenix.* His articles have appeared in *Rolling Stone,* the *Village Voice, Country Music,* and other publications.

JOHN ROCKWELL covers rock and roll, opera, and avant-garde music for *The New York Times.* He received his Ph.D. in European cultural history from the University of California at Berkeley, and has contributed to *Rolling Stone, Le Monde,* the Los Angeles *Times, Opera News, Opernwelt,* and many other publications. Lou Reed to the contrary, he does not have a bodyguard.

TOM SMUCKER was born in Chicago and now works for the New York Telephone Company. His articles on music and politics have appeared in *Fusion, Creem,* and the *Village Voice,* where he has also published the long poem "Lenin on O.T." and erratic installments of "Tom Tattles," a radical gossip column.

ARIEL SWARTLEY, who wants it noted that she writes under her real name, has contributed to *Rolling Stone,* the *Village Voice,* and the Boston *Phoenix.* She was born in Boston and lives there now.

NICK TOSCHES was born in Newark, New Jersey, and has written for *Playboy, Esquire, Rolling Stone,* the *Village Voice* and *The New York Times.* He is the author of *Country* (Stein & Day; Delta), lives in New York, and is writing a novel about Blackbeard the Pirate.

ED WARD, a former record editor of *Rolling Stone*, has written for the *Village Voice, Harper's, New West, Creem, Mother Jones*, and other publications. Now at work on *The Hot Food Cookbook: Cooking with the World's Chilis*, which will be published by Anchor, he was born in Port Chester, New York, and now lives in Sausalito, California.

LANGDON WINNER was born in San Luis Obispo, California, and rereived his Ph.D. in political theory from the University of California at Berkeley. His writing on rock and roll has appeared in *Rolling Stone, Creem*, the *Village Voice*, and the *Real Paper*. He is the author of *Autonomous Technology* (MIT) and teaches politics at the Massachusetts Institute of Technology.

ELLEN WILLIS was born in the Bronx. Her writing on music, popular culture, and politics has appeared in the *New York Review of Books, Rolling Stone, Commentary, Ms.*, and many other publications. She is the former rock critic of *The New Yorker*, the former zoo critic of *Cheetah*, and is presently a columnist for the *Village Voice*. She lives in New York.

A NOTE ON THE TYPE

The text of this book was set in Electra, a type face designed by William Addison Dwiggins for the Mergenthaler Linotype Company and first made available in 1935. Electra cannot be classified as either "modern" or "old-style." It is not based on any historical model, and hence does not echo any particular period or style of type design. It avoids the extreme contrast between thick and thin elements that marks most modern faces, and is without eccentricities that catch the eye and interfere with reading. In general, Electra is a simple, readable type face that attempts to give a feeling of fluidity, power, and speed.

W. A. Dwiggins (1880–1956) began an association with the Mergenthaler Linotype Company in 1929 and over the next twenty-seven years designed a number of book types, including Metro, Electra, Caledonia, Eldorado, and Falcon.

Composed by The Maryland Linotype Composition Company,
Baltimore, Maryland
Printed and bound by The Haddon Craftsmen,
Scranton, Pennsylvania